PERMISSIVE BRITAIN
Social Change in the Sixties and Seventies

Permissive Britain

Social Change in the
Sixties and Seventies

CHRISTIE DAVIES

Pitman Publishing

First Published 1975

SIR ISAAC PITMAN AND SONS LTD
Pitman House, Parker Street, Kingsway, London, WC2B 5PB
P.O. Box 46038, Banda Street, Nairobi, Kenya

PITMAN PUBLISHING PTY. LTD
Pitman House, 158 Bouverie Street, Carlton, Victoria 3053,
Australia

PITMAN PUBLISHING CORPORATION
6 East 43rd Street, New York, N.Y. 10017, U.S.A.

SIR ISAAC PITMAN (CANADA) LTD
495 Wellington Street West, Toronto, 135, Canada

THE COPP CLARK PUBLISHING COMPANY
517 Wellington Street West, Toronto, 135, Canada

ISBN 0 273 36032 9

Computer Typesetting by Print Origination, Bootle, Merseyside,
L20 6NS. Printed and bound at The Pitman Press, Bath.

G 4641:18

Preface

The problem in writing about a topic of such general appeal as permissiveness and society is how to treat the subject in a thorough manner without putting off the general reader. It is not a problem that a scientist would have to face, for he knows that only other specialists in his field will read his book. It is a problem unique to sociology for sociology is open to all manner of readers—and so it should be. A tome on organic chemistry will gain in precision from the use of technical terminology but a sociology text that is totally incomprehensible to the average reader is usually simply pretentious. Yet very real advantages do stem from the aspirations of sociologists to be scientific. A careful use of statistical sources *is* better than crass assertion. It *is* wise to define one's terms carefully and if necessary to invent new ones where this leads to greater clarity. Footnotes *are* useful and informative. I have tried to support my arguments in all these ways, but general readers or beginning students need not fear that they will be overwhelmed. I have cut jargon to a minimum and encased a wide range of source-material—drawn from many other subjects besides sociology—in a matrix of ordinary everyday English. Where specialized terms are used, they are used for a purpose and in a context where they alone could convey an exact and accurate meaning.

Each chapter of this book then can be read at many levels. "Buggery and the decline of the British Empire" is an attempt to describe the ways in which the social structure can influence our moral values. It is a tightly argued attempt to show how the position of the military in a society affects the society's attitudes to homosexuality. It can also be read as an historical survey of attitudes towards homosexuals or even as a series of small incidents stretching from James I's infatuation with Buckingham to Kaiser Bill and his "queer" friends. "Parliament and the Permissive Society" is an analysis of how and why the legislature's attitudes on moral issues changed over time. Yet it is also an account of how pompous Members of Parliament can be when pontificating about morality. But satirizing Parliament does not imply an attack on the institution. Parliament *ought* to be pompous, and so should bishops or professors and anyone else who claims a position of moral leadership, whether it be Field-Marshal Montgomery or Leo Abse, Germaine Greer or Malcolm Muggeridge. Pomposity is demanded by their ambiguous position in a plural society, and the mockery of their critics often only serves to legitimize that position. Moral edict and satirical response is almost our national sport, a sport we indulge in without danger precisely because we are confident that the game will always go on, that our social system is so securely anchored that the wildest gales of controversy cannot disturb it.

One position where there is, on the surface, a conflict between the demands of an academic approach and the readers' wish to revel in controversy is the issue of "ethical neutrality". Should the writer retain a dry academic detachment or should he be willing to unleash a diatribe? Feeling, after all, is the spice of thought. I have not sought to provide a trendy tirade justifying some outrageous practice nor a shout of moral indignation at the rottenness of our times. My main motive in studying the various issues of this book was in fact sheer curiosity—and I still find these social changes a fascinating subject. But I am too much a part of my own times to be neutral and I have not withheld my feelings about the different facets of the permissive society. If the reader feels alternately pleased and annoyed at the arguments in this book, then I shall be satisfied.

Acknowledgements

In writing this book I am deeply indebted to all the colleagues, students and friends who have assisted me in various ways. I must first thank all those who read and criticized various portions of the manuscript: Michael Horowitz, David Rhys Davies, Margaret Clay and Arianna Stassinopoulos. Chapter 2, "Parliament and the Permissive Society", was given as a paper to the staff seminar of the Politics Department at Leeds University and Chapter 5, "Buggery and the Decline of the British Empire", as a paper at a discussion week seminar in the Department of Sociology at Leeds. I must thank all my colleagues in both departments for the helpful comments and criticisms made on both occasions. In particular I am indebted to Diana Douglas, Geoffrey and Heather Fry and Robert Towler for drawing my attention to points I would otherwise have missed. I have used much of this book as teaching material, both at Leeds and at Reading University and I would like to thank all those students, notably Robin Roslender and Miles Hapgood, who assisted me by their criticisms of my ideas.

I have always felt strongly that sociology should be an eclectic subject drawing on the findings of other areas of research, but in an age when there is too much knowledge for even the most adventurous polymath to cover this means that sociologists must continually seek advice from specialists in other disciplines and even in unfamiliar areas of his own subject. In this context I must particularly thank my father C.G. Davies, Mark Jenkinson, Krishan Kumar and John Teasdale for their generous help and advice. Much of the work incorporated in this book was done when I was still a research student at Emmanuel College, Cambridge. I would like to thank the college and my research supervisor Professor Philip Abrams for their assistance to me at that time. I must offer my special thanks to Arianna Stassinopoulos author of *The Female Woman* (Davis-Poynter 1973) and Professor J.R. de S. Honey author of *Tom Brown's Universe* (Duckworth 1973) for allowing me to read their manuscripts before publication.

I must also thank Laurence Kenworthy-Browne for the skill, patience and kindness he has shown as editor of this book.

I have used many libraries in doing the work on which this book is based but I owe an especial debt to the staff of the Brotherton Library at Leeds University, the library of the Institute of Criminology in Cambridge, and the Library of the Union Society, Cambridge. Like many Welsh writers I also owe a great debt to "Ralph the Books" of Swansea whose bookshop provided me with many important reference works when all other sources had failed. Finally I must thank Miss Elizabeth Day and Mrs J. Imrie for typing the manuscript.

For permission to reproduce copyright material I am grateful to the authors, editors, agents and publishers of the following books: John Wilson, *Reason and Morals,* Cambridge University Press; Lord Devlin, *The Enforcement of Morals,* Oxford University Press; the (USA) *Report of the Commission on Obscenity and Pornography;* Curtis Brown for permission to quote from Konrad Heiden's *Der Führer,* Gollancz; Ernest Benn for permission to quote from Samuel Igra's *Germany's National Vice,* Quality Press; Her Majesty's Stationery Office for permission to quote from the Hansard reports of Parliamentary Proceedings.

Contents

1 Introductory

People must not do things for fun. We are not here for fun.
There is no reference to fun in any Act of Parliament.

SIR A.P. HERBERT, *Uncommon Law*

During the last twenty years Britain is said to have become a "permissive society". In 1964 C. H. and W. M. Whiteley wrote of the general change in morality that has occurred in this century:

> If the change is to be put into a few words it can be described as a general relaxation of standards, a greater permissiveness, a raising of the demands a man may make on life and a lowering of the demands life can make on him.[1]

What has happened in the last twenty years is that the pace of this change has increased. This has been especially true in the last decade. We can see changes occurring at many levels in society which reflect the erosion of traditional values and the growth of a hedonistic and anti-ascetic philosophy. This change has been greatest among young people and has resulted in a good deal of friction and misunderstanding between them and the older generation. Derek Wright carried out two surveys of 17 and 18 year-olds in 1963 and in 1970 to try to measure the changes in moral standards that have taken place. He questioned them about their attitudes to what he termed "anti-social" and "anti-ascetic" acts. He explained his use of these two terms as follows:

> Anti-social acts are those the ill-effects of which are felt primarily and most directly by others. Stealing, physical assault, and lying for personal gain fall into this category. Anti-ascetic acts are forms of

1

individual self-indulgence the undesirable consequences of which if any are felt mainly by those who engage in them—consequences such as personal deterioration and ill-health. Examples are forms of "immoral" sexual behaviour, drunkenness and drug-taking.[2]

His questions related to all these topics and also to gambling, smoking, suicide and racial discrimination. He summed up his results by saying

> condemnation of anti-social actions has declined very little and then only in the direction of a more qualified condemnation. As far as anti-ascetic actions are concerned there has been a considerable change in the direction of a position that, provided no one else is hurt, and in the case of sexual intercourse, provided the couple love each other and are responsible, it is no one's business to pass moral judgements on them.[3]

This rapid change in attitudes in the 1960s has led to a clash between the younger and the older generations. Wright does however suggest another reason for the sharp disagreement between the two groups:

> From the middle twenties [of a person's age] onwards the trend is for moral beliefs to become progressively less flexible and for people to grow less permissive in their judgements. It seems likely that the tendency for older people to think that moral standards have declined reflects this developmental trend towards greater conservatism in themselves as much as it does a genuine social change.[4]

This change in attitudes has been accompanied by changes in behaviour. In the later chapters of this book on sex, drugs, etc., I have attempted to assess what changes have occurred in people's behaviour in these areas. The general conclusion I have come to is that there has been some shift to permissiveness in all these areas and with regard to both anti-social and anti-ascetic actions. People are more likely to indulge in normal and perverse sexual activities, to take drugs of varying degrees of addictiveness and to attack their fellow citizens either in order to rob them or just for the sheer pleasure of it.

The guardians of society's morality have made little attempt to prevent or reverse these changes and indeed did much to encourage and accelerate them. Parliament freed homosexuals from prosecution, legalized abortion, made it easier to get a divorce or to lay a bet, and liberalized the law on censorship. The courts, the broadcasters, the publishers and other bodies also relaxed their attitudes as to what books, plays, films and programmes could be sold or shown. Even stuffy establishment institutions such as the BBC or *The Times* went permissive. One author described the changes in the BBC thus: "Auntie BBC didn't just hitch up her skirt, she took it off altogether".[5]

Even where society continued to condemn an action as immoral, it relaxed its penalties and made punishment more lenient. Capital punishment was abolished and corporal punishment was ended in prisons and curtailed in schools.[6] It would be a mistake, though, to see Parliament and other official bodies as motivated simply by a lust for permissiveness or even a love of freedom. In the chapter on Parliament and on censorship I have chosen rather to depict the changes that have occurred in terms of a shift of moral attitudes from "moralism" to "causalism". In the past the decision as to whether or not to forbid an activity and to punish those responsible for it, was taken on moralist grounds. Those in favour of forbidding it would argue that the activity was wrong, immoral, wicked, and that this was sufficient reason for preventing it and punishing people detected in it. Those who believed that the law should ignore the activity would argue for this position by appealing to man's basic right to be free and to order his own life. Today the arguments for and against forbidding any activity are very different and are rooted in what I have termed causalist morality. Parliament argues today about the consequences of legalizing an activity compared with the consequences of not doing so. If it turns out that more harm is done by forbidding an activity than by allowing it, then Parliament will permit it, even if most of the members consider the activity to be wrong or immoral. On the other hand, activities which no one considers wrong in themselves may be forbidden by law if Parliament or the courts decide that they constitute (through no fault of those indulging in them) an intolerable nuisance.

The distinction between moralism and causalism is not of

course a new one. It is, for example, very similar to Weber's distinction between an "ethic of ultimate ends" and an "ethic of responsibility". In an early letter quoted by Gerth and Mills, Weber wrote "The matter does not appear to me to be so desperate if one does not ask so exclusively 'who is morally right and who is morally wrong?' But if one rather asks 'Given the existing conflict how can I solve it with the least internal and external damage for all concerned?' " Gerth and Mills comment that

> Weber thus suggested a pragmatic view, a focus on the consequences of various decisions rather than on the stubborn insistence upon the introspective awareness of one's intense sincerity. His early letters and the experiences at Strasbourg clearly point to his later distinction between an ethic of responsibility and an ethic of absolute ends.[7]

A similar kind of distinction is made by John Wilson in his book *Reason and Morals* where he talks of "Moralism and Factualism". He is seeking to provide a broader distinction applicable to a wider range of situations than mine but nevertheless there is a great deal of resemblance between the two sets of categories. Wilson describes his terms thus:

> At the philosophical level we may talk of intuitionism and utilitarianism, deontological and teleological ethics, morality of motive and morality of consequence, or *Gesinnungsethik* and *Erfolgsethik*. It will be convenient for our purpose to give titles of a more general kind to either side in this distinction: and for the sake of simplicity I shall use the term Moralism for the first side, and the term Factualism for the second. . . . We can best begin, therefore, by noting some instances where the difference between these two types of ethical thinking seems plain.
>
> (1) First, a difference which suggests that the terms Moralism and Factualism are not too inapposite. Moralists and Factualists seem to defend their beliefs in different ways. Suppose we are discussing divorce by consent, or sexual promiscuity. If a Moralist were opposed to these practices, and asked to defend his opinion, he would say something like "Any decent man knows in his heart that promiscuity is wrong", or "Divorce is against the will of God", or "Your conscience tells you that you mustn't commit adultery". A Factualist would perhaps say "Easy divorce does harm to the children", or "Without sexual morality we should have social chaos". The Moralist defends his view, not by

reference to facts or social results, but by reference to a moral code, or conscience, or religion—all things which are not "facts" in the same sense that a rise in the illegitimate birth-rate is a fact. The Factualist, by contrast, looks for facts and social results, and has no time for a morality that is not closely bound up with them.

(2) Now consider a more general difference. The Moralist will defend morality as a whole (as opposed to particular moral opinions) simply because it *is* morality, not because its constituent parts fulfil any particular purpose. The moral law, some Moralists would say, is a real law which can be known: it presents itself to us as an imperative: it is written in God's commandments or our own consciences. It is not just a convenience. But the Factualist regards moral rules in much the same light as other rules—that is, as useful guides towards achieving certain ends: ultimately they are just a convenience. They have no particular validity in themselves, no absolute authority. If they serve human ends, they are good rules: if they do not, they can be scrapped. To put it briefly: the Moralist thinks you ought to do what is right because it *is* right, whereas the Factualist thinks you ought to do what is right because it is constructive or brings about a good result. Hence the Moralist will talk in terms of duty or obligation: the Factualist will talk about ends and means, the promotion of human happiness, and so on.

(3) In judging human behaviour, the Moralist will concentrate on man's intentions, on his choices, on whether he exercised free will, and on those parts of his personality which (in his view) are alone morally relevant. The Factualist will not make such a sharp division: to him, it might sometimes be just as bad to be stupid as to intend to kill somebody. He will not necessarily grant any unique importance or status to moral intentions or choices. Thus the Moralist will be interested in questions like "What did he intend to do?" or "Did he try to do so-and-so?"—questions that a judge might ask the jury to consider in a lawsuit: whereas the Factualist will consider a man's motives as distinct from his intentions, and ask "What made him do that?" or "What were the causes of his action?"—questions appropriate to a psychologist rather than a judge. The Moralist tries to get in a position where he can say "Guilty" or "Not guilty": the Factualist tries to explain, and to give an overall assessment of a man's character.[8]

Wilson speaks of the dichotomy between intuitionism and utilitarianism as being related to the division between his two "sides"—moralism and factualism. My term "causalism" is related to his "factualism" and to utilitarianism. All causalists are utilitarians, though there are utilitarians who are not causalists—as will be apparent from the discussion of

particular issues in subsequent chapters. The causalists judge
any law or rule by its consequences but they seem to restrict
their considerations of the consequences (and the utility of
the consequences) in two ways. First they consider only the
short-term consequences of their decision to enforce or to
repeal or to enact a particular law. The effect of this in
practice is that they assume that people's moral attitudes are
not affected by their decisions. For example, it was argued
by those in favour of the recent changes in the law regarding
divorce that the new law would enable people whose
marriages had broken down and who wished to remarry to
obtain a divorce and to marry a second time. Many of those
people were already living with their new partners and often
there were children of this new but unrecognized union. The
advocates of reform rightly pointed out on utilitarian
grounds that easier divorce and remarriage would benefit
many more people than it would harm. It could, however, be
argued that in the long run the change in the law would result
in many more marriages breaking up that would have been
stable and contented under the old set of rules. An opponent
of the new divorce law could have argued, also on utilitarian
grounds, that in the long run it would create more misery
than if the law had been left unreformed because it would
have the effect of weakening people's belief in the strength
and security of marriage and the family.[9] However, the
causalists, as I have defined them, would not accept this
argument. They are only concerned with the immediate and
tangible consequences of the law—with things that can be
measured and measured *now*.

Second, the causalist utilitarian is only concerned with
harm, distress, suffering, conflict, i.e. disutility or negative
utility. He is not concerned with positive utility or happiness.
He chooses to enact or to repeal or to support a law so as to
minimize suffering, not in order to maximize happiness, nor
to minimize the excess of suffering over happiness. Only
disutility "below the line" is counted. For example, when
causalists are arguing about whether or not to legalize the
consumption of cannabis, they weigh up the casualties of
allowing free use of the drug against the costs and suffering
of enforcing the law. The fact that for some of the cannabis

users the drug brings them more pleasure than pain is not part of the calculation. Only pain counts. Pleasure only enters into the equation indirectly—in so far as it provides a motive for men to break the law, to suffer punishment and to incite conflict with the authorities. All these are the kinds of "pain" that might lead the authorities to legalize cannabis on the grounds that these pains are greater than those caused by free widespread consumption of the drug. The causalist, particularly, seeks to avoid "conflict" because it is a visible tangible symptom of pain, of disutility. The group that fights to gain its ends is more likely to convince the causalist than one which suffers quietly without any external show of discontent.

Causalism is a form of utilitarianism that looks only at the short term and only at the "painful" consequences of a rule or law. These limitations possibly derive from the difficulties experienced by those who tried to apply the doctrine (of cardinal utilitarianism) in another sphere, viz. economic affairs. There are many problems involved in doing so but two in particular stand out. First it is difficult to make comparisons of the "utility" of various goods and resources to different individuals. Individuals differ in their capacity for pain and pleasure and there is a great deal of controversy about whether comparisons are possible. Those who argue that it is valid to compare and equate different individuals nearly always stress pain or disutility, whereas those who deny the validity of such comparisons draw attention to the marked differences between individuals in their capacity for drawing pleasure from similar goods or situations.[10] Second there is the problem of time. When we wish to maximize utility or minimize disutility—over what period of time do we choose to do so? In general it is held that pleasure today is worth more than pleasure tomorrow, and pain today is worse than pain tomorrow. We naturally choose to look only at the short term consequences of our economic or moral-legal decisions. If we do look at the future at all, we discount it in such a way as to make the impact of future pains, the loss of future pleasures, a matter of small importance. Eat drink and be merry, for "in the long run we are all dead".

In analysing the attitudes and decisions of Parliament and other moral authorities in British society I have often found the concepts of moralism and causalism more useful than the concept "permissiveness". The rules were relaxed in the 1950s and 1960s, but this was not simply because of a commitment to permissiveness on the part of Parliament.[11] Rather there was a more fundamental shift from moralism to causalism at this time which produced a spate of permissive legislation. There is, however, no reason why such a shift should necessarily result in changes in a permissive direction. On some occasions (e.g. when the breathalyser was introduced) the triumph of causalism over moralism resulted in legislation that was restrictive rather than permissive, and it is quite possible that over the next twenty years we shall see Parliament enact a great deal more restrictive legislation for causalist reasons.

The term "permissiveness" is not a very useful one except as a general description of the social changes of the last twenty years. In looking at particular activities such as drug-taking or homosexuality the most interesting questions do not stem from the general question "Has Britain become more permissive?" One is forced to supplement this question with other questions about international differences (in the case of drugs) or about the changing importance of the military (in the case of homosexuality). In particular I have tried to use data from other societies as well as Britain in order to throw some light on our own permissive society.

It is interesting to look at the changes that have taken place in the United States, a society that is in many ways similar to our own yet with some very different cultural traditions. In the last ten to twenty years America has similarly shifted in a permissive direction but the change has been more thorough, more drastic and more divisive than in England. Moralism, not causalism, still prevails as the predominant mode of argument in America and their society can almost be seen as two hostile camps: those committed, on moralist grounds, to permissiveness (who are chiefly young and either very rich or very poor) and those committed, on even more moralist grounds, to stamping it out.

Looking at both Britain and America, one cannot help feeling that we have been here before. The wave of permissiveness and of inter-generational conflict that swamped America in the 1960s is very similar to the earlier wave that hit that country in the 1920s. If, for example, we look at the changes in sexual *mores* of the 1960s, we can see that a very similar period of rapid change occurred in the 1920s. Kinsey in his studies of America's sex-life noted that

> During the four decades on which we have data no other aspect of the behaviour of the American female seems to have changed as much as petting and pre-marital coitus. The major change seems to have occurred in the generation born in the first decade after 1900. This was the generation that was in its teens and early twenties during the first world war and in the years immediately following that war.[12]

If we look at Kinsey's figures for what he terms "active incidence of orgasm" for women experiencing it by the time they reached the age-group 21–25 we get the following picture:

Women Enjoying Active Incidence of
Orgasm as Percentage of Age Group

Date of Birth	%
pre-1900	15
1900–09	32
1910–19	34
1920–29	37

Clearly there is a big change in the extent of female sexual experience between the first and second groups and thereafter a fairly constant situation

There was a big shift to permissiveness during and just before the 1920s and then a slow move towards even greater permissiveness in the years that followed. This sudden change naturally caused a great deal of inter-generational conflict in America between the younger generation which sought sexual freedom and the older generation which tried to uphold traditional moral values. The Lynds, in their study of a typical American town in the inter-war period, commented:

It is our impression that no two generations of Americans have ever faced each other across so wide a gap in their customary attitudes and behaviour as have American parents and children since the (first) world war.[13]

That passage sounds as if it were written today, but in fact it is taken from a book published in 1937. The literature and journalism of the 1920s and early 1930s supports the findings of Kinsey and the Lynds. In Sinclair Lewis's novel *Babbitt*, Babbitt's reaction to a party given at his home by his teenage son (in about 1921) could, with suitable amendments, be written today:

He [Babbitt] was deeply disquieted. Eight years ago when Verona had given a high-school party the children had been featureless gobies. Now they were men and women of the world, very supercilious men and women: . . . Babbitt had heard stories of what the Athletic Club called "goings-on" at young parties . . . of "cuddling" and "petting" and a presumable increase in what was known as Immorality. Tonight he believed the stories. These children seemed bold to him and cold . . . . Their stockings were of lustrous silk, their slippers costly and unnatural, their lips carmined and their eyebrows pencilled. They danced cheek to cheek with the boys and Babbitt sickened with apprehension and unconscious envy . . . . The boys and girls disappeared occasionally and he remembered rumours of their drinking together from hip-pocket flasks. He tiptoed round the house and in each of the dozen cars waiting in the street he saw the points of light from cigarettes, from each of them he heard high giggles. He wanted to denounce them but (standing in the snow, peering round the dark corner) he did not dare . . . . But he resolved, if he found that the boys were drinking, he would—well he'd "hand them something that would surprise 'em". While he was trying to be agreeable to large-shouldered young bullies he was earnestly sniffing at them. Twice he caught the reek of prohibition-time whiskey.[14]

We can see a similar scene in Scott Fitzgerald's *This Side of Paradise* (1920):

None of the Victorian mothers—and most of the mothers were Victorian—had any idea how casually their daughters were accustomed to be kissed . . . . Amory saw girls doing things that even in his memory would have been impossible; eating at three-o'clock after dance suppers in impossible cafés, talking of every side of life with an air half of earnestness, half of mockery, yet with a furtive excitement that Amory considered stood for a real moral let-down. But he never realized how widespread it was . . . until he saw the cities between New York and Chicago as one vast juvenile intrigue.[15]

The reaction of the Amorys and the Babbitts to all this was summed up by F.L. Allen (1930):

Meanwhile innumerable families were torn with dissension over cigarettes and gin and all-night automobile rides. Fathers and Mothers lay awake asking themselves whether their children were not utterly lost; sons and daughters evaded questions, lied miserably and unhappily, or flared up to reply rudely that at least they were not dirty-minded hypocrites, that they saw no harm in what they were doing and proposed to go right on doing it. From those liberal clergymen and teachers who prided themselves on keeping step with all that was new, came a chorus of reassurance; these young people were at least franker and more honest than their elders had been; having experimented for themselves, would they not soon find out which standards were outworn and which represented the accumulated moral wisdom of the race?[16]

It all sounds horribly familiar. Update the clothes and the dances, take the sexual antics a little further, substitute cannabis for the equally illegal "prohibition-time whiskey" and we are back in present-day America. We are also in present-day Britain, for the same changes took place here, only in a more moderate and dignified fashion. James Pope-Hennessy speaks of the 1920s as the "new post-war generation with its driving wish for freedom from tradition and convention whatever the cost",[17] a kind of cliché that can currently be found in any number of articles on permissiveness and the young.[18]

If we could plot permissiveness against time for either America or Britain, we would see that over time society gets progressively more permissive with particularly rapid rates of change in the 1920s and the 1960s and slower (but perceptible) rates of change in the intervening decades.

Even the explanations for the permissiveness of the 1920s have a modern ring about them. In America, at any rate, the 1920s was an "affluent" period. The rapid growth of the economy led to a general prosperity for most (but not all) of the groups in that society and to the economic independence of the young and of American women. To some extent then America became permissive because it became wealthy. The old restraints seemed unnecessary in this new rich world of high mass-consumption and the rapidity and unpredictability with which many people's incomes rose had an unsettling, anomic effect on their economic and moral outlook. It was a rapidly changing, unstable world in all senses. In Britain, by contrast, there was a great deal of unemployment and a stubborn recession. Permissiveness was limited to the more prosperous members of society such as the "bright young things" of Evelyn Waugh's novels.[19]

The other causes put forward all sound equally familiar—increased urbanization, the decline of religious belief, increased mobility, the effect of the cinema (1920s) and television (1960s). In America one must also add the effect of prohibition (cf. cannabis in the 1960s) and of the disillusionment and isolationism that followed World War I (cf. Vietnam in the 1960s).

Yet one may wonder why it should be necessary to seek an explanation for permissiveness whether in Britain or America, whether in the 1920s or in the 1960s. In a sense an easy hedonistic state of society does not call for an explanation. Rather, one wonders why it has ever been any different. It is the anti-permissive episodes in history that are baffling—the Reformation with its Puritans and Calvinists, the rise of Methodism, the transformation of the permissive and squalid eighteenth century of Hogarth into the Victorian England that strove (with moderate effect) to replace gin with temperance, the great Welsh revivals.[20] This is not merely an academic question, for only by knowing the mechanisms by which such social changes occur can we hope to control and if necessary halt and reverse the permissive society.

2 Parliament and the Permissive Society

Permissive legislation is the characteristic of a free people.

BENJAMIN DISRAELI

One demonstrable sign of the growth of permissiveness in British society has been the consistent tendency over the last twenty years for Parliament to alter laws governing moral conduct in a permissive direction. Activities which society had previously disapproved of and banned are now permitted and can be freely indulged in.[1] Perhaps the most striking of these is the abolition of most of the laws prohibiting homosexual acts between consenting male adults. As regards other matters, it is now much easier than it was to get a divorce or an abortion, to place cash bets on the dogs or the horses, to indulge in tombola or bingo or to get a drink on a Sunday west of Offa's dyke. In addition censorship of the press, books and the theatre is much less severe than it was, not simply because the censors have relaxed their standards but by conscious decree of Parliament embodied in the Obscene Publications Act and the Theatres Act. There are, it is true, some new restrictions on individual conduct such as the breathalyser and the Race Relations Act, but these do not really offset the general trend to permissiveness. Nor can it be said that the Street Offences Act has in any serious sense interrupted the ancient trade of prostitution. Rather it simply confirmed that prostitution was widespread in Britain and that Parliament did not propose to interfere with it except to prevent prostitutes being a public nuisance. Even for those acts that remained the subject of strong legal sanctions permissiveness prevailed in that punishments were reduced and to that extent such actions became more

13

permissible. Perhaps the most important change in this last category was the abolition of the death penalty for murder. All these acts of permissive legislation together with some bills that never reached the statute book but which would have pushed the country even further in a permissive direction indicate that Parliament was directly or indirectly converted to a permissive view of society.

Some of the parliamentary acts, such as those relating to censorship, to drugs and to homosexuality, are discussed in other chapters. The main issues discussed here are the changes in the laws relating to abortion, divorce and punishment for murder.

Although these changes do indicate a general shift towards permissive attitudes in Parliament and in the country at large this is not the predominant impression one gets from reading the debates in the House of Commons that preceded the enactment of individual acts of permissive legislation. Parliament was at no stage seized with a zeal for permissiveness which led it to alter eagerly all the restrictive legislation it had inherited from its predecessors (though this may have been true of a minority of new young MPs). That this is the case is shown by the relatively low correlations between Members' votes on the private Members' Bills.[2] Clearly individual MPs cannot easily be typecast as permissive or anti-permissive in their attitudes. Other factors also determine what will be their attitude on any particular issue. Again, those MPs who spoke in the debates on the "moral" issues did not on the whole use moralist language. In particular those who advocated a shift in a permissive direction did not urge such a change on the grounds that permissive values were right and should prevail. Rather each issue was debated in terms of the consequences of banning or controlling a particular activity and the consequences of not doing so. Where it was felt that to use legal means to suppress some disapproved act created more problems than it solved, Parliament was willing to amend the law and to try to use more subtle means of social control. The dominant mood of the Parliamentary debates was not one of moral clash between the permissives and the suppressers but one of factual disagreement about the consequences of legal interference in certain areas. It was suggested in Chapter 1 that there had been a shift in moral thinking in Britain from "moralism" to "causalism". How far this theory is true for the British people as a whole is debatable but it certainly seems to be true of their Parliamentary representatives. This can be seen if we consider examples of the debates as recorded in Hansard on the so-called permissive legislation of the period 1950—74 and this view is reinforced by a comparison with earlier debates on such issues.

The most obvious examples of legislation embodying the change from moralist to causalist patterns of moral thinking are the various acts altering the law relating to gambling, the Abortion Reform Act and the Divorce Reform Act. Nowhere is the shift more apparent than in the changes in the law relating to divorce. The old law relating to divorce clearly embodied moralist thinking on this issue. The new law by contrast is based on moral principles of a causalist type.

DIVORCE REFORM

Before the 1967 Divorce Act (operating from 1 January 1971) divorce was only possible if either husband or wife had committed a "matrimonial offence". The standard matrimonial offences were adultery, cruelty and desertion. To each divorce there was an "innocent" and "guilty" party. A divorce action consisted essentially of an accusation by husband or wife that their spouse was guilty of one of these offences. The spouse could either allow the divorce to go through undefended, thus tacitly admitting guilt, or could contest the divorce. If the divorce was contested then the courts settled the issue by a process in many ways similar to a criminal trial. Indeed the person accused of a matrimonial offence was described as *defending* the action. The accusatorial procedure with its two clearly separated and opposing sides, the ruthless cross-examination of witnesses by counsel, the angry recriminations, the accusations and counter-accusations, the giving of evidence by detectives and inquiry agents, all reminded the participants in a contested divorce action that the purpose and function of the court was to determine guilt and innocence. The petitioner sought to

prove to the court and to the world that his or her spouse
was guilty of a matrimonial offence. The spouse sought to
deny this, to assert his or her innocence and even to show
that it was the petitioner who was really the guilty party. A
divorce became a prize that was awarded to the innocent
party, a penalty imposed on the guilty spouse. The divorce
procedure aimed at attaching the correct moral labels to the
two parties. If no offence had been committed or at any rate
if there was no evidence before the court that proved such an
offence to the court's satisfaction then no divorce would be
awarded, however clear it was that the marriage had broken
down. In order for there to be a divorce someone had to be
found to take the blame and usually the whole blame. In
theory there could be no divorce by consent of the parties.
Where a matrimonial offence had occurred the initiator of a
divorce action had, of course, to be the innocent party.
Unless the innocent party was willing to take such action,
then the guilty person could do nothing to end the marriage
and was unable to remarry, however pressing his or her need
or wish to do so. In such a case the guilty person was felt to
have received his or her deserts and it was felt proper that the
innocent party should have the right to withhold consent to
the legal severing of the marriage tie. Fairness was seen as the
distribution of rights and penalties according to the moral
worthiness of the parties.

In practice there was of course a great deal of divorce by
consent. As the social stigma of being the guilty party in a
divorce faded, many husbands and wives were willing to
admit to a real or pretended matrimonial offence in order
that the court should grant their spouse a divorce. Both sides
gained a release from an unhappy marriage and the opportunity to remarry. The issue of innocence or guilt had
become irrelevant because people had ceased to see divorce in
these terms. There was a growing gap between what was
discussed or decided in court and the real negotiation and
agreement between husband and wife which was often settled
before the case ever came to court. At best the courts were
becoming a rubber stamp to agreements reached elsewhere.
In addition deliberate attempts to deceive the court became
widespread.

By contrast the new procedures for divorce do not seek to determine guilt or innocence, they are concerned rather to decide whether or not a marriage has irretrievably broken down. Ironically the standard matrimonial offences remain relevant not as offences but as criteria for deciding whether the marriage has or has not broken down. The new situation is well summed up by Professor Richards:

... the 1967 Bill was based on the breakdown of marriage principle, yet the standard matrimonial offences remained not as offences but as evidence of the breakdown of a marriage. Thus a petitioner has a prima facie right to divorce where the other spouse has committed adultery, has behaved cruelly, has deserted the matrimonial home two years previously, where the marriage partners have lived apart for two years and neither objects to divorce, and where one partner does object provided the separation has lasted five years. In all circumstances the court must be satisfied that the marriage has broken down irretrievably. Thus it is not sufficient to show that the respondent has committed adultery; the petitioner must also satisfy the court that he or she now finds it intolerable to live with the respondent.[3]

The new law is not a complete departure from the old since there is considerable overlap in the issues which are considered by the divorce courts. Indeed one is led to wonder whether the acrimony and recrimination associated in the past with the need to prove a matrimonial offence against one's spouse will not reappear in a new guise as the parties seek to convince the court how disastrously their marriage has broken down, citing (and perhaps inventing) matrimonial offences as evidence of this. However, the matrimonial offences no longer occupy the central position in divorce proceedings that they did in the past. They are now neither necessary nor sufficient criteria for the granting of a divorce. They are merely one cluster of reasons among many others for seeking and gaining a divorce. The "innocent" partner is no longer assured of getting a divorce simply by demonstrating that a matrimonial offence has been committed by his or her spouse. Nor is such an innocent party able to prevent the other partner from gaining a divorce and possibly remarrying provided they have been separated for five years. A marriage can now be ended whether the parties agree or

not and even against the will of the "innocent" partner.
The issue of innocence or guilt is no longer the crucial one
and the law, instead of asking the question "Who is to
blame?", asks rather "What is the best course of action to
take in this situation?" The aims of the new law are perhaps
best summed up in the Law Commission's earlier report on
this subject[4] They are:

"(i) To buttress rather than undermine the stability of
marriage.

(ii) Where, regrettably a marriage has irretrievably
broken down, to enable the empty legal shell to be
destroyed with maximum fairness and the minimum
bitterness, distress and humiliation."

In some ways this is more realistic since, when a marriage
collapses, it is rarely the case that one partner is entirely to
blame and one entirely free from blame. To attempt to sort
people into these two categories and to allocate rights and
powers accordingly was, to put it mildly, a difficult task. It
was made more difficult by the incentive it gave the parties in
a contested action to try and conceal their own faults and to
pin the blame entirely on the spouse. Even in uncontested
actions it led to collusion and to deceptions and distortions,
though of a different kind.

Since the change in the law the court is now concerned
simply to decide whether there has been a real breakdown of
the marriage or whether there is some chance of reconciliation. The aim is to find an optimal solution as fair as possible
to all the parties concerned. This solution may not be a
divorce but a prolonged and possibly successful attempt to
reconcile the parties. Indeed it is probably easier now to
effect such a reconciliation since an attempt by the parties to
make their marriage work by living together for a prolonged
trial period of reconciliation is no longer a barrier to their
getting divorced ultimately if this trial should fail. In the past
such an attempt at reconciliation would have been regarded
as condonation of the matrimonial offence. Under those
circumstances an innocent party seeking a divorce would take
care to rebuff any attempts at reconciliation, lest it
undermine his or her position *vis-à-vis* the divorce court.

However, if it is clear that a marriage has failed the court may decide that to grant a divorce is to decree less harmful consequences than to withhold it. An unwilling "innocent" party may feel aggrieved at being divorced but this may be considerably outweighed by benefits to other persons. By this time the "guilty" party may be living with a new if legally unrecognized partner and they may have children. If a divorce is granted these people can marry and thus render the children legitimate. The benefits not merely to the guilty person but to the new "spouse" and to their children of having this relationship ratified and recognized are enormous. Even where there are children of the first marriage a clear recognition of the breakdown of their parents' marriage may be more in their interest than an uncertain situation or one in which the home is rendered unhappy by continual disputes. Where a marriage has broken down in this way divorce may be the optimum solution from the point of view of the children. It is this kind of weighing up of alternative consequences that underlies the new divorce law rather than the issue of guilt or innocence.

It was considerations of this sort that dominated the Parliamentary debates on the issue. The key issues discussed and the main objections raised related not to the moral or religious issues involved but to the welfare of the children of the marriage and other dependent persons. Even the opponents of the reforms accepted the causalist framework of argument. They disputed the factual basis of the reformers' case, they queried the relative balance of consequences between the reformed and the unreformed situation. What they did not do was to take up the moralist point of view implicit in the old law. They sought rather to justify the old arrangements in terms of the new criteria being used by the reformers. Professor Richards demonstrates this by a neat piece of analysis of the voting on various amendments during the all-night sitting of 12—13 June 1969:

> During the night and the following morning many amendments were debated, most of which sought to limit the scope for divorce. Seven of the amendments were put to the vote and defeated: . . . . The highest opposition vote was 58 in support of an amendment to delete the

qualification "or the best that can be made in the circumstances" from the court's power to impose an equitable and satisfactory financial settlement as a condition of divorce. This demonstrates again that the biggest obstacle faced by reformers was not religious but concern about the material well-being of families broken by divorce.[5]

However at an earlier point Professor Richards comments that:

... one has the feeling that there is a gap between the arguments used and the driving force behind the arguments. In political debate it is common for what is said to be that which is thought to be the most acceptable and persuasive. Basic feelings and ideas are suppressed sometimes consciously for fear that they will detract from chances of success.[6]

This observation is almost certainly true. It is certainly difficult to explain the very high correlation of voting with religious belief on any other basis. It is unlikely that the cause of this association is simply that Roman Catholics and Anglicans show a greater concern for the material well-being of the broken family than do Nonconformists and Jews.

Debate on Divorce Reform Act
Correlation of Voting with Religious Beliefs of MPs[7]

Vote on Divorce	Yes	No
Roman Catholic	3	13
Anglican	32	39
Free Church	20	7
Jews	13	4
Atheist/Agnostic	29	—

Rather one suspects that many who opposed the bill on causalist grounds are moralists in disguise. This, however, does not refute the view that there has been a shift from moralist to causalist modes of viewing and discussing moral issues. Rather it shows that the victory of the causalists has been so total that not merely are they able to defeat the moralists and push through causalist based moral legislation but also they can compel the moralists to discuss it in their terms. The moralists cannot even oppose such measures in moralist terms. Had they done so their defeat would have been even more complete. In order even to try to oppose legislation put forward on causalist grounds they are forced, much against their will, to argue in terms of consequences rather than the moral standards they would have preferred to use. They cannot go down to defeat openly, fighting for their principles, but are forced into a posture where they can easily be accused of bad faith.

ABORTION

The same accusation cannot be as easily levelled at the opponents of the Abortion Act. Although for tactical reasons they constructed a mainly causalist case they also strongly put forward moralist objections to the new legislation. Indeed at times they, and even more their supporters outside Parliament, alienated opinion in the predominantly causalist legislature by putting forward strong moralist arguments. The supporters of the reform put forward a predominantly causalist case, stressing the alternative sets of consequences stemming from the law if reformed and if left as it was. They did not stress the moralist aspects of their case. They did not urge the cause of individual freedom, or of women's rights or of the permissive society. They simply stressed that legalized abortion was the lesser of two evils. As David Steel, the sponsor of the Abortion Bill, stressed in the House of Commons "We have to avoid in the Bill wording which is so restrictive as not to have the effect we are seeking, namely the ending of the back-street abortions .... Finally those who wish to oppose this Bill have to consider the effect of their opposition ...."[8] The essentially causalist nature of the reformer's arguments was also noted by one of the Abortion Bill's principal opponents, Dr Norman St John-Stevas who observed that "The case for the Bill has rested partly on utilitarian considerations—that there is a high number of illegal abortions and that this bill would reduce them."[9] The reformer's case was consistently presented in terms of the need to clarify that law and to replace the

unsafe procedures of unqualified abortionists by medically
supervised operations even if this meant allowing and
condoning an activity that many people regarded as abhorrent. Always the stress was placed on specific issues and the
limited number of alternative procedures available in particular situations. The wider moral and philosophic issues were
played down. Cause and effect dominated their arguments,
not the assertion of rights and values.

To some extent their opponents were trapped in the same
dilemma as the opponents of the divorce reforms. They
clearly felt a great deal of moral repugnance towards abortion
and yet realized that they could not successfully oppose the
Abortion Bill on this basis. Professor Richards succinctly
sums up the way in which they perceived and attempted to
resolve the dilemma:

> Equally there was no unanimity of view among those who opposed
> any extension of grounds for abortion. The strict Catholic position,
> that once a human life had been conceived it must not be extinguished,
> was put forward in both Houses. On this fundamentalist view the
> Bourne judgment (a judicial decision that the law permitted therapeutic
> abortion under certain circumstances) was unacceptable. However, no
> serious attempt was made to attack the *status quo* and the arguments
> advanced against change were essentially practical and limited in scope,
> emphasizing fears of unfortunate consequences which might follow
> from any change in the law. Such tactics were obviously good sense: a
> theological crusade against abortion was certain to fail in a pre-
> dominantly non-Catholic legislature.[10]

The opposition to the Abortion Bill was forced to
concentrate on the consequences of the new legislation—the
bad after-effects of the operation on some women, the failure
of liberal legislation in other countries to eliminate illegal
abortion, the strain on the National Health Service, the
difficulty of diagnosing abnormality in a foetus. This kind of
argument had some success. The number of MPs opposed to
the Abortion Bill rose at each stage of the debate. At the
second reading 225 members voted for the Bill and only 31
against. By the third reading only 169 remained in favour and
85 were against.[11] They also tried to cast doubt on the
general argument of the causalist reformers that liberalizing

the law in such areas tended to alleviate social problems. As William Deedes put it "I grow rather mistrustful of the doctrine that the right cure for a social abuse is to legalize it with suitable restraints. We tried that once with gambling and the experience there does not encourage me to apply that doctrine to this far more difficult subject."[1][2]

The opponents of the Bill also pressed two moralist arguments of very different kinds which served to rally the faithful but which probably harmed their cause in the context of a legislature dominated by causalist-minded members. The first of the moralist arguments was that abortion was morally wicked. This was strongly advanced in objection to two aspects of the original Bill, the social clause which permitted abortion in the interests of the general well-being of the mother and her existing children, and the eugenic clause which permitted abortion if there was a risk of the child being deformed or mentally retarded. The former was seen as objectionable since it weighed up the life of the foetus not against the life or health of the mother which might be expected to arouse comparable moral sympathy but against the apparently material criteria of social well-being. The latter was seen as the thin end of the wedge to euthanasia and as raising a further absolute moral objection. Dr Norman St John Stevas stated this objection: "It provides for abortion if there is substantial risk that the child may suffer from physical or mental abnormalities so as to be seriously handicapped. That introduces quite a new principle into the law namely that one human being can make a judgement about another as to whether that human being's life is worth living".[13] The opponents of the Bill in Parliament, however, gauging the mood and style of the House accurately, did not press these arguments too hard. It was outside Parliament that strong and, from the point of view of the opponents of the Bill, disastrous moralist arguments were pressed. Once again Professor Richards provides a good instance of this. "Even more damaging to the cause of the S.P.U.C. (Society for the Protection of the Unborn Child) was the attempt at shock tactics and the extravagance of language used at some of its meetings. Dr Margaret White was reported as saying: 'Unborn babies have no votes and they are to be sacrificed to placate extreme left-wing members of the party who are restive about the slaughter in Vietnam and the wages freeze. Rather than melt frozen wages too quickly the Government is preparing to allow thousands of unborn children to be burned in incinerators'. The tactical stupidity of a speech of this kind needs no emphasis."[14] It is not just the language and the imagery on their own that display stupidity but the way in which this kind of outburst cuts right across the dominant causalist mode of argument. It is simply shrugged aside by the undeterred causalist. As Angus Maude put it in the House of Commons when referring to the kind of moralist argument that spoke of "killing unborn babies": "It concentrates attention in the most emotionally possible way on the act of termination of pregnancy without considering what is much more important—the results of doing it and the circumstances in which it is done."[15]

The other objection by the moralists to the Abortion Bill was that it gave abortions to the wrong people—to people who did not deserve an abortion. On this view abortion ought to be granted according to the moral deserts of the mother and child. The foetus ought not to be destroyed not because it is human but because it is innocent. The innocent foetus can, however, have its rights disregarded if the mother is even more innocent and sinned against than the embryo, for example where she is the victim of a rape. The chief exponent of this view was Mrs Jill Knight who found abortion abhorrent but was prepared to allow this abhorrence to be overridden by her even greater abhorrence of rape. The following two quotations from her speeches in the debate taken from Hansard illustrate this:

(1) Once we accept that it is lawful to kill a human being because it causes inconvenience where do we end? Society or at any rate the majority in this house has already conceded that the life of a convicted murderer shall be preserved. How can we possibly agree to that and yet kill the most innocent of all things, an unborn baby? It just does not seem to be logical.[16]

(2) .... when I outlined the method of operation required for this horrible abortion, I said that one must have good reason for it. I said that it was not enough that the child was not wanted. An act of rape

completely changes the character of this ordeal. If the right honourable Lady reads my speeches she will see that I have said consistently that rape must be regarded as a horrible experience and that it was quite unfair to ask a woman to carry through a pregnancy resulting from rape[17]... The right honourable Lady pointed out that cases of rape are covered by Clause 1 (i,a) (i.e. the victim of a rape could get an abortion on the grounds that to bear the rapist's child would damage her health or well-being) and she quoted what I said in committee but again she did not quote all I said. I then made it clear that I regarded these circumstances as meriting special consideration. I want to see rape spelled out clearly as a particular reason for abortion. If women know that without any argument they could get an abortion after rape if they reported it immediately, they would be much more ready to report it.[18]

The implication of this argument is that a woman who has been raped deserves an abortion not because she is liable to suffer most but because she is free of all blame. Rape was an involuntary act from her point of view. She did not will it. She is indeed in the most deserving of the moralist's categories. She is a victim. The essentially moralist aspect of Mrs Knight's arguments was stressed by Roy Jenkins who noted "(abortion) is a very nasty business which should be resorted to only in certain circumstances but one does not necessarily take the easy view that she does that an abortion may be for a good or a bad reason."[19]

The House of Commons, however, rejected both this clause and the clauses granting an abortion automatically where the mother was under 16 or a mentally defective. (These cases are very similar to that of rape. A criminal offence is involved because the woman could not in any real sense be said to have consented. Thus the young girl or the defective can be regarded as innocent victims of circumstances beyond their control.) In all these cases they preferred to let the criteria be one of harm to the mother or her family rather than one of guilt or innocence. Both Angus Maude and Sir John Hobson argued that the problems of the innocent were dealt with under other clauses, i.e. they did not deserve different and special consideration because of their moral position.

Angus Maude on the case of the girl under 16 argued:

Nor do I accept that it automatically follows that the results of the pregnancy will be disastrous. After all if the girl is liable to suffer serious physical or mental damage she is covered by paragraph (a).[20]

Sir John Hobson similarly argued against automatic abortion for the "defective" mother:

I have a great deal of doubt about whether it is right to terminate a pregnancy because the mother is defective. If, however, the reason is given that there is a strong possibility that the mother being a defective may suffer serious consequences as a result of having the child why cannot she be dealt with under paragraph (a)? If on the other hand the reason is the risk that the child itself will be seriously handicapped, then the point is already dealt with under paragraph (b)[21]

Sir John Hobson also chaired a committee that published a booklet entitled *Abortion, A Conservative View*, in which a general causalist view on such cases was firmly stated:

. . . our proposed second ground would, however, enable the doctors to consider fully whether the circumstances in which the conception had or was believed by their woman patient to have taken place were such as to make it desirable for the sake of her future mental or physical health to terminate her pregnancy.

We think this to be sufficient. It would permit operation in almost every case of very young or immature girls according to their actual mental and physical condition—which is the right test—and not according to the age limits rigidly fixed by the criminal law or the knowledge which the man had or ought to have had of the girl's age—which we think is the wrong test. No doubt most cases of rape and many other cases of criminal conception would justify operation by reason of the risk of injury to the mental health of any woman who had conceived a child in such circumstances. We repeat our view, however, that the effect on the woman and not the criminality of the man ought to be the test which doctors should consider and apply.[22]

Interestingly the great British public seemed to be in favour of this kind of moralist argument. In general public opinion as measured by the pollsters was strongly in favour of reforming the abortion laws—thus a National Opinion Poll Survey in 1965 showed 72 per cent in favour of reform.[23] But people were far more in favour of abortion for deserving categories of women than for the feckless or promiscuous. There was a strong majority in favour of abortion where the mother's mental or physical health might suffer if she bore the child and for cases where a woman became pregnant as a result of rape. But there was no majority in favour of abortion where the woman was under 16 or unmarried or liable to suffer financial and material hardship. A clear line seems to have been drawn between cases where the woman is innocent or not in control of her situation (ill-health is generally regarded as unwilled and unlucky and hence such a person *deserves* sympathy) and cases where her condition and prospects are seen rather to stem from her own past or future wickedness, carelessness or folly.

CAPITAL PUNISHMENT

The debates on capital punishment in Parliament are interesting because of the variety of both moralist and causalist arguments which occur on both sides. Among those in favour of retaining the death penalty are moralists who see it as a just retribution for the crime of murder or as a means of reinforcing society's moral abhorrence of such a wicked crime by emphatically denouncing and condemning the murderer and causalists who believe that fear of the death penalty deters those who are tempted to commit murder. Among the abolitionists are moralists who see the death penalty as so wrong in itself that it should be done away with regardless of whether or not it deters and those who see the very existence of the death penalty as having a harmful effect on society in general, and on the attitudes of ordinary people. There are also causalists among the ranks of the abolitionists—those who regard the death penalty as an ineffective deterrent or who fear that an error in the course of a trial for capital murder could lead to an innocent man being hanged. For this last group it is the irreversibility of the death penalty that renders it incompatible with an ethic of responsibility.[24] In the past there have even been those who have argued that the death penalty should be abolished in order that the guilty should be more easily convicted since, if the consequences of a guilty verdict were less drastic, not so awesomely irreversible, juries would be more willing to convict. Capital punishment is an issue in which the retentionists and the abolitionists cannot be labelled respectively "moralists" and "causalists". The situation is summed up in the Table below.

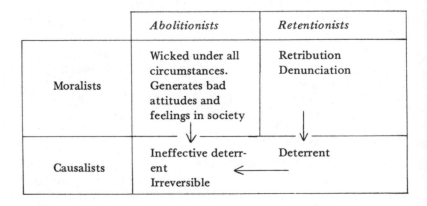

	Abolitionists	*Retentionists*
Moralists	Wicked under all circumstances. Generates bad attitudes and feelings in society	Retribution Denunciation
Causalists	Ineffective deterrent Irreversible	Deterrent

The process by which the legislature moved towards abolishing the death penalty is shown by the arrows in the Table. There is a general shift over time from moralist to causalist attitudes towards the issue by both sides so that the issue of deterrence became more and more crucial. Finally there is a change in factual beliefs about the effectiveness of capital punishment as a deterrent and this gives the final victory to the abolitionists. It is of course much easier to change one's opinion on an issue of fact in this way, than to make the more difficult jump from being a believer in retribution to finding capital punishment totally abhorrent. The issue is also correspondingly less divisive since individuals simply disagree about the facts of deterrence, rather than taking up totally irreconcilable moral positions. The various moral positions taken up by individuals who see morality in terms of consequences lie on a continuum, whereas those who see morality in terms of ultimate moral ends are often totally separated by their opposed and dichotomous views. In a society dominated by causalist modes of moral thinking it is not merely easier for individuals to change their views but also easier for general social changes to occur without undue disruption and opposition. If those who do not believe that capital punishment is a deterrent defeat those who do and succeed in abolishing capital punishment, there is no great clash of moral values, the retentionists do not feel that their unique moral views (which they may also see as being basic to their society's overall pattern of values and traditions) have been overturned and a new and heinous moral outlook imposed on their country. If the same change (abolition) occurred in a society dominated by moralist attitudes, then the very process of change would polarize the society into two totally opposed moral camps. The losers would see the change as utterly disastrous and would either continue in strident opposition or totally withdraw from participation in the society and lapse into apathetic alienation from the new moral order. Societies characterized by intense moral senti-ments of the moralist kind are very cohesive so long as there is general consensus about the values of the society and the ways in which they are applied through particular procedures. However, if a disagreement does arise—say over whether or not to abolish capital punishment—then the society finds it very difficult to resolve the issue, even where the moral feelings of both sides may stem from similar basic moral values—in this case the sanctity of human life and an abhorrence of taking it. Any moral disagreement can easily lead to a polarization of attitudes in this way and reveals the potential instability of such a society, despite the apparent strength and vitality of its collective conscience. In a causalist thinking society moral sentiments are less intense and the ties which bind its members together less coherent. But the moral solidarity of such a society lies elsewhere—it lies rather in the common procedures of thought, debate and action through which its moral sentiments are expressed. Its members are united by a common disposition to see moral issues and their relation to law in terms of cause and effect, by jointly considering (and even disagreeing about) the consequences of particular measures and by compromising over the details of what action to take. In such a society a change over an issue such as capital punishment is less drastic, more likely to be settled by compromise and it is always possible that at some future time the change may be reversed.[25] Neither the change nor the possibility of its failure or reversal is seen by either side as a moral disaster. The recent history of legislation on capital punishment in Britain is one of compromise and slow change precisely because the legislature had come to be dominated by causalist attitudes. Two such interesting compromises during the last twenty years were the Homicide Act of 1957 which abolished capital punishment for certain categories of murder but retained it for others and the clause in the Murder (Abolition of the Death Penalty) Bill 1965 which provided that the Bill should only remain in force for five years, after which it should only continue to apply if both Houses of Parliament voted to renew it. This was the only clause on which the abolitionists were defeated (by a big majority—176 votes to 128)[26] which indicates the tendency of causalists to keep all options open, to allow themselves the possibility of reversing a piece of legislation if the hypothetical cause and effect relationships on which it is based turn out to be invalid.

The 1957 Homicide Act is based entirely on causalist arguments. It prescribed the death penalty for certain categories of murder only, not because they were the most heinous but because it was postulated that murderers of this kind were the most likely to be deterred from killing by the threat of execution. The capital murders were: killing in the course of theft; the killing of policemen and prison officers; killing by shooting or an explosion; and committing (i.e. more than one) murder on separate occasions. These were seen as "rational" murders, murders as a means to an end, by criminals who were presumed to calculate the rewards and penalties involved in any criminal enterprise that might involve killing. This was in contrast to the impulsive murders, often in a family context, by people who simply found an emotional situation unbearable and used murder as a way out. Certain types of murder which are generally thought to be the most vile did not carry the death penalty—the child murderer, the sex murderer, the poisoner, could all be found guilty only of non-capital murder. When Parliament debated the Murder (Abolition of the Death Penalty) Bill, which was to replace the Homicide Act and render all kinds of murder free from the death penalty, the abolitionists rather unfairly played on this fact, viz. that certain murders which excited relatively little moral abhorrence were more severely punished than other more heinous crimes. In effect the abolitionists imputed moralist arguments to the retentionists and then pretended to be surprised at the gap between moral feeling and the punishment prescribed by the law. Their use of the differences between the retentionists on causalist grounds and the retentionists on moralist grounds is perhaps best illustrated by placing together a number of relevant quotations from the House of Commons debates.

Sidney Silverman: No one could think that the exceptions in the 1957 Act were the worst murders. Those who accept the position of the 1957 Act accept that the murderers of children shall not be hanged. Those who accept the 1957 Act accept that foul sexual crimes shall not be capital. Those who accept the 1957 Act accept that, if a man waylays his enemy around a dark corner of a back street and stabs him in the back with a knife, that shall not be capital murder, whereas if he waits for him with a revolver and shoots him in the front, that is capital murder. Anyone who tried to justify the exceptions in the 1957 Act on the grounds that it was a successful attempt to distinguish between the gravest kinds of murder and crimes which were not so grave would have an impossible task. Let the House remember that Ruth Ellis [killed her lover] would still have committed a capital crime under the Homicide Act because she used a revolver instead of a knife.[27]

Tom Iremonger: It was not that the government purported to draw a line between those kinds of murder which were most heinous and those which were less heinous. They attempted to distinguish between types of murder as to the degree to which they contributed to the disturbance of public order . . . .[28]

Sir Peter Rawlinson: [The important argument is what would be] the effect of abolition and what the result would be on the practices of the professional criminal if there were total abolition. Would there be an increase of violence or an increase in the use of firearms? . . . It [the 1957 Act] said "death where you kill in the course of committing a crime and death where it affects law and order".

Leo Abse: . . . will he [Rawlinson] explain how a rapist or a poisoner does not disturb the peace in the sense he means as distinct from a robber?

Sir Peter Rawlinson: My argument is that one should use this penalty

only where one believes that one can deter. I do not believe that one
can deter a poisoner or a rapist . . . . These [people whose murders
would be capital offences under 1957 Act] are professional criminals.
They weigh up the circumstances and the risks involved . . . . I do not
believe we can deter the poisoner or the sexually perverted but I do
believe that we can deter the professional criminal who acquires a pistol
and goes out to rob as an occupation, weighing risk against risk . . . .[29]
Henry Brooke: The [Homicide] Act as has been said was designed to
protect society by a special deterrent against carrying of lethal weapons
or compounding theft with murder and to protect public servants such
as police officers and prison officers in their dangerous duties. It
produces anomalies at the sentencing stage. There can be no doubt of
that. However sound the principles of the Act when they are tested
against the criterion of motive, nevertheless, it results in most heinous
murders not being capable of attracting the death sentence whereas the
law requires that the death sentence passed on others who have
committed what is defined as capital murder even though it would be
almost universally felt that they had in fact been offences of a less grave
kind . . .[30]
Emlyn Hooson (interruption): Is the Hon. gentleman arguing that the
basis of the justification for retaining capital punishment is retribution?
Iremonger: With great respect, I should have thought that it was the
very opposite. I am not fundamentally interested in retribution,
perhaps I should be. I am interested in protecting those who have the
right to come to me and say "This [a murder victim] was my husband
and you have a share of the responsibility for his death". If that is
anything to do with retribution, I do not think the words can have very
much meaning.[31]

It is difficult to see quite why the abolitionists keep
imputing moralist arguments to the retentionists. It may be
because they suspect that the retentionists are only adopting
causalist modes of argument in order to fit in with the
dominant style of the House of Commons in the 1960s
and that this masks their real moralist arguments and
feelings. This seems to be Professor Richards' view for he
comments

Indeed by 1965 the deterrence theme seemed so flimsy that one
suspects that many of those who struggled to keep the death penalty
did in fact subscribe to some form of retribution theory, although this
was rarely evident because retribution is not intellectually respectable
and may be classed as unchristian.[32]

I doubt if that is true as specifically argued by Professor Richards since the kind of people who support retribution are not concerned about intellectual respectability. Further the avowed Christians in the House of Commons were much more likely to support retention than were the atheists or the Jews.[32]

Percentage of a Religious Group
Voting "No" to Abolition

Group	%
Roman Catholic	11·5
Anglican	42·6
Free Church	7·5
Jews	3·5
Agnostic/Atheist	3·7

Some abolitionists may derive their convictions from Christian principles but few people would argue that retribution is necessarily unchristian. When the Homicide Bill was being debated the then Archbishop of Canterbury, Dr Fisher, specifically rebutted this point saying

My Lords, in the debate of July of last year, last session, both the most reverend Primate the Lord Archbishop of York and I, made as clear as we could what the doctrine of the Church is in the matter of capital punishment. We said that the state has a right in the name of God and of society to impose the death penalty, *whether as an act of justice, or for the protection of its own citizens from violence.* I repeat that not least because the noble Lord, Lord Silkin, said that in his view the imposition of the death penalty was immoral, and I feel bound to repeat what I said last time: that there is no immorality in it at all. It may be wise or unwise, expedient or inexpedient but it is not against the laws of God or the doctrines of the Christian church.[33] (My italics.)

But Professor Richards' point could be true at the general level, i.e. moralist arguments on either side carry little weight so everyone phrases their views in causalist terms. The predominance of causalist arguments is certainly seen in the care that abolitionists take to couch their own arguments within the causalist framework. At times they seem to be saying "were the facts about deterrence different, we would be in favour of capital punishment". Again this is perhaps best illustrated by quotation from leading abolitionists in the debates on the Homicide Act 1957 and the Murder Act 1965.

Sidney Silverman: The Hon. gentleman [Sir H. Lucas-Tooth] said, and I agree, that if we can prove that with the death penalty there are fewer murders than without it then the death penalty is justified. I agree . . . He went on to say "you cannot *prove* that with the death penalty there are fewer murders than without it" . . . I agree . . . but when he said: "therefore, I shall vote to retain the death penalty", I thought this was a complete *non-sequitur* and that he ought to have drawn exactly the opposite conclusion. The onus surely is not on those who wish to abolish the death penalty. The onus is on those who wish to retain it. Every jury is told "Do not convict this man if you have a reasonable doubt of his guilt." We are entitled to say to the House of Commons, "Do not retain the death penalty if you have a reasonable doubt of its effectiveness." Surely that is right. If there are those Hon. and Rt Hon. members in the House tonight who are left in doubt at the end of the argument, if they are not sure, if they feel that the argument rests in the end on a fine balance and cannot conscientiously decide for themselves where it comes down, I beg of them: do not by your votes or by neglecting to vote continue a penalty which in your hearts you know you cannot hold to on the evidence that would be necessary . . . those who want to abolish the death penalty are just as much concerned for the protection of society as those who want to retain it. The argument is not about that. It is about whether or not the death penalty is a necessary or useful protection to society.[34]

S.C. Silkin: Even if it be shown that this is a more effective penalty, a more effective deterrent, none the less, is the difference so great as to amount to this imperative need in a civilized community to kill other human beings? I pray in aid also the great authority of the chairman of the commission, Sir Ernest Gowers (Royal Commission on Capital Punishment 1948) who in his little book which repays study, *A Life for a Life*, confessed that when he began his task he thought that the abolitionists had larger hearts than heads and that when he ended it after four years of study of the figures all over the world he came to the conclusion that sentiment was on the side of the retentionists and reason on the side of the abolitionists.[35]

Henry Brooke: I do not share the view that the taking of life by the state is contrary to moral principle. I think that, if it can be shown that by retaining the death penalty for some or for all types of murder one is lessening the likelihood of innocent people suffering death by murder, then there is no ground of moral principle on which one can dismiss the death penalty ... But I believe that retention of the death penalty can be justified only on the grounds that it is a unique deterrent. If it is a unique deterrent there is justification for it. If it is not, I do not think that the case for it can be upheld.[36]

In each of these quotations the abolitionists take a strong causalist line, conceding the morality of the deterrence argument, criticizing it only on the facts. For Henry Brooke, this is the whole of the argument. He is a pure causalist who feels there is no moralist argument for abolition. As Home Secretary he had upheld capital punishment. Now on rational reflection he has changed his mind on the facts of the situation. If new facts were presented showing that it was a "unique" deterrent one feels that he would (quite reasonably) support the reintroduction of capital punishment. For Silkin and Silverman one feels that this is not the whole argument, that somewhere beneath the causalist arguments lurks moralist feeling. They are prepared to agree to capital punishment if it could be shown to be a deterrent because they feel confident that this will not happen. They give this hostage to Fortune because they know Fortune will not take it. But is there not some anxiety revealed in Silverman's odd argument about the burden of proof, in Silkin's smuggling a quasi-moralist argument into the content of a causalist argument? Silkin's argument really is a strange mixture of cardinal utilitarianism ("is the difference so great") and an appeal to the absolute values of "a civilized community". He half concedes the case for deterrence, half admits a gap in the factual case for abolition and then closes it by a disguised appeal to moralist considerations. He then firmly repudiates such emotional considerations and appeals to the House to be hard-headed and unsentimental and to support the strong causalist case of the abolitionists.

Thus on both sides causalism prevails, not merely as the prevailing mode of thought but as the prevailing mode of argument, even to those who retain some moralist notions. Indeed, the causalist arguments were taken even further by some abolitionists, notably Leo Abse, who declared

Most solicitors with anything like a criminal practice will usually be able to say, "I believe there is a man in prison who is about to come out

or who is temporarily free and who is likely to commit murder."
Experienced police officers say exactly the same thing. "So and so,"
they say, "will one of these days commit murder." Why do we wait?
Why when a man is put in prison for assault or unlawful wounding do
we not realize immediately that this is not normal behaviour? Why is he
not screened? Why at the point when it is clear that the man is a danger
to himself and the community is he not psychiatrically examined?[37]

This passage shows how the causalist whittles down the area
of freewill, replaces choice by causality, punishment by
treatment. It also shows that causalism is not necessarily a
permissive doctrine. If the level of violence in the community
is to be reduced the causalist is willing to screen out and treat
the abnormal before they go on to commit serious crimes. It
is difficult to see this as more permissive than punishing them
afterwards. Either way their freedom to act is restricted in
the interests of community safety.

To find full-blown moralist arguments on either side one
must go back to an earlier period of debate on the issue
before causalist thought came to dominate the legislature in
the 1950s and 1960s. The earlier debates on capital
punishment in 1948 and 1949 illustrate well the kinds of
moralist argument that could have been made on either side
in the later debates but were not. Either because old
moralist members were placed by new causalist ones or
because the old ones were converted to the causalist modes
of thought and argument, this whole moral outlook disappeared from the debates between the earlier and later
controversies about capital punishment.[38] Even if it only
became disguised and muted this in itself is significant.
People do not take the trouble to disguise their thoughts and
feelings unless they feel these are likely to meet with
disapproval or misunderstanding from some dominant group
thinking in a different way, arguing in a different style. But
in 1948 the moralists did not have these inhibitions. The
following quotations speak for themselves.

Mr. Paton: I am no detached scientifically impartial person on this
issue. I am a red-hot partisan and I make no pretence at all of any
soaring to the heights of ideal impartiality. I believe capital punishment
is a foul thing. I believe it to be an unmitigated evil in our community,

a centre of pollution sending out constantly-spreading ripples throughout our whole community. I believe that every time we hang a criminal
guilty of a foul murder, we are striking at the real defences of social
order in any community—a high regard for human life and personality—
that is equally as grave in its effects upon the community as is the crime
it seeks to punish .... I want to suggest to this house as the
representative assembly of a country of free men and women that
instruments of repression have no proper place in the institutions of a
free democracy. By their very nature, by their inherent quality
repressive punishments belong to the systems of totalitarian states and
not democracies. It was no accident that the chief exponents of
violence and severity in the treatment of criminals in modern times
were the Nazi and Fascist states ...[39]

Quintin Hogg: ... although human life is sacred it has not that
indefeasible sanctity which makes it wrong in all circumstances and for
all persons to take it ... we have just been hanging our defeated
enemies after the trials of Nuremburg. The Attorney-General who is not
here today prosecuted them not as an act of war but as an act of what
was claimed to be justice .... If we were going to say as some hon.
members think we ought to have said that it was at all times and in all
circumstances wrong to take human life, whatever evil-doing the
malefactor may have committed, then the time to say so was before
Nuremburg and not immediately after. Only two days ago I saw in *The
Times* that we were hanging some more members of the S.S. ...[40]

Mr Maude: After all, all these persons [convicted murderers] were
absolutely worthless persons. No evil was done to this world so far as I
know by any one person being hanged in all the twenty-five years I
have been at the bar. I cannot think of one individual by whose hanging
the community genuinely suffered a loss. May I put the matter in this
way—think of the thousands who are killed in traffic accidents, people
who are really worth while and by whose death we suffer a tremendous
loss. Here we are considering the possibility of hanging each year eleven
absolutely worthless people who thoroughly deserve what they
get ...[41]

Leslie Hale: I want to argue the case on the basis of public morality and
public ethics and the effect that the retention of this barbarous
principle has on the people associated with it—the people who read
about it, the people now in contact with it, our children and our
populace generally ... Nuremburg has been mentioned. I do not
complain. I want to say frankly that I have much agreement with the
views expressed. It may well be that none of us has the right to
criticize who did not criticize at the time. In some measure Nuremburg
was a tribute to public indignation and public lust for vengeance but in
connection with this it is right to remember what happened in Belgium.

Many years ago they abolished capital punishment but they have reinstated death—by shooting—in respect only of war crimes for the collaborator and the quisling. That cannot be justified on the ground of any argument about a deterrent effect. There is no question about wanting to deter people from collaborating in any future war in which one's country may be involved. This is a kind of yielding—and one can understand the yielding—to popular sentiment of the moment, to popular lust for vengeance and the indignation to which the populace is subject . . . the bad old days of public execution when

> Thousands of hearts beat horrid hope
> Thousands of eyeballs lit with Hell
> Turned one way all to see the rope
> Unslacken as the platform fell.

The Hon. member for Oxford shakes his head. I am glad he does if he feels the horror of that scene as we do. It is right to do so if we loathe this thing, if this inspires us with detestation and induces us to turn our heads away from it and not to look at the hangman and his apparatus and not to think of the chaplain chanting his psalm as he accompanies the half-dead man to the scaffold. If we feel this horror then this is the *real reason* for abolishing it . . . . However, I would say that it may be when the *idealism of the forties gives way to the empiricisim of the sixties* there will be solid ground for thinking the forties were right, there will be solid ground for thinking the sixties wrong . . . .[42]
George Porter: . . . I feel that the actual carrying out of the penalty of hanging is a crime against humanity and a crime against the social conscience of the whole nation.[43]
Sir Ronald Ross: . . . The interesting thing about the debate tonight and about the whole question is the crusading fervour of those sincere people who wish to abolish capital punishment . . .[44]
Elwyn Jones: I cannot believe that the morbid publicity and interest that attaches to these murder trials—and anyone who takes part in them is very conscious of it—can be of any advantage to the people of this country; nor in particular can it be of any benefit to our children to read the squalid and sordid details in the newspapers. The circumstances that attend hangings are frequently horrible. Lord Buckmaster has stated that at one execution there were people leaning with their ears against the walls of the prison so that they could hear the thud of the falling body. I cannot believe that experiences of that kind can do anything but debase the character and standards of our people . . .[45]
S.N. Evans: We must see these things in correct perspective. Is it seriously suggested that someone who rapes a little girl and kills her to

destroy the evidence should be kept alive for any reason whatever? I do not think so . . . . It [public opinion] accepts the Biblical injunction and I share that sentiment—eye for eye, tooth for tooth.[46]

It is clear that in the austere days of 1948 there were moralist thinkers on both sides. Those in favour of capital punishment saw murderers as "absolutely worthless persons" who deserved to be hanged and especially those murderers who had committed the most horrid of murders (e.g. after a sexual assault on a child). Those against capital punishment were also preoccupied with the effect it had on the moral tone of the nation. The very sense of justice having been done, of righteous official vengeance having been carried out, which appealed to the supporters of capital punishment, appals the abolitionist. Both sides are concerned with the state of Britain's collective conscience in a way that later retentionists and abolitionists are not. There are causalist arguments about deterrence and the possibility of error in the 1948 debates but they do not dominate the scene in the way they do later. Indeed the debaters of the class of '48 are well aware both of the centrality of the moralist issues and with a curious prescience of the way in which these issues would lose their importance in the future. Members boast of being "no detached scientifically impartial person" and of wishing "to argue the case on the basis of public morality and public ethics" in a way quite foreign to the later debates. As Leslie Hale so rightly predicted "when the idealism of the forties gives way to the empiricism of the sixties . . . ". Yet we still have the problem "why were the forties moralist?" Why did this give way to the empiricism of the sixties? Why did Leslie Hale predict the change that in fact occurred? The main reason for the general change to "causalist" thinking was (as I have argued elsewhere in this book) that in other important sectors of society—in industry, in the economic ministries, in social welfare—men's thinking had come to be dominated by considerations of cause and effect, of technical rationality. The solution to Britain's problems came to be seen not in moral uplift but in "social engineering"—the very phrase conveys the new image men had of their society and the ways it could be manipulated. Socialism and *laissez-faire* liberalism, the great moral dogmas about the control of industry and the economy, ceased to have any force. Both Labour and Conservative governments sought rather to "manage" the economy. The key question became, for the economist or the social reformer as it had much earlier for the engineer, "does it work?" This way of looking at the world inevitably spread to such moral issues as abortion, divorce or capital punishment. Men could not keep social and economic issues in one sector of their minds to be analysed by the law of cause and effect and in another separate sector moral issues to be judged by moralist criteria. The pressure towards consistency that exists in even the most closed-minded person proved too great. Moreover, the visible success of pragmatic thinking in the practical worlds of science and industry, of production and welfare, caused people to feel that here was a method, a technique, a way of weighing up issues that could profitably be applied to moral questions.

The question of why the "moralists" were still important in 1948 when moral issues were being discussed, at a time when causalist thinking was already dominant in other spheres, is a more difficult one. A simple but not very illuminating answer is that there was a lag—moral issues did not present themselves as candidates for causalist analysis as obviously as did social and economic questions. The feelings and prejudices that had to be overcome were perhaps more basic, deeper-rooted. Also the experience of World War II and its aftermath had reinforced any tendency people had to view the world in moralist terms. At a later date historians and dramatists might come to see the war in terms of cause and effect but at the time it was a great moral struggle between our side (the good ones) and the other side (the bad ones).[47] This view had been reinforced by the war crimes tribunals to which many speakers in the debates referred. This was an act of retribution and denunciation. Deterrence and reformation did not come into it. No one argued that the Nazi leaders' fate would deter future dictators or aggressors. No one pleaded for leniency on the grounds that it was their first offence. For some these experiences vindicated their view that malefactors should receive exemplary punishment; for others the fact that the war criminals had used harsh methods during their period of success rendered all use of harsh methods for whatever purpose unacceptable. From these roots stemmed "the idealism of the forties". As the memory of the events of the forties faded it was inevitable that the idealism would fade too, and that the long-term trend towards "the empiricism of the sixties" would prevail.

The issue of capital punishment, more than any other moral issue, raises problems concerning the relationship between Parliament and the electorate. Parliament has abolished capital punishment but the British people clearly did not agree with this. They wished to retain the death penalty at the time and they wanted it restored after it was abolished.

Public Attitudes to Capital Punishment[48]

Date of Opinion Poll	Pro-abolition	Pro-retention or restoration
	%	%
June 1962	19	
July 1964	21	
February 1965	23	
June 1966	18	76

At the 1966 General Election the very real strength of public opinion in favour of hanging was shown by the success of a pro-capital punishment independent candidate who stood against Sidney Silverman (the leader of the abolitionists who introduced the Bill to abolish capital punishment in the House of Commons) in Nelson and Colne. The independent, who fought the election entirely on this issue, gained over 5,000 votes and 13 per cent of the total votes cast.[49] This was an outstanding performance by an independent candidate at a general election. It demonstrated that people were not merely prepared to support the retention or restoration of capital punishment in answer to a questionnaire but felt strongly enough to allow this issue to determine their vote at a general election when other important issues were at stake. Indeed the people's view at this time was best expressed by

Brigadier Terence Clark who told the House of Commons of the letters he had received on the issue: "I received over 200 replies by last Saturday saying 'Hang the murderers'. Many of them said, if you can hang the hon. member for Nelson and Colne as well, we will be delighted."[50]

This raises the crucial point—was Parliament justified in ignoring the wishes of the electorate and altering the law in a way directly opposed to the opinions and feelings of the vast majority of the British people? The answer to this question depends on whether one assumes the dominant mode of considering such an issue both in Parliament and in the nation at large is moralist or causalist. If we assume both Parliament and the people see the issue in causalist terms then Parliament is probably justified in overriding the views of the people. The disagreement between them is over an issue of fact, or of interpretation of facts. Members of Parliament believe that capital punishment is not a deterrent, the people believe that it is. Under these circumstances Members of Parliament may justifiably argue that they are better informed or more intelligent than their constituents and therefore better able to judge an issue of this kind. Parliament in effect sets itself up as an intellectual élite that "knows better" than the common people. This is not to say that Members of Parliament are either well-informed or intelligent but simply that they possess these qualities to a greater extent than their constituents. It is doubtful whether many Members of Parliament understand the intricate statistics that are used to test whether or not capital punishment is a deterrent. However, we can be sure that an even smaller proportion of their constituents have even heard of these data, let alone understand them. Under these circumstances Parliament is perfectly justified in arrogantly riding roughshod over the wishes of the people.

If by contrast both Parliament and the people consider the issue in moralist terms, then it is clearly disgraceful for Parliament to flaunt the wishes of the people in this way. The disagreement between them is one of moral feeling. Members of Parliament find capital punishment morally repugnant. The people feel it is right and proper that people convicted of the horrid crime of murder should be punished by hanging.

There is no way of saying that one view is better than another and it would be intolerable for Members of Parliament to impose their own personal moral impulses on the people. Any group that sets itself up as a moral élite in this way must be fiercely resisted in the name of democracy. Our democratic system does not assume that people are intellectually equal—indeed it is very easy to show that they are not and that there is a clear division between that small number of highly intelligent people who are the country's intellectual élite and the vast majority of ordinary people. But we do as a basic principle of our democracy assume that people are equal in their capacity for making moral preferences. As Lord Devlin has eloquently stated:

> Those who do not believe in God must ask themselves what they mean when they say that they believe in democracy. Not that all men are born with equal brains—we cannot believe that; but that they have at their command—and that in this they are all born in the same degree—the faculty of telling right from wrong. This is the whole meaning of democracy, for if in this endowment men were not equal it would be pernicious that in the government of any society they should have equal rights.[51]

If Parliament arrogantly asserts that the moral impulses of its members are superior to those of the electorate and that therefore these can serve as the basis for legislation that is morally repellent to the ordinary man, then democracy is dangerously undermined. We can only urge that the "dear old peasants stand up for themselves"[52] and replace the present morally élitist membership of the legislature with men whose moral perceptions are more in line with those of the common people or who are prepared to vote according to the people's will whatever their own private views.

Thus, when Burke describes the duties of the Member of Parliament as being that of a representative of his constituents, not a delegate, he is right in part only. We can in fact break his argument into its constituent parts and agree or disagree with these as we choose. Burke said:

> But his [the Parliamentary representative's] unbiased opinion, his mature judgement, his enlightened conscience, he ought not to sacrifice

to you, to any man or to any set of men living . . . . Your representative owes you not his industry only but his judgement; and he betrays instead of serving you if he sacrifices it to your opinion.[53]

There is a world of difference between a member's "mature judgement" and his "enlightened conscience". He is indeed as Burke stresses elected to Parliament in order to exercise his mature judgement since this is a quality we may reasonably expect him to have to a greater extent than his electors. They choose him for this reason. But they do not choose him so that he may exercise his enlightened conscience as and when he pleases. The implication is that their consciences are unenlightened and may be ignored. One man's judgement may be better than another's but one man's conscience is as good as that of the next. We elect a representative to exercise his own judgement in Parliament but on issues of conscience we send to Parliament a mere delegate whose duty is simply to express the collective conscience of his constituents.

In practice the matter cannot be resolved in this simple manner since Parliament and people probably differ not merely as to whether there should be capital punishment but also as to the kinds of argument they feel are relevant. Parliament wishes to abolish hanging on causalist grounds (it is not a deterrent and mistakes can occur) whilst the people wish to retain it on moralist grounds (murderers are wicked and should be hanged). This presents a much more complicated problem for the political theorist and one that would need a whole book to analyse fully.

3 Permissiveness and Censorship

Speaking against the motion was Christie Davies, former President of the Cambridge Union and now a BBC producer, who made the rafters shake in a tirade reminiscent of the thirties, which left me branded as a Fascist and a reactionary.

MRS MARY WHITEHOUSE, *Who does she think she is?*

During the last twenty years society has demonstrably come to exercise less and less (overt or indirect) censorship over books and magazines, plays and films, speeches and pamph- lets, radio and television. Writers, speakers and broadcasters are allowed to deal with subjects formerly taboo and they are allowed greater freedom of style and language. Scenes from plays, films or broadcasts that in the past would have been cut by a censor (or by the producer himself in an act of prudent or masochistic pre-censorship) are now freely shown. However, the change has not been a total, an even or a regular one. Some things formerly uncensored such as horror comics or racialist publications are now subject to censorship for the first time. There has been a steady diminution in censorship of material relating to sexual or religious matters but even here there have been occasions when the trend appears to have been halted or even reversed. As on many other issues discussed in this book thinking on this subject has shown a shift from what we have termed "moralism" to what we have termed "causalism" and the greater permissive- ness is in many ways associated with this. However, on this particular issue it is much less easy to divide individuals or their arguments into moralists and causalists. Nor is it automatically possible to state that on any particular issue the causalists will dominate the argument or defeat the moralists. Nor are causalists necessarily in favour of permissive legislation on censorship or permissive actions by the censor or moralists opposed to this. Even more than on most issues there seems to be a gap between the way people argue and the way they *really* think. Sometimes this is because they are humbugs but often they are simply confused. There is a general trend to causalist thinking but it is no more than that and it is often indiscernible in particular cases.

The shift towards less censorship occurred on at least four levels. First, the law was altered by Parliament in a more permissive direction by the Obscene Publications Act of 1959 and by the Theatres Act 1968. The former Act, sponsored by Roy Jenkins, made the law relating to censorship of published material on the grounds of obscenity much less restrictive. The latter abolished the right of the Lord Chamberlain to exercise censorship of stage plays.

Secondly, the courts came to apply the criminal law relating to obscene publications in a more permissive way. Juries in particular became less willing to convict authors or publishers of obscenity. The 1960s was a period in which there was a series of spectacular trials in which publishers and prosecutors (both public and private) sought to test out how the new law would be interpreted by a jury. Almost invariably the jury decided the book concerned was not obscene and these books (from *Lady Chatterley's Lover* to *Last Exit to Brooklyn*) enjoyed the dual advantage of being judged not obscene—which made them legal—and yet of being sufficiently salacious to merit a big, highly publicized trial—which made them sell.

Thirdly, as prosecutors, both private and public, realized that the juries of the 1960s were remarkably permissive in their approach to literature (or at any rate could be persuaded to be so by a skilful defence counsel and a string of articulate defence witnesses testifying to the book's freedom from obscenity or redeeming literary merit) they ceased to bring prosecutions. The authorities in general—magistrates, local councils, watch committees, police, pressure groups, local moral and religious leaders—seem also to have become more permissive (or to have lost their nerve). They simply are less willing or able to take action against such "enormities" as dirty bookshops, strip-clubs, blue-film shows, sex shops or indecent theatrical performances. This is especially true in London and other big urban centres.

Fourthly, as the external pressures were removed, authors and publishers, producers and directors ceased to censor (or pre-censor) themselves. Their concept of what was permissible, or what they could get away with, itself shifted. There was a particularly remarkable change within the BBC and the independent television companies. Their whole sense of what could be broadcast without offending the susceptibilities of the public shifted radically. Also it came to be questioned whether offending the public or a section of it mattered anyway.

Thus far the offerings of the last twenty years are simply a continuation of a trend that has gone on since the early part of the century. It has been a regular feature of the cultural and moral history of the last sixty years at least that books that were banned as obscene at one time are accepted a little later and later still become compulsory examination reading for schoolchildren. Plays that were refused a licence by the Lord Chamberlain's office survived this ban and were granted a licence after a suitable lapse of time to enable the attitudes of theatre audiences and Lord Chamberlain to catch up with those of playwrights and producers.[1] The degree of nudity permitted on the stage or on films has steadily increased. All that can be said of the 1960s is that the pace of change accelerated and that at times conflicts arose because there were those who wished to go even faster. The censor steadily retreated but was occasionally overtaken by those impetuous for his total abolition. However, there were some checks to and reverses of this general tendency. On the issue of obscenity the rapid changes that had occurred spurred into existence powerful pressure groups who sought to stop further changes and called for more, rather than less, censorship in the future. In 1964 Mrs Mary Whitehouse set up the "clean-up TV campaign" which grew into the National Viewers and Listeners Association. She was able to mobilize a large body of individuals and organizations who took offence at the change in the BBC's policy as to what was and what was not fit material for broadcasting. The BBC, which had been attacked in the 1950s as part of the Establishment[2] and as the official purveyor of society's conventional attitudes and values, was now attacked for being a source of obscenity and irreverence.[3]

The "clean-up TV campaign" has since then provided the inspiration for further organizations dedicated to fighting the permissive society and its manifestations in literature, plays and films. Lord Longford's Commission on Pornography and the Festival of Light rapidly followed Mrs Whitehouse's lead. These later developments have sought to use the style of the permissive society in their attempts to defeat it. Rallies of noisy teenagers in Trafalgar Square and pop concerts in Hyde Park characterized the Festival of Light, which demanded a "reform of the censorship laws" to "protect the citizen from being offended" and to "establish sound standards and control commercial exploitation".[4] Lord Longford's Commission which visited Copenhagen and examined the effect of pornography and sex shows on the state of Denmark was careful to include among its members young and trendy persons.[5] Predictably, the Commission has been unable to agree on the effects or offensiveness of pornography or to issue a report acceptable to *all* its members.

The general shift to permissiveness in the last twenty years with regard to what people are allowed to say, write or publish is subject to two marked exceptions. Although, in general, legislation has removed censorship, in two important areas it has imposed it. The first was the Children and Young Persons (Harmful Publications) Act of 1955. The second and more substantial imposition of censorship was the Race Relations Act of 1965, which curtailed speeches or written propaganda of a racially abusive nature.

It is not easy to demonstrate a consistent moralist or causalist style in the statements made by people arguing about these issues nor a trend from one to the other over time. It is particularly difficult to tell whether there has been a shift from one kind of attitude to the other. The main evidence that there is has is the immense amount of expensive research that has been done, especially in the United States, to try to test and measure the effects of pornography or of television violence on the attitudes and behaviour of people exposed to them. Only people wishing to test out causalist arguments would wish to finance research of this nature, research which has been deliberately geared by its sponsors to try and answer questions such as "Does television violence cause viewers to behave aggressively?" or "Does the wider dissemination of pornography result in fewer or more sex crimes?" Millions of dollars have been spent in America, England and Denmark by the American Commission on Obscenity and Pornography and the Surgeon General's Commission on the Effects of Television Violence to try and find answers to these questions. In part this reflects distinctively American factors—their increasing anxiety about their social problems, their love of quantitative social science research, the almost unlimited resources they have to squander on these things. Nevertheless the results of such research have come to dominate arguments in England too. For the first time the causalists have got data they can use and we can expect an acceleration in both Britain and America of the spiral:

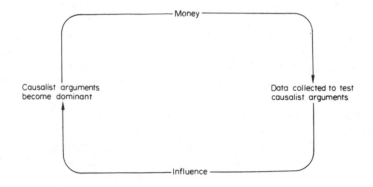

The beginning of one version of the spiral in America and the shift from moralist to causalist arguments there is well illustrated by the dissenting minority report of Commissioners Morton A. Hill, SJ, and Winfrey C. Link of the American Commission on Obscenity and Pornography in their section "History of Creation of Commission":

For several years prior to 1967 legislation to create a Commission on Obscenity and Pornography was introduced into the Congress. It passed the Senate each time and each time died in House Committee. Legislation was vigorously opposed by the American Civil Liberties Union which reads the First Amendment in an absolutist way. Their position that "obscenity as much as any other form of speech or press, is entitled to the protection of the First Amendment" can be found in an amicus brief in *Jacobellis* v. *Ohio* (1964) among others. In 1967, however, the feeling of the Congress was such that legislation to create a Commission was certain to pass. Now, the ACLU strategy changed. In April of that year, the Director of the Washington office of the American Civil Liberties Union testified on such legislation before the House sub-committee on Education and Labour. He called for "scientific studies" into effects on the part of such a Commission and maintained that the public and private groups should not be involved in the workings of the Commission. A bill to create the Commission was considered by the Senate in May of 1967. The bill made no mention of effects studies and drew for membership from both houses of Congress, from various governmental agencies, education, media, state attorneys general, prosecutors, and law enforcement. It provided for public hearings and power of subpoena. The bill which ultimately passed the Congress called for effects studies, drew heavily from the behavioural sciences for membership and the power of subpoena had been removed.[6]

At one level this can be read simply as a description of the Machiavellian tactics of the American Civil Liberties Union. Like most trendy liberal Americans they are clearly prepared to use any means to impose their values on society. But there is another and more important level of analysis. The ACLU clearly saw that success lay not in a moralist invoking of the First Amendment but in swimming with the causalist tide and calling for "scientific studies into effects". They chose this tactic because they saw the trend of opinion and the dominant mode of argument shifting in that direction. I doubt if the ACLU had as much influence in shaping the nature of the bill to create the Commission as Hill and Link suggest. Any overt and obvious pressure from them would have only stimulated opposition from such hostile groups as the Citizens for Decent Literature who, according to the Commission report, had 11 senators and 126 Congressmen among their Honorary Committee members, including such powerful figures as Senator Barry Goldwater, Senator Thomas J. Dodd, Senator Strom Thurmond, and even Congressman John N. Happy Camp (*sic*).[7] What is more likely is that the ACLU chose to support a trend in opinion that would have won anyway. It is entirely in keeping with the shift from moralist to causalist thinking that I have postulated as a general trend that they should set up a Commission which "drew heavily from the behavioural sciences" and emphasized "effects studies" rather than one which called on politicians and other public leaders to testify their moral feelings at public hearings.

All this of course occurred in America, but America is traditionally a much more moralist country than Britain. America is the land of the Constitution, a set of moral pieties about freedom that have no equivalent in England. It is also the land of Prohibition and tough laws against heroin addicts, of innumerable acts of legislation in individual States against all sexual practices whatsoever from fornication to buggery, from fellatio to adultery, the land where Anthony Comstock raged against indecency and William Jennings Bryan fought against evolution. For all their love of quantitative research they are less likely to put any of it into practice than we are in England. We may well end up basing our legislation on the research that they have financed, while they revert to "gut reactions" of a liberal or a puritanical kind. British society is possibly less moralist than America at all levels, less inclined to assert abstract rights or freedoms, less inclined to condemn and persecute deviance. This is certainly true as far as our legislators and politicians are concerned. We are a more causalist society than America and perhaps always have been. If America goes causalist on this issue then it is likely that we shall too, since our cultural traditions are more likely to reinforce and allow such a tendency than are theirs. At the same time there are indications that we might take a different line. The section of the Race Relations Act dealing with censorship is an essentially moralist piece of legislation. When it went through Parliament in 1964-65 it called forth arguments from both supporters and opponents of the clause that were essentially moralist and not causalist in nature.

MORALIST ARGUMENTS

The moralist arguments for censorship centre round the fact that certain books, films, plays contain words, scenes, ideas or emotions that either give rise to feelings of indignation and disgust in the breasts (or chests) of decent citizens or encourage improper thoughts and feelings in the susceptible reader (or both). This in itself is sufficient reason for banning such a work, normally on the grounds that it is obscene or indecent (but also possibly because it is blasphemous or seditious). No manifest illegal or flagrantly anti-social behaviour need stem from the dissemination of such a work. No tumult or violence need result. It is sufficient that the work is offensive to the reader or produces thoughts and feelings in the reader that others find offensive.

The best examples of this attitude to censorship come from America, that home of moralism, whose judges, politicians and moral leaders are more willing than ours to make explicitly moralist statements of the need for censorship undiluted by concessions to causalist modes of argument. The following extracts from the minority report of Commissioner Charles H. Keating Jr to the American Commission on Obscenity and Pornography are about the best examples I have seen of hard-core moralism:[8]

No, the state cannot legislate virtue, cannot make moral goodness by merely enacting law but the state can and does legislate against vices which publicly jeopardize the virtue of people who might prefer to remain virtuous . . . . Since 1967 the flaunting of immorality in the states, i.e. the forcing of immorality on the states by the United States Supreme Court has gone on unabated insofar as obscenity cases are concerned . . . . The Eden Theatre is located in East Greenwich Village. This is a sleazy, disreputable part of New York. The theatre is old and dilapidated. *Oh Calcutta* plays at the Eden Theatre. *Oh Calcutta* is pure pornography—a two-hour orgy principally enacted in the nude. It is not possible to verbally depict the depravity, deviation, eroticism or the utter filth of the play. Male and female players fondle each other, commit or simulate intercourse, sodomy, cunnilinctus, masturbation, sadism *ad nauseam*. This abomination, at the time I write this Report is proposed to be televised live or by video-tape across the nation via lines of American Telephone and Telegraph and various telephonic communications systems. Never in Rome, Greece or the most debauched nations in history has such utter filth been projected to all parts of a nation. If there is or ever was any such thing as public decency these actions offend it. If there is or ever was a constitutional prerogative of the American people to have the exercise of police power in the interests of the public health and welfare this is it . . . . Many of the shops (in America) have display cases containing artificial sexual devices—penises, vaginas, french ticklers, vibrators etc., as well as penis-shaped candy and inflatable rubber dolls with built-in vagina, etc. Certainly ancient Sodom and Gomorrah couldn't have been as obsessed with sex as America is today. What is rotten in Denmark is already positively putrid in this country . . . . It is possible for me and every reader of this opinion to bespeak decency, morality, God—indeed sanctity and purity throughout this land. This to me is a positive approach which I encourage everyone to take . . . .

Pornography is for Commissioner Keating an evil *per se.* His disagreement with the other Commissioners is a straight moralist one. As such he sees his colleagues not as mistaken but as wicked. He says of them and their advocacy of a repeal of America's laws against pornography:[9]

Such presumption! Such an advocacy of moral anarchy! Such a defiance of the mandate of the Congress which created the Commission! Such a bold advocacy of a libertine philosophy! Truly it is difficult to believe that to which the majority of this Commission has given birth . . . . The Commission majority report can only be described as a travesty, preordained by the bias and prejudice of its Chairman, closely followed by his staff, who has long advocated relaxation of restraints for the dealers in pornography. The Report of the majority of the Commission does not reflect the will of Congress, the opinion of law enforcement officials throughout our country and worst of all flaunts the underlying opinions and desires of the great mass of the American people.

CAUSALIST ARGUMENTS

In a causalist era the arguments of the moralists tend to be unconvincing unless backed up with causalist arguments and data. This tends to be true of both the pro-censorship and the libertarian variety. Lord Devlin in his book *The Enforcement of Morals* has effectively attacked the moralist libertarian position, sometimes from a moralist position of his own but also from a causalist point of view. His book is a classic statement of the unfashionable moralist case for restricting individual liberty, yet even he is enough a man of his time to back it up with some causalist reasoning. It is primarily an affirmation of moralism and an attack on causalism—yet within this book is a very solid causalist demolition of moralist libertarianism. The following passages (atypical of the book as a whole) illustrate this latter theme:

> Freedom is not a good in itself. We believe it to be good because out of freedom there comes more good than bad. If a free society is better than a disciplined one it is because—and this certainly was Mill's view—it is better for a man himself that he should be free to seek his own good in his own way and better too for the society to which he belongs, since thereby a way may be found to a greater good for all.[10]
> ... Is this [Hart's moralist libertarian case] the sort of result that is really worth striving for on a high theoretical plane? Any law reformer who raises this sort of issue must be the sort of man who likes to bang his head against a brick wall in the hope that he will be able to get through on his own terms and so avoid a little argument at the gate. It will not improve his chances of getting through the gate if he tells the janitor that there ought not to be a wall there at all. So it is much easier to obtain the repeal of a law by persuading the lawmaker that on balance it is doing more harm than good than by denouncing him as a meddler who ought to be minding his own business. Whether or not I am right in thinking that this is the only way in which the case for reform can be put, it is certainly the most attractive way. It is put thus cogently by Professor Hart in the preface to his book where, after mentioning proposals for the reform of the law on abortion, homosexuality and euthanasia he refers to them as cases where "the misery caused directly and indirectly by legal punishment outweighs any conceivable harm these practices may do". This is the balancing process. There are other factors besides human misery (which inevitably accompanies any serious punishment for any breach of the law) to be taken into account; .... This applies to every exercise of the criminal law. If the law on abortion causes unnecessary misery, let it be amended not abolished on the ground that abortion is not the law's business ....[11]

For Mill's doctrine is just as dogmatic as any of those he repudiates. It is dogmatic to say that, if only we were all allowed to behave just as we liked so long as we did not injure each other, the world would become a better place for all of us. There is no more evidence for this sort of utopia than there is for the existence of Heaven and there is nothing to show that the one is any more easily attained than the other. We must not be bemused by words. If we are not entitled to call our society "free" unless we pursue freedom to an extremity that would make society intolerable for most of us, then let us stop short of the extreme and be content with some other name. The result may not be freedom unalloyed, but there are alloys which strengthen without corrupting.[12]

In these passages Lord Devlin develops a causalist critique of the libertarianism of the moralists. Freedom is seen as something to be sought because it brings good consequences rather than because it is good in itself. Law reform should be justified by discussing the relative consequences of amending and not amending the law—"if the law on abortion causes unnecessary misery"—not by appealing to abstract moral principles about freedom—"abortion is not the law's business". Lord Devlin is not a causalist—the "other factors besides human misery" to which he refers are primarily moralist ones—but he does explicitly recognize that causalist arguments are "the most attractive way . . . in which the case for reform can be put". He also implicitly recognizes that they are the most attractive arguments against legal and other reforms by choosing to use them even in the context of a very moralist book. He even espouses the moral values and styles that are characteristic of causalism. He criticizes Mill as being dogmatic and for putting forward arguments for which there is "no more evidence than for the existence of Heaven". He criticizes Professor Hart for talking of general moral issues rather than the specific problems associated with the particular matter under discussion. He urges moderation, compromise, the use of factual evidence specific to the issue and eschews dogmatism, assertion and general moral principles. In this way he is able to put the libertarians in a very difficult position. He is able to attack them in terms of procedural values that they themselves share, which they cannot repudiate and which they are not used to seeing used in this way. He is also able subtly to shift the burden of proof. Instead of laws having to be justified on the grounds that citizens are entitled to be free unless there are good reasons for restricting their freedom, it is *changes* in the law that he claims must now be justified. Unless the critics of the law can show good reason

for altering the present state of affairs then the law must
stand. The moralist gap that must occur at the end of all
causalist arguments (*a*) in the sense that when all the facts are
in, there is still a need to weigh up the claims of competing
values, and (*b*) in the sense that the facts are never complete,
that we give one view or another the benefit of the doubt
when we make a decision, is closed by him in favour of the
enforcement of morals rather than freedom.

In this way Devlin exposes the weaknesses of moralist
arguments—weaknesses as inherent in such arguments about
censorship as about the issues he looks at in the passages
quoted. In addition to these problems for the moralist—and
yet connected with them—are the problems stemming from
the fact that, for a moralist policy to be effective, it must
have the overwhelming agreement and support of the
community. This is very much a problem for the would-be
censor. If there is a diversity of attitudes to the question of
what is obscene or otherwise offensive or if attitudes are
changing over time then it is very difficult for the censor to
do his job. His authority soon either ceases to be effective or
it ceases to be legitimate. If he ceases to be effective then he
might as well cease to exist. If he chooses to be effective and
as a result ceases to be legitimate, then in the long run the
opposition to him and the erosion of his edicts will
undermine the very effectiveness he asserts today. In a
diverse society the censor cannot win.

The causalist weighs up the decision as to whether to
censor or not on a different basis from the moralist. He is not
concerned with whether a work excites moral outrage or vile
thoughts and feelings. He is not interested in abstract rights
and freedoms. He simply asks the question "will censoring
works of this type lead to a greater or lesser incidence of
actions which we can agree ought to be illegal?" He is
concerned simply with the direct effect of books or films,
magazines or television on people's public activities as
compared with the effect of censoring such works. Those in
favour of censorship on causalist grounds argue that works
dealing with sex and violence often incite their readers to
anti-social and illegal acts they would otherwise not have
committed. A pornographic book inflames some disturbed

adolescent to go out and rape a passing housewife, dirty old men are tempted to assault children by the magazines they read, violent television programmes lead to violence in real life. Against this it is argued that such books and programmes have a cathartic effect. The man who reads dirty books gets a vicarious satisfaction from them that provides a viable substitute for real-life sexual assaults and by allowing him to read them we actually reduce the incidence of such assaults. The expression of perverse impulses in this way provides a safety-valve where suppression of them might lead to an explosion. To block the fantasy outlets of sexually disturbed or aggressive individuals is seen as dangerous for the individual and for society. A further argument against censorship of a causalist kind is that the works you seek to eliminate are ineradicable. If you do try to censor out of existence books or films for which there is a strong demand, you simply create a black market and more serious social problems than those you are seeking to eliminate. Criminals and racketeers move in to supply the prohibited books, films and photographs, and the purchasers who may be otherwise perfectly respectable and law-abiding citizens are arbitrarily turned into a kind of criminal.

These arguments are old and familiar ones but only in the last decade, the decade of permissiveness and of causalism, have large-scale attempts been made to test them, notably with respect to pornography and television violence. On both these subjects extensive research has been carried out in America, Britain, Denmark, Italy, Australia and many other countries. The results are complex and often contradictory and the methods used often suspect, but two interesting conclusions do emerge. First, the free availability of pornography seems to reduce rather than increase the number of sex crimes. The cathartic effect exceeds the incitement effect and censorship does not seem to be justified.[13] Second, television violence does seem to result in the viewers being more violent in their everyday lives.[14] The incitement effect exceeds the cathartic effect and the censors seem to have a good case. These are the general conclusions of the extensive research in these two areas, conclusions that point in opposite directions in the two cases.

Thus the causalists' victory over the moralists and their determined collection of data to test their arguments in the 1960s have led to two very different implications for censorship. Pornography turns out to be harmless and even beneficial and censorship to be a mistake. Television violence is found to be a source of real violence and tougher and more effective censorship is called for. This still leaves the question: "Why is there such a contrast between the two sets of findings?" The answer probably lies in the difference between sex and violence. If a person is excited by an erotic work and needs to find release from the tension this creates, the answer lies in his or her own hands. The more erotically exciting the pornography, the more likely people are to find an outlet in the various forms of masturbation available to them. Indeed the availability of pornography may enable tense but inhibited individuals to masturbate to orgasm who otherwise would need to seek some direct outlet such as an assault on a young child. This is probably also true of those who like kinky sex or sadistic violence. The free availability of pornography may well result in fewer outbursts of sadistic violence rather than more.

There is no such simple mechanism for tension release in the case of people who are excited by violence or aggression except through some form of aggression itself. Television violence excites people but it does not provide any outlet for this excitement or release from it. Casual brutal violence on television (which usually lacks any sexual component) therefore results in casual brutal violence in real life.[15]

A problem associated with pure causalism in the matter of censorship is that it may prove impossible to uphold censorship on causalist grounds if people do not find the matter to be censored morally offensive. The categories of things that shock the public and things that have harmful consequences may not overlap very much. It is easy to get public approval to ban things that shock but if they are harmless there is no point in doing so and a causalist-minded legislature will refrain from instituting such a ban. Things that cause harm ought to be banned by such a legislative body but they may not be able to get the public support necessary to institute such a ban. It is clear from the research on televised violence that such violence in general has harmful consequences. What we do not yet know for certain is what sorts of violence have the worst effects and which are relatively innocuous. It is by no means clear that shocking kinds of violence such as sadism are those that cause harm. It may well be that the routine brutality of the boxing contest has far more harmful consequences because it is nearer to the everyday experience of those viewers prone to aggressive behaviour. But precisely because it is more everyday, it is more acceptable and perhaps it would be impossible to get public support for a ban on it.

In general the causalists have won the day, but there is one area where the moralists do seem to have a case—over the distinction between public and private display of offensive materials: books, pictures, films and even speeches. This it seems to me is a distinction that should be more widely applied. If on a causalist basis we decide that offensive books or pictures are to be sold without hindrance that does not mean that society should not seek to regulate the place or manner in which they are sold. The moralist may justifiably argue that society is entitled to protect its members from the flaunting of offensive materials and that the sale of such materials should be under conditions which remind the seller and producer of society's disapproval. At present this is achieved by restricting their sale to certain shops in clearly delineated areas of large towns only, and by imposing restrictions on the kinds of material the shop may display in the window and on public sale as distinct from in its sleazier back rooms to which only those who desire "something a little stronger" are admitted. The pictures and books, shop displays and advertisements for strip shows and blue films openly displayed in Soho would certainly not be permitted in the main streets of Hereford or Pontardulais, Inverness or Winchester. The artefacts on sale in London's sex-shops are not always displayed in the window because this might prove offensive to passers-by. Moreover a warning in the window provides a strong enticement to potential purchasers rather than horrified bystanders.

All these restrictions are indications of the admirable hypocrisy of British society. You can get dirty books, you can watch indecent shows, you can see blue films but only if you go to certain prescribed areas and do so clandestinely. You cannot do so openly in your village emporium or church hall but if you put on a long raincoat and take the train to London you can procure all these things by joining a club under a false name or wrapped in a brown paper bag behind a wooden partition. The need is not to sweep this hypocrisy away but to institutionalize it. Society should choose clearly what kinds of literature it wishes to encourage and which to regulate and which to ban; and pictures whose sale is to be "regulated" should be subject to the kind of licensing arrangements that apply to films or to indecent shows. The sale of such items should be *explicitly* restricted to a limited number of official "dirty" book shops located in the less salubrious parts of major cities. Any attempt to sell them elsewhere or to press them on unwilling customers by lurid displays or the sending of unsolicited samples and catalogues through the post should be strictly illegal. In this way the person who wishes to buy such items can do so and, provided there is free competition between the shops so licensed—the licensing authority could use its power to enforce this—he would be able to do so at far lower prices than at present.

The person who finds such material offensive can avoid it totally and it can be largely kept out of the reach of children. Further, the State, although permitting the sale of all books, pictures, films, magazines of this sort, emphatically demonstrates its disapproval of them by the way in which it designates the points of sale. If those who want total permissiveness in the publication and sale of pornography have any sense they will support the hypocrites behind bills such as the Cinematograph and Indecent Displays Bill. If such an Act were passed and enforced it would rob the moralists of their only strong argument and prevent them from introducing other tougher restrictions that might have far more serious consequences for the pornographer and his customers.

4 Sexual Behaviour and Sexual Attitudes in the Permissive Society

... Epicurean is a much misused word. Whenever you want to say that someone is inordinately greedy, lewd, sensual, or just a plain swine, you say he's an Epicurean.

Innokenty Volodin in Alexander Solzhenitsyn's
The First Circle

When the term "permissive society" is used of the present day, most people associate it with the drastic changes in sexual behaviour and attitudes that they believe have taken place in the last ten to twenty years. Paradoxically this is the area of which we have least direct evidence either about how people behave or about how behaviour and attitudes have changed. No one in England has conducted a survey as large, as detailed and as rigorous as the Kinsey studies in America.[1] Such data as we do have do indicate a trend towards increasingly permissive attitudes and behaviour but the data are fragmentary, and often contradictory. There probably has been a growth in willingness to tolerate and indulge in sexual behaviour previously regarded as taboo or immoral but the nature and extent of this change remains largely unknown. In many ways this is not surprising for sexual activities are not conducted in public in our society and are not susceptible to direct observation. Other kinds of behaviour are easier to record and measure since they are either public and measurable, or deviant and hence recorded whenever sanctions against them are invoked. In this way we can have some idea of the production of motor-cars, or the number of murders, the level of attendance at church or the number of working days lost in strikes, the fall in cinema-going or the rise in drug addiction. But we cannot know with any degree of precision,

61

how much premarital sexual intercourse occurs or what the number of lesbians is. Sex is a private matter between the partners concerned and the world rarely intrudes either to measure and encourage or to curb and prevent. It is an issue about which people are reticent to describe their behaviour and attitudes and yet not an issue about which the authorities can compel disclosure of the facts through investigation by census or courts of law. Even when a conscientious researcher is able to question people about their sexual habits and attitudes he may not get any reply and the reply he does get may not be the truth. Until we have an English researcher with the resources and shock-tactics of the Kinsey team we will continue to be uncertain about the sexual antics of the British people. Even then, many of us will have doubts about the accuracy and validity of his results.

One issue which has excited society and stimulated research is whether there has been a marked increase in premarital sexual intercourse (particularly among young people) and if there has, whether this implies that we have become more promiscuous. Perhaps the best study (though it contains some methodological errors) in this field to date is Michael Schofield's *The Sexual Behaviour of Young People*.[2] This study indicated that premarital sexual intercourse is common but by no means universal among young people. Of the sample surveyed the following proportions had experienced sexual intercourse at least once though unmarried at the time.

Experience of Premarital Intercourse[3]

	Boys	Girls
15–17 years old	11%	6%
17–19 years old	30%	16%

The picture that emerges is not one of riotous promiscuity for, as Schofield puts it "Our results have made it clear that premarital sexual relations are a long way from being universal among teenagers as over two-thirds of the boys and

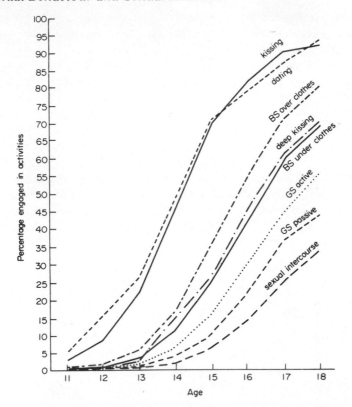

1 Accumulative incidence curves of eight activities for boys

three-quarters of the girls in our sample have not engaged in sexual intercourse".[4]

A broader picture of teenagers' sexual habits is indicated in Schofield's diagrams on pages 63 and 64 which summarize his findings as to the incidence of deep kissing, breast stimulation (BS) and genital stimulation (GS) among boys and girls at different ages as well as full sexual intercourse.[5]

It is of course possible that these findings under-estimate the amount of premarital sex that actually takes place. Thus the teenagers in the sample may have been reluctant to disclose the full extent of their sexual experiences to the interviewers. This would be especially true of the girls. Also it was a survey simply of teenagers. One might reasonably expect that premarital sexual experience is much greater among older unmarried people in their twenties who are more mature and more likely to be living away from home. Finally the survey was conducted at one point in time (1964) and thus can give us no idea of whether patterns of sexual behaviour were changing and if so how fast. Since *attitudes* to sex seem to have changed very rapidly in the 1960s a survey of sexual behaviour conducted in 1964 may by now be totally out of date. There are earlier surveys of sexual behaviour than Schofield's but it is doubtful whether the samples and techniques used are sufficiently similar for a meaningful comparison to be made. However, compared with Chesser's survey of the sexual behaviour of women in Britain in 1956, Schofield's study does seem to show that there has

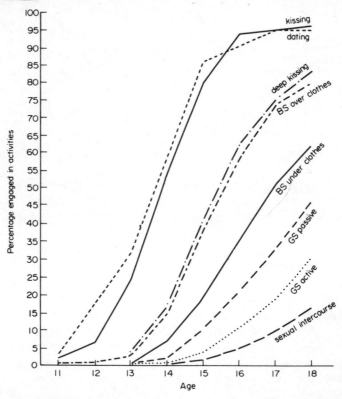

2 *Accumulative incidence curves of eight activities for girls*

been an increase in premarital intercourse. Schofield cal-
culates from Chesser's data that about 10 per cent of the
single girls in Chesser's samples were sexually experienced at
the age of twenty, compared with Schofield's own figure of
17 per cent so experienced at the age of eighteen.[6]

An interesting study by Wright and Cox again of teenagers
(but restricted to grammar-school sixth-formers) shows that a
remarkable change has taken place in *attitudes* towards
premarital sex during the 1960s. Wright and Cox asked their
boys and girls to rate various activities on a scale as to when
and whether they thought them wrong. The percentage of
the sample who endorse the different rating categories for
premarital sexual intercourse in 1963 and in 1970 is as shown
below.[7]

		Always wrong	Usually wrong	Sometimes wrong	Never wrong	Undecided
1963	Boys	28·6%	27·6%	20·5%	10·2%	13·1%
	Girls	55·8%	25·2%	6·6%	2·4%	10·0%
1970	Boys	10·3%	12·8%	30·4%	33·7%	12·8%
	Girls	14·6%	19·5%	30·0%	17·7%	18·2%

For comparison we can add Schofield's own (1964) figures
relating to attitudes to sexual intercourse before marriage.
The statement put to his sample was "sexual intercourse
before marriage is wrong".[8]

		Agree	Don't know	Disagree
1964	Boys	35%	20%	45%
	Girls	62%	14%	24%

Clearly there has been a massive change in attitudes in a
permissive direction and especially among the girls. The view

that premarital sex is wrong is rapidly disappearing. The survey by Wright and Cox also looked at the teenagers' attitudes to other activities often disapproved of, such as gambling, drunkenness, smoking, lying, stealing, suicide and the colour bar. In none of the other cases had there been anything like as great a shift of opinion as on the issue of premarital sex. There is no general shift towards permissiveness, the change is only concerned with sex. There is some tendency to be less ascetic and more permissive of (other) anti-ascetic acts but the changes are small in comparison with the very large change in attitudes to premarital sex.[9]

Changes in attitudes do not necessarily mean changes in behaviour but, since Schofield's study shows empirically that there is a close relationship in this area between attitudes and behaviour (and especially for girls), it would seem reasonable to infer that the period 1963–70 may have seen a very large increase in actual premarital intercourse. Schofield's sexually experienced girls have very low scores on his attitude factor "opposition to sexual intercourse". i.e. they "tend to reject the view that girls acquire bad reputations by having sexual experience",[10] "disagree that intercourse before marriage is wrong and do not believe that most boys want to marry a virgin". Since the Cox and Wright figures indicate that there is a decline in these views among teenage girls, it seems probable that there has also been a rise in the proportion of sexually experienced girls. If that is the case then there will certainly have been a concomitant rise in the numbers of sexually experienced boys and probably a greater degree of sexual experience among older unmarried people in their twenties as well.

That this is the case would seem to be supported by other pieces of indirect evidence on the subject. The rise in the illegitimacy rate, notably among groups one would expect to be most affected by the shift towards permissiveness, is one such fact. As Sillitoe puts it in his book *Britain in Figures* "The recent rising trend in illegitimacy seems to be characteristic of different social groups from the 'old' nineteenth century rates. The trend has started in the cities, especially in London and the South, is commoner among unmarried than

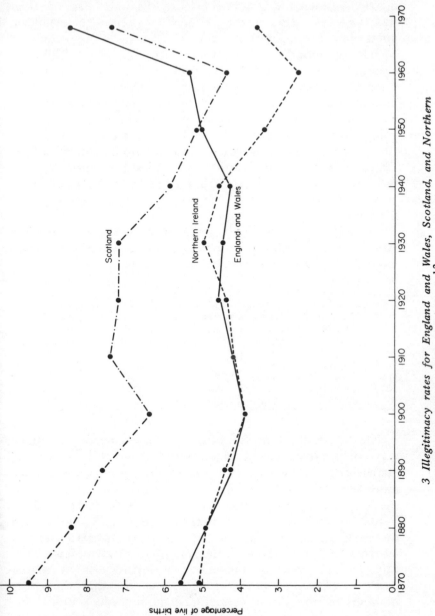

3 Illegitimacy rates for England and Wales, Scotland, and Northern Ireland over the last 100 years (Sillitoe[12])

married women and is more a feature of middle class life than was the case earlier in this century".[11] Although as Sillitoe points out one must be cautious in drawing inferences about social and moral changes from these figures (cf. Sillitoe's graph),[12] it is likely that they reflect an increase in premarital sexual intercourse notable among the permissive middle classes of London and the south-east. Some of the rise, though, is probably the result of fewer pregnant women going through a "shot-gun" wedding with the father of the child. Fewer premarital conceptions are now "concealed" by marriage and the proportion of brides pregnant on their wedding day has fallen. This change in itself indicates a greater degree of permissiveness in regard to sex and illegitimacy.

As well as the rise in illegitimacy rates there has been a large rise in the number of legal abortions to unmarried women since the law was altered in the permissive direction in 1967.[13]

	Total number of abortions	Number to single women	Number to divorced, widowed, separated women	Number to girls under 16	Number to single girls 16–19
1968	23,641	–	–	–	–
1969	58,819	25,499	4,762	1,231	–
1970	83,851	39,532	7,387	1,791	14,250
1973	169,362	83,001	13,666	3,476	30,164

The rise in the numbers of single women getting abortions may of course simply be a result of doctors becoming increasingly willing to perform the operation. In consequence more women have their abortions legally (and thus get into the official figures) rather than go to a back-street abortionist. But whether the rise in the number of abortions given to single women is real and due to rising premarital sex or whether it simply reflects changing medical attitudes—either way it indicates an increasing permissiveness in sexual matters. There is some evidence, though, that the rising numbers of unmarried women having abortions is in fact the result of a change in sexual behaviour. Dr J. Slome in his study of unmarried women who had wanted abortions seems to come to this conclusion. He says that "The kiss of the 1940s and 1950s has now become the sexual intercourse of the 1960s and 1970s . . . That is intercourse is practised where previously a kiss would have been appropriate."[14]

It seems likely then that a change in sexual habits has occurred in recent years as great as the changes which Kinsey describes as having occurred early in this century:

> During the four decades on which we have data, no other aspects of the sexual behaviour of the American female seem to have changed so much as petting and premarital coitus. The major change seems to have occurred in the generation born in the first decade after 1900. This was the generation which was in its teens and early twenties during the first world war and in the years immediately following that war.[15]

Given that the first World War disrupted British society even more than American it is possible that a similar change in sexual behaviour occurred in England and notably among women. In that case we seem to have had two separate marked shifts towards sexual permissiveness in the course of this century. The products of the first permissive generation are now aged between 60 and 70 and are the grandparents of the second one!

Although there has been a large and rapid increase in premarital sexual intercourse in our permissive society, it would be wrong to deduce from this that there has been a corresponding increase in promiscuity. In Schofield's study less than 12 per cent of the boys had had more than one partner in the last year while 6 per cent had only one partner and 3 per cent, though they had experienced intercourse, had had no such experience in the previous year. Only a quarter of the experienced boys, 6 per cent of the sample, had had four or more partners. Further, less than a quarter of the experienced girls had had more than one sexual partner in the previous year. Schofield concludes that "promiscuity though it exists is not a prominent feature of teenage sexual behaviour".[16]

The Cox and Wright study, while showing a marked change in attitudes towards premarital intercourse, does not show any similar change as regards promiscuity. Wright says "But the preliminary indications are that there has been little or no

Experience of Sexual Intercourse[17]

	Proportion of sample of boys having sexual intercourse	Proportion of experienced boys having sexual intercourse (est).
	%	%
At all	20	100
Experienced intercourse but not in last year	3	15
With only one partner in last year	6	30
With more than one partner in last year	12	60
With four or more partners in last year	6	30

increase in the condoning of promiscuity. The change has been rather in the direction of an increase in the number who adopt what Reiss has called the 'permissiveness with affection' standard".[18]

This would also seem to be true of older people, for a survey of students by Dr A. Gunn, senior assistant medical officer in the University health service, showed that of the girls:

(a) 78 per cent had experienced intercourse with less than three males;

(b) 51 per cent had experienced intercourse with one only;

(c) 73 per cent said that, given the opportunity, they would like to marry their present partner.

Dr Gunn concluded:

This is hardly in keeping with the myth of the promiscuous student and the results moreover refer to a complete three-year cross-section of the university population . . . . It is fair for parents to assume that a girl going away from home will be likely during her undergraduate years to form a stable and probably permanent relationship with a male colleague of the same institution.[19]

Given that a shift from abhorrence and restraint to "permissiveness with affection" has occurred in our attitude towards premarital sex, we now have the problem of explaining it. I would suggest that two relevant changes have occurred in recent years. First the general shift in the structuring of our moral attitudes from moralism to causalism that I discussed earlier. Although these categories were devised for analysing the behaviour of legislators debating how to control various types of deviance, it is possible to apply them in a modified form to an analysis of changing patterns of personal sexual morality. The moralists, who were formally the dominant group, discuss premarital sexual relations in terms of such acts being right or wrong *per se* and determine their own behaviour accordingly. For most of this group premarital intercourse is "degrading", "cheap", "disgusting", "polluting", "despicable", though there is also a minority that regards it as "natural", "liberating", "progressive". The causalist by contrast will have a much less emotive response and will simply ask the question "what are the results of premarital intercourse?" and assess whether on balance they are harmful or beneficial. On the one hand sex is very enjoyable, on the other it can result in an undesired pregnancy which could be disastrous for the couple concerned and especially for the woman. Clearly then the second factor affecting sexual behaviour in the 1960s has been the improvement in methods of contraception—notably the coming of the contraceptive pill. The pill is safer than previous contraceptives, it is taken by the woman and it is premeditated—a girl who desires premarital sexual intercourse can "go on the pill" and provided she takes it regularly need not worry about becoming pregnant. The pill avoids the woman having to rely on the man (often with disastrous consequences). It is removed from the seedy masculine world of barbers ("anything for the weekend, Sir?") and drug stores selling the traditional male sheath. As a result of the pill women have potentially gained the same degree of sexual freedom as men.

Even if contraception fails the consequences of pregnancy are less drastic than in the past. Abortions are much easier to obtain and much safer and the unmarried mother is much less harshly treated. Although the illegitimacy rate rose in the 1960s and has remained at the same higher rate in the 1970s, there are fewer babies (other than Roman Catholic ones) available for adoption, homes for unmarried mothers are being closed down[20] and, as pointed out earlier, the number of "shot-gun" weddings is declining. Thus, although there has been a rise in illegitimacy, it is probably true to say that the social problems stemming from it are decreasing. By relaxing our sanctions against the unmarried mother we have created more of them (i.e. more unmarried mothers) and yet reduced the aggregate amount of suffering entailed. Much of the suffering was not caused by the act of illegitimacy but by society's responses to it. One probable reason for the decline in the sanctions against illegitimacy has been the falling age of marriage. In a sense, when the age of marriage is low there is less need for the taboos. Although as a result the illegitimacy rate has risen, it is still much lower than it would have been if we had combined our present permissive outlook with the earlier pattern of deferring marriage for a few years. It is, though, a paradox that illegitimacy should rise at the same time as contraceptive techniques improve and become more widely diffused. The reason probably lies in the wide differences in rationality and foresight that exist among different individuals. Whereas all girls could understand the simple condemnation and prohibition of sexual intercourse of the moralist era, they do not all have the intelligence and prudence necessary to a rational use of contraceptive methods. The intelligent unmarried professional woman in her twenties goes on the pill and declares to the world that sexual restraint is no longer necessary. "If you can't be good, be careful". Less competent women understand her general message and like her indulge in premarital intercourse but lack her knowledge of contraception and her rational planned outlook and become pregnant.

In a study of women who had had an abortion, J. M. Williams and K. Hindell noted that:

... the unmarried women in our sample were generally sexually inexperienced. Sexual intercourse was a very infrequent occurrence. It was something that our youngest respondents had only experienced once or twice. Not only were they not "promiscuous" in the sense that they did not sleep around, but moreover they did not have regular sexual activity even with one man. Thus the sexual act giving rise to the pregnancy was usually unexpected and certainly on their part unplanned. It was the result of excessive petting, excessive demands from the boy friend or excessive drinking and they did not expect it to happen when these exercises were initiated, however amazing this lack of awareness may seem to an outsider.

Their sexual morality was indeed such that they believed it wrong to plan cold-bloodedly for sexual intercourse within the types of relationships they had as opposed to a spontaneous hot-blooded response to a particular set of circumstances. Thus their romanticism was in direct conflict with reality or at least practicality. Within their morality premarital sexual intercourse was permissible as long as it was a spontaneous act of love with a loved one, but implicitly contraception was not permissible because it denied spontaneity. The idea of stopping half-way to fit a cap for instance offended their romantic ideas. It was "unnatural" and "contrived". Moreover they said they did not know that they were going to let it happen. Until it did so they found no point at which to stop.[21]

These findings are interesting for two reasons:

(a) They confirm that there is little truth in the popular view "that young unmarried women have been seeking abortions mainly as a direct result of an increase in promiscuity and immorality coupled with a crude, cynical, hedonistic attitude to sex".[22] Once again the evidence points to the prevalent moral attitude to sex being one of "permissiveness with affection" and not one of wild promiscuous hedonism.

(b) They show that there are grave difficulties in the transitional period when moralism is giving way to causalism and that many people mix together aspects of the two moralities in a manner that leads to personal disaster. It is not the causalist who gets pregnant but the woman who confuses foresight and prudence with cold-bloodedness and a lack of spontaneity.

As the pill becomes more easily available to single women and with the development in the future of the new "do it yourself" abortion pill or pessary the number of illegitimate births will probably fall again.[23] These new drugs will not require the rational foresight involved in taking the present oral contraceptive, for the woman need only take it if she discovers she is late with her period. As Dr Malcolm Potts, the medical secretary of the International Planned Parenthood Federation, put it "they will by their sheer availability and cheapness mean that every woman who wanted to could have the means of abortion—either legally or illicitly—in her own hands . . . we shall see a complete rethinking of our moral and social attitude towards birth control and abortion."[24]

The change in attitudes and behaviour in relation to premarital intercourse stems then from a combination of a general change in our moral attitudes, coupled with a particular change in the technology of birth control. Without the former, the "pill" would be irrelevant to the needs of the unmarried since their decision as to whether or not they will sleep with someone would be determined by factors other than the simple consequences of doing so—by factors of taboo and total moral prohibition. Without the pill unmarried couples might hesitate to sleep together because of the consequences of an error with earlier, more fallible contraceptive methods. That people have come to see the world in terms of cause and consequence is shown by their changing attitudes to the pill itself. In an opinion research poll conducted for the *Evening Standard* in 1971 the following results emerged:

Should the pill be available to single women?[25]

	All	Men	Women	Women 15—24	Women 25—44	Women 45—64	Women 65+
Yes	59%	68%	51%	76%	62%	46%	24%
No	32%	23%	39%	20%	33%	46%	53%
Don't know	9%	9%	10%	4%	5%	8%	23%

There is a strong and growing belief (the pollsters say there is a "rapid shift" but do not give the earlier figures) that single women should be permitted to take the contraceptive pill and this view is especially strong among the younger women (more of whom will be unmarried). This would indicate the prevalence of moral views of a causalist nature.

The respondents to the poll are probably arguing: "The consequence of intercourse for single women who are not allowed the pill is possible pregnancy. They should take the pill to avoid this consequence." By implication they are saying: "It is a good thing for single women to have sexual intercourse if they want to" and "moral considerations other than consequential ones are irrelevant."

Contrary to many writers in this field I would also argue that the lack of support for promiscuity in present-day attitudes may also be a manifestation of utilitarian attitudes. It does not seem to be a new version of the old moralist view "sex in marriage is holy but outside it it is disgusting", now put forward in a revised form as "sex is good provided you are in love with your partner but promiscuity is degrading". Rather permissiveness with affection is simply a recognition that sex under these circumstances is more pleasant and rewarding and that promiscuous people tend to be unhappy. The reasons for not being promiscuous are prudential rather than based on moral condemnation.

To take this argument any further it is necessary to clarify the distinction I made earlier between causalism and other forms of utilitarianism.[26] The causalist is only interested in those consequences of his actions which are visible, tangible, measurable. As such it is a viewpoint likely to be popular among legislators and Government bureaucrats who are only provided with information of this kind. They are forced to take notice of unhappiness (of certain kinds) because unhappy people often express their misery in visible (and sometimes harmful) ways—by political organization, by anti-social behaviour or by becoming a charge on the State. Happiness or contentment by contrast is not visible (except in the negative sense that people are not rioting or organizing or getting drunk) and it cannot be legislated for except indirectly by encouraging faster growth and greater material prosperity, and even here people are beginning to have doubts.

Thus a causalist-minded legislator is only interested in the measurable and harmful consequences of people's sexual behaviour such as unwanted pregnancies. He is concerned to measure the cost of these and to weigh this up against the cost of legislative intervention. A good example of this attitude is seen in the document *A Birth-Control Plan for Britain*[27] where the cost to society of unwanted children is weighed up against the cost of a free birth-control service. They estimate that a completely free birth-control service would cost about £40 million a year and note that

> every year that we continue to allow perhaps 150,000 live births as a result of unwanted pregnancy through lack of an efficient birth-control service, we are committing ourselves to an expenditure of another £300 million of tax-payers' and rate-payers' money during the following two decades. That money is well spent once the children are born, but most of it could have been saved by better birth-control provision and publicity.

The main items in this calculation for Great Britain in 1969 are as follows:

		£ million
50,000 illegitimate children @	£4,350 each =	217
14,000 fourth children @	£ 500 each =	7
10,000 fifth children @	£ 500 each =	5
13,000 sixth and subsequent children @	£ 500 each =	6
	Total =	235

This is a perfectly valid and worth-while way of looking at such a problem and the causalist legislators have now in effect accepted the plan and ignore moralist criticisms about "sex on the rates" and "subsidizing immorality". However, it is not a basis on which individuals can plan their own lives. For the individual, pleasure is as important as pain, and his or her own subjective feelings are the indices of these on which most reliance is placed. Accordingly a utilitarian philosophy for individuals takes many other kinds of consequences into account and not simply pregnancy or venereal disease. An individual can and does take into account inward states (happiness, love, affection) in a way that a strict view of causalism does not. I shall term this *personal utilitarianism*. The moral view opposed to this I shall term *ritualism* because of the central importance in it of notions of pollution and degradation. The relationship between the two dichotomies, causalism-moralism and personal utilitarianism-ritualism can be shown in a diagram as follows. In each box of the diagram are the most important reasons for not sleeping with someone for a person holding that pair of moral views.

	Causalism	Moralism
Ritualism	V.D. ←	Pollution Degradation
Personal Utilitarianism	↓ Pregnancy	↓ Affection Absent

→ = Changes over time

The boxes marked "pregnancy" and "pollution" are straightforward but some explanation is needed for the other two. For the moralist it is wrong to have intercourse without affection and this is a rule that can be generally applied. The test of whether the rule applies is personal but the rule itself is not. The individual who holds to a philosophy of personal utilitarianism seeks affection in a relationship because he or she knows from experience that such relationships are more rewarding. He is not concerned except in a peripheral sense with other people's behaviour in this respect. Thus there are two alternative reasons for the behaviour that is termed "permissiveness with affection". I would suggest that personal utilitarianism is more likely to be the basis on which people justify an attitude of "permissiveness with affection" and the behaviour that stems from it.

The other attitudes noted in Carr and Wright's survey also seem to fit in with a philosophy of personal utilitarianism better than with one of diluted moralism.[28] I say diluted because the criterion of "affection absent", when the moralists use it, seems still to have a ritualistic flavour. It is as if they feel they can no longer justify chastity on the grounds that sex is degrading and therefore seek to do so on the nowadays more acceptable grounds that promiscuity is wrong because no love is involved. The real reason for their abhorrence of promiscuity is not the stated one.

VENEREAL DISEASE

A similar point can be made about venereal disease. The
consequences of V.D. are real, tangible and unpleasant, and
for that reason I have placed it in the column marked
causalism. Some indication of its costs is given by R. S.
Morton in his book *Venereal Disease:*

> The US Public Health Service considered the costs of maintenance of
> the syphilitic blind to be 6 million dollars per annum and hospitalization
> of the syphilitic insane to be no less than 49 million dollars. This works
> out at about £18 million for the US population of about 180 million.
> In England and Wales in 1962 there were about 138,210 new
> patients attending special clinics. The total number of out-patient visits
> was 791,000. According to the Ministry of Health, costing depends on
> the type of hospital concerned. If all the visits had been made to
> London teaching hospitals the cost would have been £1·13 million. If
> all the visits had been made to non-teaching hospitals the cost would
> have been £830,000. Thus without much error we can say that
> day-to-day venereal disease out-patient services cost £1 million per
> annum. To this must be added in-patient costs both short and
> long-term. If these approached the American figure of £1 million per 10
> million population, they must amount to £4·7 million. The estimated
> total of £5·7 million is for the year 1962 and for that part of the Health
> Service in England and Wales only. The loss to the nation in output and
> taxes from those crippled and unable to contribute and the loss to
> industry implicit in the 791,000 out-patient attendances is anybody's
> estimate.[29]

Thus the causalist-minded legislators should regard V.D. as
a serious problem that requires to be faced and eliminated.
For the individual it is a less immediate matter since the risk
of infection to any one person is low and the chances of
being cured are high. The chief moral to be drawn is that
partners known to be promiscuous—homosexuals, sailors,
tarts, immigrants—are to be avoided. In general it is not the
main reason for a utilitarian decision about whether or not to
sleep with someone. It is subordinate to such considerations
as the risk of pregnancy and the fact that relationships
involving affection are more satisfying than promiscuous
ones. However, V.D. is not seen in this way, nor is it regarded
as a disease like other diseases, to be treated and prevented in

the same kind of way. Morton gives an instance of the emotional and moralist response to V.D. that still prevails:

> When for example a factory-worker's fellows learn that he or she has V.D. the news spreads rapidly. The contagiousness of the condition is liable to be magnified. Everything the victim has touched is rumoured to be fouled. Demands are made on the management for the victim's removal. The works lavatories are declared unusable. Threats of strike action may follow. Common sense is challenged and overrun. Emotions crystallize in a threatening communal synthesis. Such situations are not uncommon even today. In a span of four years aid was sought from the authorities in the settlement of four such upheavals. In one the victim, a laundry worker, did not have and never had had venereal infection. Vicious and hostile feelings prevailed in these circumstances. The vehemence of both men and women was intense and their condemnation often vitriolic. "Lock him up": "Whip her": "Lack of moral fibre": "Dirty bitch": "Force him to have treatment": "Sack her". There is no ambivalence here: no hint of compassion, pity, or even humility. We can only sense, beneath the heat, the smugly satisfying glow of self-righteousness and wonder at the near-hysterical demands for ostracism.[30]

This is not the way in which we usually react to disease. Polio or tuberculosis are as harmful diseases but do not evoke such a marked moral response. The style and content of the response is not that of the causalist mode of argument. What is probably true is that V.D. is simply a symbol of and a surrogate for pollution and degradation. We no longer speak of sex openly as dirty so we get hysterical about V.D. instead. It is yet another case of the moralist putting on causalist clothes in order to win an argument in a society tending more and more to use causalist and not moralist modes of arguing and acting. One way to test whether a person's fear of and hostility to V.D. is genuinely causalist or really moralist-ritualist is to find out what his reaction is to the possibility of curing it. If in the future it becomes possible to eradicate it then in Carstairs' phrase "moralists might soon be confronted with the alarming prospect of a world in which sexual promiscuity was freed of its age-long attendant threat of disease".[31] This might occur as a result of a combination of new super antibiotics and more rapid and certain means of detection (i.e. an extension of the way we tackle the problem now) or by some form of vaccination. Morton sees the chance of discovering vaccines for all forms of V.D as remote, but notes that:

> Dr John Knox speaking at a seminar in Denver in January 1965 gave it as his considered opinion that if as much money was put into syphilis research as went into research on poliomyelitis—which did not kill or cripple as many people—a vaccine could be found in a few years.[32]

A genuine causalist would welcome such a discovery and would be willing to allocate the research funds needed. A "secret" moralist would be at best ambivalent about such a discovery, would be very unwilling to regard syphilis in the same way as polio and quite unwilling to see as much money spent on preventing it.[33]

ABSENCE OF AFFECTION

Thus the decline of the moralist-ritualist view of premarital sex as polluting and degrading has led those who still hanker after some such approach to sexual morality to retreat in two directions. At the legislative level (and in personal encounters) they fulminate about V.D., i.e. they put forward a pseudo-causalist argument which I have categorized as ritualistic in the same sense as arguments based on the notion of pollution. The other retreat is to attack premarital sex as loveless, an approach which appears similar to the notion of permissiveness with affection but probably reduces to the tautology that all premarital sex *must* be promiscuous and lacking in true affection. This is in fact simply the old ritualist position clad in new language to render it more acceptable to a present-day audience which is disinclined to accept ritualist moralities of any kind. In fact the category "causalism-ritualism" does not exist since those who appear to occupy this position are either really moralist-ritualists or personal utilitarians; the latter happen to be also causalists because their philosophy tends to be reduced to causalism when they are asked to play a political or bureaucratic role. Thus there is a tendency for the four boxes to collapse into a two-box model with moralist-ritualists being seen as the only alternative to causalist-personal utilitarians. What prevents this from happening entirely is the limitations on the uses of the term causalism as I have defined it and the unwillingness of the moralist-ritualists to stick to a "losing" argument and a moral position that is under considerable attack.[34]

My main purpose in analysing people's reasons for caution in sexual matters is to show that the rational desire to avoid pregnancy has little in common with the emotional revulsion involved in condemning promiscuity as degrading. There is no real problem in incorporating considerations about the nature of a relationship into a framework of a morality of consequences. A morality of consequences does not imply a constant egocentric calculation of the pleasures and draw- backs of indulging in particular sexual relationships. In this context it simply says that, in general, steady affairs tend to be happier for those concerned than wild promiscuity and that it is therefore better to aim at the former than the latter. To criticize such a moral position as being merely hedonistic or instrumental and unconcerned with the quality of human relationships is to commit the same kind of error as the critics of the utilitarians or earlier still of Epicurus.[35]

This charge, whether levelled at the epicureans or at the utilitarians, is perhaps best refuted by the arguments assembled by Mill:

Human beings have faculties more elevated than the animal appetites and when once made conscious of them do not regard anything as happiness which does not *include* their gratification ... there is no known Epicurean theory of life which does not assign to the pleasures of the intellect of the feelings and the imagination and of the moral sentiments a much higher value as pleasures than to those of mere sensation .... It is quite compatible with the principle of utility to recognize the fact that some kinds of pleasure are more desirable and more valuable than others. It would be absurd that while in estimating all other things quality is considered as well as quantity the estimation of pleasure should be supposed to depend on quantity alone. If I am asked what I mean by difference of quality in pleasures or what makes one pleasure more valuable than another merely as a pleasure except its being greater in amount there is but one possible answer. Of two pleasures if there be one to which all or almost all who have experience of both give a decided preference, irrespective of any feelings of moral obligation to prefer it, that is the more desirable pleasure. If one of the two is by those who are competently acquainted with both placed so far above the other that they prefer it even though knowing it to be attended with a greater amount of discontent and would not resign it for any quantity of any other pleasure which their nature is capable of, we are justified in ascribing to the preferred enjoyment a superiority in quality so far outweighing quantity as to render it in comparison, of small account.[36]

Here stated at a general level is the reason why in an era of a morality of consequences most people prefer "permissiveness with affection" to promiscuity even though the latter is no longer a taboo or condemned activity. Given the simplicity of Mill's argument and the breadth of his sympathies it is difficult to see why for many authors "utilitarianism" as applied to sexual behaviour implies some kind of impoverishment of human relationships. For example in their study *Sex and Society* Walker and Fletcher declare that "This attitude is a direct consequence of the transposition of utilitarian standards of judgement into the realm of personal action and its results are uniformly disastrous"[37] and again ". . . It was a disastrous assumption because as we have tried to show personal relationships are reciprocal, utilitarian relationships are not and the logic of utilitarian action cannot be extended into personal action without destructive effect."[38]

Given the preceding specific statement of what is involved in a morality of consequences and given the general defence of utilitarianism it is very difficult to see what meaning or validity these statements can have. Quite simply there is no such dichotomy between love and utility. Utilitarianism, far from not applying to sexual relationships, is probably more appropriate here than in any other field of human behaviour.

Another way of looking at the question of the nature of "permissiveness with affection" is in terms of conditioning. In childhood people have strong ties of love and affection to particular individuals, especially their parents, and in adult life they automatically seek relationships of a similar kind. Those individuals who are promiscuous are probably those who lacked strong and stable relationships with their parents when very young and who failed to acquire this capacity for loving a particular person. Most people refrain from promiscuity not because they find it abhorrent but because they desire something quite different. For people in our kind of society permissiveness with affection is simply more satisfying than promiscuity.

INCEST

Perhaps I can make this clearer by digressing to look at those aberrant sexual relationships between primary kin known as incest. In his book *Kinship and Marriage*, Robin Fox suggests two types of theories about incest, viz. those that postulate:

> (a) people have repressed desires for incestuous relations which are very strong and hence they institute stern penalties for incest to keep them repressed.

and those that postulate:

> (b) people reared in close familiarity from childhood do not develop sexual feelings for each other and are therefore averse to incest.[39]

If I rewrite Fox's categories so as to deal rather with the kinds of sexual behaviour we have discussed earlier they will read:

> (c) people have repressed desires for premarital sexual relations which are very strong and hence they institute stern penalties to keep them repressed.

and

> (d) two people who lack ties of love and affection for each other do not develop strong sexual feelings for each other and are therefore averse to promiscuity.

What I am suggesting *by anology* is that we have moved from a society in which all premarital sexual relationships were treated as in category (c) to a society in which such relationships are permitted but where promiscuous behaviour does not occur for reasons put forward in category (*d*). These reasons of the (*d*) type were always true but in the past they were masked by the occurrence of social processes of type (*c*) towards all premarital sex, whether promiscuous or not.

Fox's categories for discussing incest are of course of great interest in their own right. Incest does not occur or is forbidden or both in almost all societies but societies vary greatly in the way they eliminate incestuous behaviour. In some societies incest is suppressed by type (*a*) methods; in others it does not occur because the state of affairs described in (*b*) prevails. The preventing of incest is a universal problem for society, but societies differ almost totally in the ways in which they deal with this problem.

However, the ways in which incest is prevented in a society may also differ systematically depending on which family role (mother-son, father-daughter or brother-sister) is involved. Within a given society mother-son relationships may not be prevented in the same way as brother-sister relationships. The *difference* between the way these two particular aberrant sexual relationships are dealt with remains fairly constant in societies with similar family structures to our own, even though the overall patterns of prevention of incest are very dissimilar. Although societies may differ greatly as to whether mechanism (*a*) or mechanism (*b*) is invoked against incestuous relationships as a whole it does seem likely that—at any rate for societies similar to our own[40]—mother-son relationships are more likely to be dealt with by mechanism (*a*) and brother-sister relationships by mechanism (*b*). Father-daughter relationships will tend to fall between the two categories and for this reason (among others) are in our type of society the commonest form of incest and the one regarded with least abhorrence.

This differential mechanism for preventing incest explains the centrality of the Oedipus complex in Freudian psychology. Any psychology having as one of its most important concepts the notion of "repression" was bound to concentrate its attention on the mother-son relationship, i.e. that family relationship where society was most likely to control incestuous desires by invoking and then suppressing them. By contrast, the corresponding Electra complex based on the father-daughter relationship is not worked out in anything like the same detail, has a very unsatisfactory explanation and occupies a much more peripheral place in Freudian thought. Brother-sister relationships which on this hypothesis are simply not desired rather than repressed are rarely dealt with by the dynamic psychologists except in terms of sibling rivalry, notably rivalry for parental attention and affection. It seems to me that this does not represent so much a deficiency in Freudian psychology (except in so far as it shows the limited use of the concept of repression) as real differences in the nature of European family relationships. Freud in his discussion of infantile sexuality is able to point to the erotic aspect of mother-son/child relationships involved in such activities as breast-feeding and the need to repress this later in order that the son may make the transition to adult sexuality. However, he is unable to show any corresponding mechanism whereby a similar process occurs in relation to the father-daughter relationship. The idea put forward by some dynamic psychologists that the daughter somehow comes into erotic contact with the father's genitalia seems ludicrous. It would have been even more absurd in the era of the distant upper-middle class Edwardian paterfamilias who saw relatively little of his children. Brothers and sisters also do not come into any *structured and systematic* erotic contact with each other, and the effect of their being brought up together "in close familiarity from childhood" seems rather to prevent their developing sexual feelings for each other. Reinforcement of this view comes from the fact that children brought up in small groups (from various families) on a kibbutz are also in later life averse to sexual relationships with other former members of their group.[41] The fact of people being brought up together as small children, whether blood relatives or not, does seem to prevent them from developing sexual feelings towards each other as adults.

Mother-son sexual relationships then do not occur because the desire for them is strongly repressed as part of the child's normal process of growing-up. Brother-sister sexual relationships do not occur because neither side is interested in them.

Familiarity has bred sexual indifference. Father-daughter sexual relationships do not fit easily into either category and since the two methods of incest avoidance are incompatible this probably weakens the mechanism of incest prevention in this case. This would account for the fact that father-daughter incest is in most European societies the most common form and the least abhorred. Another and more powerful reason is that a sexual relationship between father and daughter probably poses the least threat to the authority structure of the family and certainly to the authority of the father as head of the family. Also in this relationship the authority roles associated with the age and sex of the partners are compatible. The father possesses authority both by reason of his age and by reason of being a male, and correspondingly the daughter is in a subservient position in both respects. It is easier for a sexual relationship to occur under these conditions than say between mother and son where there is a clear clash of authority roles. This clash and the torment and uncertainty associated with it will of course add to the horror with which such a relationship is viewed and the rigour with which any temptation in that direction is supressed.

It is difficult to predict what will happen to incestuous behaviour in the permissive society and what effect this would have on the family as an institution. However, it is probable that this will be the very least of the challenges that the family will have to face in the future. The menacing rise of the so-called women's liberation movements is a much more serious threat to the stability of the family and one which we must now deal with.

WOMEN'S LIB

It is a mistake to analyse a movement such as women's lib either in terms of the psychological oddity of its members or in terms of the legitimate grievances women have in our society. Most observers have tended either to dismiss the movement as the work of a minority of twisted females who have failed as women and who somehow both hate men and yet want to be men themselves, or to see it as a pressure group making specific bread-and-butter demands on behalf of women as a whole. The first approach points to the odd traits of some of the leaders of the movement for the following reasons:

First, some of the leaders are by their own admission unable to have any children and hence unable to fulfil the most important of female roles. Their participation in the movement and their attack on woman's child-bearing and child-rearing role stems from their understandable frustration at being unable to fulfil it. They naturally wish to attack a system in which a woman's status and importance is tied so closely to her capacity as a mother. Such a system excludes the sterile woman and deprives her life of meaning. It does though seem rather suspect when such women suggest that children are more of a burden than a pleasure for all those women who do have families.

Secondly, some are exceedingly aggressive. Indeed, women's lib leaders tend to provide the only really good female debaters, because they alone can provide the *public* verbal aggression necessary to that otherwise decorous activity. Aggressive behaviour in women tends to be strongly disapproved of in our society. For most women this does not create any problems since they are constitutionally less aggressive than men and glad to avoid the problems that male aggression creates for its participants. For these few women, however, who even by male standards are abnormally aggressive, society provides no outlets and the social constraints on women exhibiting aggressive behaviour are especially onerous for them. They cannot state their problem directly, for demands that (for instance) our society should permit the recruitment of female combat troops or encourage women to make direct physical passes at men who attract them would be met with refusal and ridicule. Whatever changes occur in other aspects of the economic and political roles of women and of men, the sexual division of aggressive labour is unlikely to vary. As Tiger puts it "organized aggression remains an all-male phenomenon in part as a result of human evolutionary history"[42] and "almost universally war is an all-male enterprise. In various communities females participate in police activity, but they usually do so in clearly defined and quite specialized circumstances."[43] Institutions which foster aggression are an extreme case but they are closely connected to most of the other key sources of power in our society and the values and attitudes necessary to their functioning are widely diffused throughout our culture. As a result the notion that aggressive behaviour is a male prerogative is continually reinforced, and in view of the importance and power of institutions for aggression (armies, police, etc.) it is unlikely to be successfully challenged. Nor is there any evidence that many women want to challenge it. The aggressive woman is doomed to perpetual frustration, and as women become more equal to men in other respects her frustration will intensify.

Thirdly, many of the aggressive leaders of women's lib seem to be married to men who, far from being the passive complementary consorts one might expect, are even more pathologically aggressive than their wives. They are often of lower social status than their wives, have held jobs of a distinctly tough and masculine kind, such as coal-mining, and even have criminal records involving violent offences. It is as if in a last desperate attempt to play a submissive female role the aggressive women's "libber" deliberately marries a thug. His brutal and insensitive behaviour within the marriage naturally confirms her opposition to a society based on male dominance. She only knows of two kinds of male-female relationship, the total domination (or else bitter struggle) that is her own experience or the total equality idealized in her theories. She cannot realize that there are an infinite number of positions between these two extremes and that most couples happily create relationships which, whilst not egalitarian, are by no means authoritarian. Some kind of mild and diluted male dominance is probably the chosen experience of most married couples. This of course is precisely the kind of relationship the aggressive women's "libber" can never have. For her, total dominance of one partner by another is the only realizable possibility. This explains her exaggerated longing for an egalitarian world in which dominance ceases to be an issue and in which the central problem of her life is apparently resolved and removed.

These psychological explanations, though valid and

interesting, do rather miss the point. There have always been maladjusted women of the types discussed, but only now in the 1960s and 1970s have they been able to gather a following of ordinary normal women. In the past they had to find other and different outlets for their frustrations.

A similar criticism can be made of the view that women's lib is simply a pressure group for women putting forward legitimate demands for free contraception and abortion, for equal pay and job opportunities, for nurseries and play groups and for the tailoring of career patterns to meet the needs of the intelligent woman who wants both children and a career. All these are reasonable reforms which should be instituted as quickly as possible and which will probably be achieved during the course of the 1970s. However, it is difficult to see why the need to achieve such bread-and-butter reforms (which are widely supported by people to whom women's lib is anathema) should call forth a radical movement which dares to attack the sacred institution of the family and to suggest that differences between the sexes should be eliminated. Whereas the emancipation of women implies that women should have equal formal institutional opportunities to men and that distinctively female roles should enjoy parity of esteem with male ones, the liberation of women means that such roles should cease to exist and that equality should be achieved through sameness. Women should not merely have access to male opportunities but should not feel inhibited from grabbing them by a desire to be women; i.e. to behave as they feel women ought to. The bread-and-butter demands of women's lib listed earlier are not more likely to be achieved by this new approach than by the earlier reformist tradition. If anything they are likely to alienate potential support and postpone reform, rather in the way the more militant suffragettes prevented women from getting the vote earlier than they did.[44] The sources of female radicalism must be sought elsewhere.

One possible source of women's discontent is the fact that we are in the process of changing from a society that is repressive about sex to one which is repressive about birth (as a source of over-population). The strong male dominance necessary to a society insisting on sexual repression (and by the

operation of the double standard especially restrictive for
women) is crumbling and this has given women's lib its
opportunity. Birth control has made "birth repression"
possible without sexual repression and the world-wide population crisis has made such birth repression essential to our very
survival. Already we are at the stage where a medical expert has
posed the drastic alternatives of an intelligent overall plan to
curb the population explosion or legislation compelling future
generations to limit their families. An expert in another field,
Britain's leading sociologist of contraception, John Peel, has
predicted that within a few years parents having more than two
children will be thought as anti-social as people who drink
and drive.[45] Although society is becoming increasingly
permissive about sex it is simultaneously becoming much less
permissive about birth. In Sweden, where this process has
gone furthest, sexual permissiveness coexists with a declining
birth rate that is now so low that the Swedes are in danger of
dying out.[46] In other countries too, notably Japan, the drive
to reduce the birth rate (plus the ready availability of
contraceptives and abortion) to avoid population growth has
been overdone and the population may be failing to
reproduce itself. Under these circumstances the basic female
role in society, that of producing children, is devalued. The
very process for which women were once praised and valued
is now seen as a threat to mankind. Giving birth is seen as an
activity to be controlled and prevented rather than freely and
joyfully indulged in. As a result, the very significance of a
woman's life is threatened and challenged, her status and
security eroded. The decline of sexual repression gave
women's lib its opportunity, the rise of birth repression gives
women's lib its impetus. From the devaluing of child-bearing
stems woman's radical dissatisfaction with her traditional role
and her desire to seek a new one. Since her distinctively
female task can never again be held in equal esteem with male
tasks, so equality is sought instead in the obliteration of sex
differences. It is unlikely, though, that this is anything more
than a temporary phenomenon. In time, as we achieve full
control over the size and growth of our population, we will
cease to need the urgent propaganda against more births,
indeed against birth itself, that characterizes the present

crisis. Birth control will become a purely routine administrative matter, rather than a subject calling forth strong emotion and dogmatic moralizing. As this happens the crisis of meaning in women's lives will resolve itself. Child-rearing will again become a respectable and admired vocation though with the emphasis on quality and not quantity. In any case, the family is too strong and durable an institution to be damaged by the attacks of women's lib.

Nor is the growth of premarital sex liable to undermine the family, for even these individuals who are most permissive in this direction continue to disapprove of extra-marital sexual affairs by married people.[47] The family is durable because it is irreplaceable as an institution for bringing up children and it is unlikely to be damaged by the attractions of such rival institutions as communes. The twentieth century has seen many attempts to undermine or supplant the family as an institution from the Russian experiment in anti-family permissiveness in the 1920s to those hideous co-educational monasteries, the Israeli kibbutzim. The Russians, appalled at the social disorder and juvenile delinquency that followed their attack on the family, rapidly reversed their policies which now seek to preserve and strengthen family life.[48] The kibbutzim do not seem to attract the current generation of Israelis,[49] the overwhelming majority of whom enjoy a properly gemütlich family-dominated existence. If the family can survive and prosper in such unfavourable circumstances, I do not think we need fear for its future in England. Above all the family is a self-reinforcing unit. Most people experience their earliest affectionate relationship within the family and in our society this means that they have a small number of very strong and exclusive ties with particular individuals, notably their mother and father. This produces the kind of adult personality that needs a strong and exclusive relationship with another adult, i.e. one who will easily fit once again into a family structure, this time as spouse and parent. Such people will not be attracted to the multiple and diffuse relationships offered by communal living. Even if a move could be made to some sort of radical alternative to the family the benefits are vague and unproven and we might well be worse off if we adopted them; moreover, even if there were substantial benefits to be gained from such a change, these would be more than outweighed by the transition costs involved in making the change. The uncertainty and chaos of the period of transition might even create so much havoc that a stable substitute for the family would never emerge. Even in the permissive society family life is here to stay.

5 Buggery and the Decline of the British Empire

> *O! withered is the garland of the war*
> *The soldier's pole is fallen: young boys and girls*
> *Are level now with men.*

Cleopatra in·William Shakespeare's *Antony and Cleopatra*

As society has become more tolerant of normal sexual behaviour under conditions where it was formerly condemned, it is perhaps inevitable that there should also be a growing tolerance for sexual activities traditionally regarded as perverted, notably homosexuality. Indeed in the debate in the House of Commons on the Sexual Offences Act which legalized male homosexual behaviour Leo Abse explicitly used this as an argument:

It [the law against male homosexual behaviour] leaves the homosexual feeling that he is almost a selected minority specially chosen for persecution. Within the wider community he sees increasingly permissive attitudes, he sees more permissive attitudes adopted to fornication and adultery. He sees franker and often salacious advertisements on the screen and television.[1]

It is obviously more difficult for the heterosexual majority to try and compel the homosexual into sexual abstinence at a time when the restrictions on their own behaviour are being relaxed. If "normal" people can have queer and kinky sex why shouldn't homosexuals?[2] The homosexuals themselves see it this way as is shown by the emergence of organizations such as Gay Liberation and the Campaign for Homosexual Equality. They are also campaigning for the right to come out into the open and behave in public with the same degree of freedom as heterosexuals.

Now that the law against homosexual behaviour between consenting male adults in private has been repealed, it is very difficult to see why such behaviour should ever have been subject to legal sanction. Why should anyone want to persecute this harmless, powerless and rather pathetic minority? One reason that is often suggested is that homosexuality must be suppressed in order to protect family life, for without the restraining influence of social and legal sanctions men would choose the free gay life of a homosexual rather than take on the onerous responsibilities of the paterfamilias.

Another reason that can be put forward is that homosexuality has been traditionally regarded as an abomination because it cuts across the distinction between men and women. Mary Douglas's commentary on the abominations of Leviticus seems relevant here.[3] In the Old Testament the Jews are instructed to avoid certain objects, animals and situations as being unclean. They are told to avoid eating unclean animals of apparently diverse kinds and origins. The rules are summed up in the Books of Leviticus (11: 1—31) and Deuteronomy (14: 1—12). If we take examples from the text of the King James authorized version it becomes clear both that the rules cover an apparently unrelated set of circumstances and yet have a certain coherence.

(2) For thou art an holy people unto the Lord thy God, and the Lord hath chosen thee to be a peculiar people unto himself, above all the nations that are upon the earth. (3) Thou shalt not eat any abominable thing. (4) These are the beasts which ye shall eat: the ox, the sheep, and the goat, (5) The hart and the roebuck, and the fallow deer, and the wild goat, and the pygarg, and the wild ox, and the chamois. (6) And every beast that parteth the hoof, and cleaveth the cleft into two claws, and cheweth the cud among the beasts, that ye shall eat. (7) Nevertheless these ye shall not eat of them that chew the cud, or of them that divide the cloven hoof; as the camel, and the hare, and the coney: for they chew the cud, but divide not the hoof; therefore they are unclean unto you. (8) And the swine, because it divideth the hoof, yet cheweth not the cud, it is unclean unto you: ye shall not eat of their flesh, nor touch their dead carcase. (9) These ye shall eat of all that are in the waters: all that have fins and scales shall ye eat: (10) And whatsoever hath not fins and scales ye may not eat; it is unclean unto you.[4]

(20) All fowls that creep, going upon all four, shall be an abomination unto you. (21) Yet these may ye eat of every flying creeping thing that goeth upon all four which have legs above their feet, to leap withal upon the earth; . . . (29) These also shall be unclean unto you among the creeping things that creep upon the earth; the weasel, and the mouse, and the tortoise after his kind, (30) And the ferret and the chameleon, and the lizard, and the snail, and the mole. . . .(41) And every creeping thing that creepeth upon the earth shall be an abomination; it shall not be eaten. (42) Whatsoever goeth upon the belly, and whatsoever goeth upon all four or whatsoever hath more feet among all creeping things that creep upon the earth, them ye shall not eat; for they are an abomination.[5]

(19) Ye shall keep my statutes. Thou shalt not let thy cattle gender with diverse kind: thou shalt not sow thy field with mingled seed: neither shall a garment mingled of linen and wool come upon thee.[6]

The question Mary Douglas asks is "what have all these in common?"

Defilement is never an isolated event. It cannot occur except in view of a systematic ordering of ideas. Hence any piecemeal interpretation of the pollution rules of another culture is found to fail. For the only way in which pollution ideas make sense is in reference to a total structure of thought whose key stone, boundaries, margins and internal lines are held in relation by rituals of separation. To illustrate this I take a hoary old puzzle from Biblical scholarship, the abominations of Leviticus and particularly the dietary rules. Why should the camel, the hare and the rock badger be unclean? Why should the frog be clean and the mouse and the hippopotamus unclean? What have chameleons moles and crocodiles got in common that they should be listed together?[7]

Her answer seems to be that all the forbidden animals and indeed all things that are abominated are ambiguous, they are hybrids, they break down the categories used to describe the world or at any rate fail to fit neatly into a particular category. The mixing of different kinds of seed, the cross-breeding of different animals, the wearing of cloth made from both wool and flax are all explicitly forbidden. To do these things is to break down the correct ordering of the world. Mary Douglas notes that

All these injunctions are prefaced by the general command "be holy for I am holy". We can conclude that holiness is exemplified by completeness. Holiness requires that individuals shall conform to the class to which they belong. And holiness requires that different classes of things shall not be confused.[8]

Being a pastoral people the Israelites defined wild animals in terms of their resemblance to cattle. The true animal is the beast which chews the cud and has a cloven hoof like the ox, the sheep and the goat. Animals outside this class are not proper animals and not a proper source of food. Those animals which are singled out and named as abominations are those which are ambiguous, which resemble cattle in having one of their key characteristics but not the other. Thus the pig, which has a cloven hoof but does not chew the cud, is particularly abominable.

Animals can also be divided into categories according to whether they inhabit the earth, the water or the air. Ambiguous creatures such as birds that cannot fly or molluscs which live on the margin of the sea and the land are rejected. Mary Douglas sums up their qualities as follows:

... in general the underlying principle of cleanness in animals is that they shall conform fully to their class. Those species are unclean which are imperfect members of their class or whose class itself confounds the general scheme of the world. To grasp this scheme we need to go back to Genesis and the creation. Here a three-fold classification unfolds, divided between the earth, the waters and the firmament. Leviticus takes up this scheme and allots to each element its proper kind of animal life. In the firmament two-legged fowls fly with wings, in the water scaly fish swim with fins. On the earth four-legged animals hop, jump or walk. Any class of creatures which is not equipped for the right kind of locomotion in its element is contrary to holiness. Thus anything in the water which has not fins and scales is unclean . . . . The only sure test for cleanliness in a fish is its scales and its propulsion by means of fins . . . . The last kind of unclean animal is that which creeps, crawls or swarms upon the earth. This form of movement is explicitly contrary to holiness . . . whether we call it teeming, trailing, creeping, crawling or swarming, it is an indeterminate form of movement. Since the main animal categories are defined by their typical movement, "swarming" which is not a mode of propulsion proper to any particular element cuts across the basic classification. Swarming things are neither fish nor flesh nor fowl. Eels and worms inhabit water though not as fish; reptiles go on dry land though not as quadrupeds; some insects fly though not as birds. There is no order in them.[9]

Abomination and pollution then have their roots in a dislike of ambiguity. This notion can be extended to many other circumstances. The current campaign against industrial pollution for example is concentrated very much on an ambiguous class of chemicals called colloids. Colloids are mixtures of two substances in which the two substances are too finely mixed to be easily separable and yet not so finely mixed as to constitute a solution. Often the two substances are in different states—a solid adhering to a gas or a gas to a liquid. Smokes, froths, foams, jellies, emulsions are all colloids and are particularly abhorrent to the campaigner against pollution.

A similar dislike of ambiguity underlies much of sexual morality. Intercourse with animals is strictly forbidden because it breaks down the divisions between the human and animal worlds—it creates confusion.

> Neither shalt thou lie with any beast to defile thyself therewith: neither shall any woman stand before a beast to lie down thereto: it is *confusion.*[10]

Mary Douglas notes that

> Holiness means keeping distinct the categories of creation. It therefore involves correct definitions, discrimination and order. Under this head all the rules of sexual morality exemplify the holy. Incest and adultery (Leviticus 18: 6–20) are against holiness in the simple sense of right order. Morality does not conflict with holiness but holiness is more a matter of separating that which should be separated than of protecting the rights of husbands and brothers.[11]

Surprisingly, Mary Douglas does not extend this argument to cover homosexuality. Yet the homosexual, by his behaviour and indeed simply by his very existence, breaks down that most basic of categories of differentiation, the division of all human beings into men and women. The Old Testament clearly regards such people and such behaviour as abominable:

> Thou shalt not lie with mankind, as with womankind: it is abomination.[12]

This injunction comes immediately before the prohibition of bestiality quoted earlier. The two are clearly associated in the minds of the chronicler.` They are still associated in English legal terminology, for the crime of buggery includes two separate offences, bestiality (involving animals) and sodomy (usually involving male homosexuals).[13]

Homosexuality is roundly condemned in several places in the Old Testament (e.g. Leviticus 20: 13). The Israelites attacked and destroyed the Benjamites because they practised homosexuality (Judges 19 and 20) and Sodom and Gomorrah were destroyed by God for the same reason (Genesis 19). The destruction of Sodom is a particularly good example of an act being abhorrent because it broke down the boundaries between categories.

> (1) And there came two angels to Sodom . . . and Lot seeing them rose up to meet them; and he bowed himself with his face toward the ground; (2) And he said, Behold now, my lords, turn in, I pray you, into your servant's house and tarry all night . . . . (4) But before they lay down the men of the city, even the men of Sodom, compassed the house round, both old and young, all the people from every quarter: (5) And they called unto Lot, and said unto him, Where are the men which came in to thee this night? Bring them out unto us, that we may know them. (6) And Lot went out at the door unto them, and shut the door after him, (7) And said, I pray you, brethren, do not so wickedly. (8) Behold now, I have two daughters which have not known man; let me, I pray you, bring them out unto you, and do ye unto them as is good in your eyes: only unto these men do nothing; for therefore came they under the shadow of my roof.[14]

The crime of the Sodomites, sodomy, was particularly heinous in this context because they wished to practise it on angels. Thus not merely was the boundary between men and women broken down but also that between the human and the divine.

According to this theory then we may assume that homosexuality is abhorred in our society because we have inherited through the scriptures the Jewish tradition of rejecting and avoiding objects or situations that involve categories of separation being blurred or confused. If this is so, it would go a long way towards explaining the furious conflict that was provoked by Darwin's theory of evolution in nineteenth-century England. It would be difficult to explain the hostility to the theory of evolution on the part of many religious people simply on the grounds that it contradicted the story of the creation in the Book of Genesis. It is, as later Christian apologists have shown, a fairly simple matter to reinterpret the story of the creation in symbolic terms in such a way as to fit in with the Darwinian theory of evolution. The threat posed by Darwinism was much more subtle, much more fundamental than this: it broke down the view of the universe that divided animals into separate distinct species that fitted into neat categories. All living creatures were now seen to be the descendants of other creatures in different categories. Even man himself was seen to descend from ape-like creatures that would not be classed as human. Biologists who believed in evolution concentrated their studies on those very ambiguous creatures that the Old Testament found abhorrent, flightless birds like the ostrich, peculiar inhabitants of the sea like the coelacanth and the famous "missing link" between man and the apes. Opponents of evolution, by contrast, concentrated on "the difficulty of reconciling the suddenness with which new types appear in the geological record with any theory of slow mindless evolution, the impossibility of tracing any family into another family by means of true lineage series of fossils".[15]

Clearly there is a clash between two world views, one based on the clear separation of different animal species, the other stressing that there are no definite and permanently separated categories. For our present purposes it is sufficient to note that we have inherited the Jewish abhorrence of blurred categories. Today we do not observe the prohibitions regarding food or clothing or work but owing to St Paul's influence we have preserved the sexual taboos (Romans 1: 3—32). In a sense homosexuals are the gentile's traife.

Even today then confusion of categories is basic to our concept of dirt and pollution whether meant literally or metaphorically (as when we speak of a dirty book). Even ordinary household grime or air- and water-pollution is simply matter in the wrong place messing up a neat category. We display the similarity of our attitude to the homosexual when we abuse someone as a "dirty bugger", an expression much used by the English lower orders. Homosexuality arouses disgust because it breaks down the boundary between the two most basic categories we know—male and female. We learn very early in life to abhor dirt and as early to distinguish people according to sex. Anything that cuts across or seems to destroy these "basic beliefs" that structure our world has to be eliminated because it threatens our very perception of how the world is.[16] The earlier and less rationally we acquire a notion of how things are and should be, the more reluctant we are to part with it.

ASYMMETRY

The trouble with both the family argument and the pollution argument is that they fail to explain the asymmetry of our attitudes and sanctions to male homosexuality and lesbianism. The lesbian has not been subjected to legal prosecution in the way the male homosexual has, nor are the social sanctions against two lesbians living together anything like as strong as against two male homosexuals. A similar discrimination existed in the past between male and female prostitutes and male and female transvestites. As Walker and Fletcher (1955) put it:

The difference in the attitude of the law to male and to female homosexuality is reflected again in the penalties attached to importuning on the part of the two sexes. Whereas a woman prostitute [note that this is *pre*-1959] is liable to a maximum fine of £2 for importuning, a male prostitute can be imprisoned for two years as a "rogue and a vagabond" .... If a male of any age is found dressed in female clothes he is promptly arrested and charged with masquerading for improper purposes. If he endeavours to qualify for wearing female clothes by undergoing a serious operation the law again steps in to forbid it. Yet a woman is entitled to dress as she likes and if she wants to masquerade as a man, don a moustache and beard.[17]

It is fairly certain that few women would choose to don a beard or to grow one. Even so, they are allowed to do so if they wish. The male transvestite by contrast cannot wear female clothes in public without causing offence and possibly prosecution. He cannot even buy his female garments openly. Women who buy men's clothes and underwear create no comment. A man trying to buy female clothes and especially underclothing (even as a present for a woman) is subjected to embarrassing obstructiveness by the sales girls. The transvestite is forced to go to specialist kinky shops in Soho for his underwear.

It is perhaps noticeable that in the abominations of Leviticus and elsewhere in the scriptures very little notice is taken of female homosexuality or transvestism. There are a few references such as the moral edict in Deuteronomy that

> The woman shall not wear that which pertaineth unto a man, neither shall a man put on a woman's garment: for all that do so are abomination unto the Lord thy God[18]

and also St Paul's description of the sins of the gentiles in his epistle to the Romans:

> For this cause God gave them up unto vile affections: for even their women did change the natural use into that which is against nature: And likewise also the men leaving the natural use of the women, burned in their lust one toward another; men with men working that which is unseemly. . . .[19]

But on the whole these condemnations of lesbianism are few and ambiguous (does the phrase "that which is against nature" above refer to lesbianism or to heterosexual sodomy?). The really abominable abominations are male and these are referred to far more frequently. When the chroniclers of abominations do mention lesbianism or female transvestism as above, they seem to feel obliged to put in a reference to the equivalent male vice as well. Male vices by contrast are frequently referred to on their own in the absence of any reference to the female equivalent.

In our society, a society based on the Judaeo-Christian tradition of abominations, this scale of relative abominableness is preserved and if anything accentuated. Women are permitted to dress and behave like men and nowadays literally wear the trousers everywhere. In the past this was disapproved of but not really very strongly. When a woman

did adopt the clothes or behaviour of a man in order to avail
herself of the greater freedom and opportunities of the male
sex this was seen as daring, perhaps shocking, but not
grotesque or disgusting. A good example of men's reactions
to such a woman is given in Thomas Hardy's novel *Far from
the Madding Crowd:*[20]

Lingering and musing here he [Gabriel Oak] heard the steps of a
horse at the foot of the hill and soon there appeared in view an auburn
pony with a girl on its back ascending by the path leading past the
cattle shed, she was the young woman of the night before....
[Gabriel] returned to his hut. Here he ensconced himself and peeped
through the loophole in the direction of the rider's approach.

She came up and looked around—then on the other side of the
hedge. Gabriel was about to advance and restore the missing article,
when an unexpected performance induced him to suspend the action
for the present. The path after passing the cowshed bisected the
plantation. It was not a bridal-path—merely a pedestrian's track and the
boughs spread horizontally at a height not greater than seven feet above
the ground, which made it impossible to ride erect beneath them. The
girl who wore no riding habit, looked around for a moment, as if to
assure herself that all humanity was out of view, then dexterously
dropped backwards flat upon the pony's back her head over its tail, her
feet against its shoulders, and her eyes to the sky .... The performer
seemed quite at home anywhere between a horse's head and its tail and
the necessity for this abnormal attitude having ceased with the passage
of the plantation, she began to adopt another, even more obviously
convenient than the first. She had no side-saddle and it was very
apparent that a firm seat upon the smooth leather beneath her was
unattainable sideways. Springing to her accustomed perpendicular like a
bowed sapling, and satisfying herself that nobody was in sight she
seated herself in the manner demanded by the saddle, *though hardly
expected of the woman* and trotted off in the direction of Tewnell Mill.

Later Farmer Oak meets her and returns the hat she had
lost and had been searching for.

She went on "I had to ride to Tewnell Mill"
"Yes you had" [Oak]
"How do you know?"
"I saw you"
"Where?" she inquired, a misgiving bringing every muscle of her
lineaments and frame to a standstill. Here—going through the plantation

and all down the hill said Farmer Oak, with an aspect excessively knowing with regard to some matter in his mind, as he gazed at a remote point in the direction named and then turned back to meet his colloquist's eyes.

A perception caused him to withdraw his own eyes from hers as suddenly as if he had been caught in a theft. Recollection of the strange antics she had indulged in when passing through the trees was succeeded in the girl by a nettled palpitation and that by a hot face. It was a time to see a woman redden who was not given to reddening as a rule; not a point in the milkmaid but was of the deepest rose colour.

Here we have a woman who defied conventional dress and behaviour and rode a horse like a man. Yet good Farmer Oak clearly found this erotically exciting. That he found the woman attractive is clear from the rest of the novel—she is described as outstandingly beautiful, he early on falls in love with her and eventually marries her. It is also clear that the beginning of this attraction lay in her unconventional behaviour on the back of the horse—in her adoption of the freer masculine way of sitting on horseback. Farmer Oak was *not* disgusted by this—he was amused, astonished and captivated. The entire passage is filled with erotic hints and images, symbols and allusions. She is the woman "of the night before". She "wore no riding habit". She rode the horse first flat on her back, then astride it with her legs apart. Here are sufficient indications of both a direct and a disguised erotic symbolism. What after all does a man do with a woman "the night before" or one who wears no riding habit (i.e. a lack of clothes is stressed, not what she wears) or one who lies flat on her back or has her legs apart? This may not be the immediate obvious meaning of the phrases used but it is not straining the meaning to put an erotic connotation on these words and phrases. No doubt a more determined searcher for erotic symbols would make much of the implication of a girl on a horse or the "smooth leather beneath her". There is also a strong erotic element in the secretiveness, the covert quality of the whole incident. Farmer Oak hid in his hut and "peeped through the loophole", the girl assured herself "that all humanity was out of view". They are both embarrassed when he reveals to her later that he saw everything—an embarrassment of the kind

felt at a mention of sexual matters. But at the centre of this
beautiful and erotic description is the unconventional "masculine" behaviour of the girl. The implication is that a girl
who is unconventional in one way might be unconventional
in other (more directly erotic) ways, that a girl who seized
masculine freedom in one context might do so in another. As
indeed she does for she later pays an unchaperoned visit to
Oak and practically proposes marriage to him. Farmer Oak
tells her that there is gossip in their locality about his wishing
to marry her:

[Oak:] "The top and tail o't is this—that I'm sniffing about here, and
waiting for poor Boldwood's farm, with a thought of getting you some
day".

"Getting me! What does that mean?"

"Marrying of 'ee in plain British. You asked me to tell, so you musn't
blame me".

Bathsheeba did not look quite so alarmed as if a cannon had been
discharged by her ear, which was what Oak had expected. "Marrying
me! I didn't know it was that you meant" she said quietly. "Such a
thing as that is too absurd—too soon—to think of, by far!"

"Yes; of course, it is too absurd. I don't desire any such thing; I
should think that was plain enough by this time. Surely, surely you be
the last person in the world I think of marrying. It is too absurd as you
say".

" 'Too—s-s-soon' were the words I used."

"I must beg your pardon for correcting you but you said 'too absurd'
and so do I."

"I beg your pardon too!" she returned with tears in her eyes: " 'Too
soon' was what I said. But it doesn't matter a bit—not at all—but I only
meant, 'too soon'. Indeed, I didn't, Mr Oak, and you must believe me!"

Gabriel looked her long in the face but the firelight being faint there
was not much to be seen. "Bathsheeba" he said tenderly and in surprise
and coming closer: "If I only knew one thing—whether you would
allow me to love you and win you after all—If I only knew that!"

"But you never will know" she murmured.

"Why?"

"Because you never ask."

"Oh—oh!" said Gabriel with a low laugh of joyousness. "My own
dear—"[2][1]

Before she paid the visit to Oak's house, Bathsheeba had
"thought it doubtful if it were right for a single woman to

call upon a batchelor who lived alone."[22] Having successfully proposed to him she declared

> "I must be going now or I shall be missed. Why Gabriel" she said with a slight laugh as they went to the door, "it seems exactly as if I had come courting you—how dreadful!"[23]

The word "dreadful" exactly describes her quasi-masculine behaviour throughout. It is dreadful in a literal sense because it breaks down the taboos which restricted female behaviour in Victorian England. It is dreadful in an ironic sense because it is bold and exciting and by implication erotic.

By contrast a man who behaved or dressed as a woman, even if this were necessary to a disguise and no sexual impulse was involved, was regarded as somehow defiled by the experience. There is an interesting example of a man's attitude to such an incident in Jim Corbett's autobiographical tales *The Man-Eaters of Kumaon*. Corbett was a soldier, a big-game hunter and an official of the British Empire in India. He was noted for his courage and expertise in tracking down and killing man-eating tigers. On one occasion in order to tempt a tiger to attack him he dressed himself up as an Indian woman hoping the tiger would try and eat this apparently harmless (but in reality well-armed) "bait". He describes the incident thus:

> For a month I had lived in an open tent, a hundred yards from the nearest human being and from dawn to dusk had wandered through the jungles and on several occasions had disguised myself as a woman and cut grass in places where no local inhabitant dared to go.[24]

It is quite clear that the aim of the exercise was to make the tiger think he was a woman and that the more accurately he looked the part the more likely the tiger would be deceived. He has a perfectly legitimate reason for dressing as a woman and most people would admire his willingness to go to such lengths to kill a man-eating tiger and thus protect the lives of the people of the area. Yet Corbett is clearly uneasy about such incidents for earlier he wrote:

> I would like to interrupt my tale here for a few minutes to refute a rumour current throughout the hills that on this and several subsequent

occasions I assumed the dress of a hill woman and, going into the jungle, attracted the man-eaters to myself and killed them with either a sickle or an axe. *All I have ever done in the matter of alteration of dress* has been to borrow a sari and with it draped round me cut grass or climbed into trees and cut leaves.[25]

Thus even though he had a good excuse for wearing a woman's sari he insists that he didn't really do so—it was merely "draped round" him. This was all he had ever done. He hadn't really *worn* such clothes. His uneasiness about this necessary disguise indicates a strong taboo on men wearing women's clothes. Women who have worn men's clothes in adventurous situations such as this have by contrast almost boasted of the fullness and success of such a disguise. Perhaps, however, this uneasiness about dressing up as a woman to act as a decoy is on the way out. The New York police readily consent to being photographed "in drag" when out trying to catch the robbers or rapists who molest the women of that city.

We can perhaps also see this curious double standard working in our theatrical conventions. Drag shows of the Danny La Rue type with men impersonating young attractive women have only become acceptable in recent years. Before that men were only allowed to play old and ugly women as pantomime dames, the ugly sisters and in *Charley's Aunt* and even then only for comic effect. Women by contrast could impersonate young and (supposedly) attractive and virile men on the stage and frequently did so in Edwardian and Victorian music-hall and pantomime.

Even *Charley's Aunt* was considered *risqué* by some. Gwen Raverat who was born in 1885 was greatly shocked at seeing the play when a child:

And then there was *Charley's Aunt.* This was the first real play we ever saw. It did not seem to me at all funny, only tremendous and exciting; and at one point dangerously improper. I have never seen the play since then, but as I remember it, one of the young men dressed up as Charley's Aunt and ran across the stage, lifting up his petticoats and *showing his trousers underneath.* Nothing since then has ever shocked me so much. [26]

It might be objected at this point that in Elizabethan times female parts were played by boys; indeed they were exclusively played by boys. However, this was regarded as indecent by many people at the time, notably by the Puritans. The Shakespeare critic Halliday comments on the Puritan hostility to the theatre that "The [puritan] attack was not only on the immorality of the plays themselves but also on the actors (on) the dressing up of boys as women."[27] He also notes that the use of boys to play female roles imposed considerable restrictions on the dramatists. Because the women were played by boys they were not allowed to be women in a full sense:

> It is worth noting that there is no passionate love-making in Shakespeare's plays. In the comedies hero and heroine keep their distance, on guard with the rapier of their wit; in the tragedies they are rarely seen alone; Romeo once as he leaves Juliet; Othello once when he murders Desdemona; Anthony and Cleopatra never. This no doubt is Shakespeare's happy solution to the *problem* created by a boy's playing the heroine's part.[28]

There is of course another happy solution and that is to turn them back into boys again, or even into men. This is easy for Shakespeare to do precisely because there is no taboo against women disguising themselves as men in this way. Portia and Nerissa in *The Merchant of Venice*, Viola in *Twelfth Night*, Julia in *The Two Gentlemen of Verona*, Rosalind in *As You Like It* and Imogen in *Cymbeline* all discard their female role and clothes and dress up as and pretend to be men or boys. No one sees anything indecent in this. If by contrast men had disguised themselves as young and attractive women for the purposes of the plot this would have caused great offence. Shakespeare does have men disguise themselves as women but only in gross comic situations, i.e. where indecency is hinted at and made the object of knockabout humour. Where grown men dress up as women, as when Falstaff disguises himself as the old witch of Brentford or Parson Sir Hugh Evans as the Fairy Queen in *The Merry Wives of Windsor*, Shakespeare makes sure that the women are perceived by the audience as old, unattractive and ludicrous—almost pantomime dames. There are also a few rare instances where a boy briefly impersonates a young woman as when in *The Taming of the Shrew* Christopher Sly's page dresses up as his wife in order to fool him or when in *The Merry Wives of Windsor* Slender and Caius are tricked into eloping with boys, each thinking the boy is Anne Page. However, it must be stressed that these incidents are very brief, peripheral to the play and the subject of a good deal of lewd humour. The audience laughs at Caius when he finds he has eloped with a boy, because it is indecent. Also all the incidents where boys disguise themselves as women are curiously hidden from the men who are deceived. When Christopher Sly is deceived into thinking a page is his wife he is very drunk at the time. When Caius and Slender elope with boys, the elopement takes place on a very dark night. The implication is that Shakespeare is unwilling to portray a man being deceived by a boy dressed as a woman when he is sober and in daylight. This would seem to be too indecent to be shown even as a joke. A pretext such as drunkenness or darkness has to be found for his audience to be able to relax their inhibitions sufficiently to allow a potentially indecent situation to be a comic one. On the other hand it must still be perceived as rather *risqué* or the audience will not laugh.

The contrast with his women who impersonate men is clear—they do so openly and over long periods of time, their disguise is central to the plot of the play, and at no time is their masquerade seen as improper or comic because it is indecent—though it may be comic for other reasons. Also the men who are fooled by their disguise are fooled remarkably easily. The impersonators do not need the assistance of drink or the dark, even where they are well known to the men being deceived.

Thus the conventions of the Elizabethan theatre, far from going against my view that our notions of indecency are asymmetrical, in fact buttress it. (Whether, of course, this is true for non-European cultures is another matter. In Japanese Kabuki drama male actors play both male and female parts and have done so for several hundred years. Originally Kabuki, which means "trendy", was all-female with women dressed in male clothes playing the male parts. In 1629 the

Shogun banned the female Kabuki on moral grounds. It may have been simply that the theatre was considered an unsuitable place for women as it was in Elizabethan England. Alternatively it may have been that the Japanese, with their different cultural response to the problems created by male homosexuality and transvestism, saw female impersonation of the male as more heinous than the reverse.)

LESBIANISM

Now clearly women who are lesbians or who dress up in men's clothes blur the distinction between men and women (as in their own way do women's lib) as effectively as a male homosexual or transvestite. Yet historically the man alone has been punished and community sanctions have operated against male homosexuality and transvestism only. Also it is difficult to see why male homosexuality should threaten family life while lesbianism does not. As the Wolfenden Committee concluded in its report: "we have had no reason shown to us which would lead us to believe that homosexual behaviour between males inflicts any greater damage on family life than . . . lesbian behaviour."[29] It is sometimes argued (as by William Shepherd in the House of Commons debate on the Sexual Offences Act)[30] that male homosexuals live a promiscuous existence which could entice men into a life of "sexual gratification without responsibility" whereas lesbians "on the whole find it agreeable and acceptable to live together for long periods of time". Even if this is true, it is a very double-edged argument. If lesbian relationships are more stable and more like the family and offer something of the emotional security and gratification of family life then lesbianism is a much more serious rival to the family than homosexuality. Few people are going to choose the lonely, promiscuous, unstable world of the homosexual in preference to family life but many women could be tempted by the pseudo-family offered by a lesbian relationship. If one of the partners is willing to have a casual affair with a man in order to get pregnant, then a lesbian couple can have children and bring them up just as if they were married. This is something no male homosexuals can do. Lesbianism seen in this light is a much more serious threat to the family than male homosexuality.

THE MILITARY

In order to explain fully the strength of social sanctions and prejudices against the male homosexual alone, it is necessary to locate attributes and activities unique to men as distinct from women and to seek the cause there. The main area reserved for men in our society is, as my earlier quotation from Tiger showed, organized aggression (see page 87). According to Tiger institutions for this purpose such as armies, police, etc. (as well as many other all-male groups such as public schools, gentlemen's clubs, the Free-masons, team-sports, which do not have female equivalents that are anything like as durable or as important), are characterized by what he calls "male bonding". For Tiger, "male bonding" describes the

> particular relationships between two or more males such that they react differently to members of their bonding unit as compared to individuals outside of it. Inherent in this is the notion that, except for some exceptional cases, males and females are not interchangeable in the process of forming and maintaining bonds.[31]

Male bonding is the basis of those incredibly strong ties of comradeship and loyalty between man and man that grow up in all-male institutions, and notably in those geared towards aggression, defence and the maintenance of social order. In some societies these ties have taken on an erotic quality and homosexual behaviour within the all-male group is allowed and even encouraged. This seems to have been the case among the Samurai of medieval Japan, the war-like Pathans of the north-west frontier district and the Nazi S.A. when under Ernst Röhm. In our society, however, homosexual bonds are regarded as a very aberrant form of male bonding and destructive of the unity and morale of the military units in which they occur.

The reason for this must lie in the character of our armed forces which are and have been since the army reforms of the nineteenth century essentially bureaucratic organizations where the loyalties I have described coexist with and are structured by the demands of a large organization. They are thus very different from the small bands of Samurai or Pathans or S.A. men tied to a traditional or a charismatic leader. Homosexuality might be permissible in a pre-bureaucratic army but not in a modern highly organized mass army, for the reasons discussed below. It might be noted though that even in an earlier era homosexuality could create problems for the armed forces. We can see this for example in the tensions created when homosexual kings such as Edward II or James I conferred military commands on their favour-ites, Gaveston and Buckingham. With a heterosexual king who has mistresses this problem doesn't arise in such an acute form simply because women are not interested in military matters or in commanding an army. For a comparable hiatus we must look to Elizabeth I's favourites Leicester or Essex, both of whom were placed in high military commands because the Queen was attracted by them and both of whom were incompetent soldiers.[32] But owing to the operation of the Salic law in varying degrees we have had far more kings on the throne than queens. The queen problem is a rare one though a serious one as one can see from Henry VIII's frantic efforts to father a male heir or Stephen's seizure of Matilda's throne and indeed from the existence of the Salic law itself. Society avoids having queens precisely because they cannot command armies themselves and are liable to give such commands to favourites. Where the queen is married of course it can be less of a problem since provision can be made for her consort to take charge of the army. If he himself is not gifted militarily he can delegate power to one of their loyal subjects who is, and since he will presumably not be romantically or physically involved with any of the possible candidates he has the possibility of making a choice unbiased by this factor at any rate.

No such provision can be made in the case of a homo-sexual king—he can hardly hand over command to the queen. Here we have the acute problem of sex getting mixed up with military power. The king's military judgement is likely to be distorted in a way that is not possible for a heterosexual monarch—he can become romantically involved with someone who may legitimately desire military power and use his relationship with the king to gain it. Military commanders are ideally chosen for their qualities as soldiers. If other factors such as political faction or family loyalties or the old school tie intrude this can and does create conditions inimical to military efficiency. Homosexuality is simply an irrelevant and intrusive factor that is especially strong and yet potentially unstable and unpredictable and is therefore perceived as being especially dangerous.

The favourites of James I and Edward II mentioned earlier were resented and disliked by the other powerful subjects of these Kings. Simply because the Kings found them sexually attractive the favourites had access to military and political power which the barons and territorial magnates thought should be their own. The Kings' homosexual favourites were seen as flatterers and plotters who had attained power by unfair means. Gaveston, Edward II's favourite, was regarded as an upstart who had risen above his station because of his attraction to the king. He was felt to have unfairly taken precedence over more worthy and substantial men who provided the military support on which the crown's authority was ultimately based in a feudal society.[33] James I's favourites, Somerset and Buckingham, were similarly disliked and their influence on military matters and foreign policy was felt to be disastrous. Somerset's unpatriotic friendship with Spain was seen to influence James's foreign policy in a manner inimical to the interests of the country. Buckingham's incompetence in the handling of foreign military adventures was seen as proof that a man's sexual attractiveness to the King was a poor criterion for selecting military leaders. These resentments were widely felt among the politically conscious groups in Jacobean England and played some small part in the downfall of his son. Robert Ashton comments "In the opinion of many of his contemporaries the king's passion for his male favourites was the greatest and most disastrous of his vices and some of them were emphatically of the opinion that he was a pederast".[34] He also quotes a contemporary source as saying:

And these . . . his favourites or minions . . . like burning glasses, were daily interposed between him and the subject, multiplying the heat of opressions in the general opinion, though in his own he thought they screened them from reflecting upon the crowne: Through the fallacy of which maxime his son came to be ruined; . . . Now, as *no other reason* appeared in favour of their choyce but handsomnesse, so the love the king shewed was as amourously convayed; as if he had mistaken their sex, and thought them ladies; which I have seene Sommerset and Buckingham labour to resemble, in the effeminatenesse of their dressings; though in whoreson lookes and wanton gestures, they exceeded any part of woman kind my conversation did ever cope withall. Nor was his love, or what else posterity will please to call it, (who must be the judges of all that history shall informe), carried on with a discretion sufficient to cover a lesse scandalous behaviour; for the kings kissing them after so lascivious a mode in publick, and upon the theatre, as it were, of the world, prompted many to imagine some things done in the tyring-house, that exceed my expressions no less than they do my experience: . . .[35]

Another contemporary of James I noted that:

. . . he was very constant in all things, (his favourites excepted), in which he loved change, yet never cast down any (he once raised) from the height of greatnesse, though from their wonted nearnesse and privacy; unlesse by their own default; . . . he naturally loved not the sight of a souldier, nor of any valiant man, . . .[36]

The dislike of military men and his tendency to place them in subordinate positions to his favourites is James I's chief weakness in the eyes of some of his contemporaries. A particularly unfortunate aspect of James I's weakness for homosexual favourites is the inconstancy of his affections for them. Not merely is his choice of advisers and commanders irrational, it is also unstable and unpredictable. Yet another source, quoted by Ashton, noted that

The true fall of Somerset [an early favourite] was this,—that love and affection, though they are the *strongest* passions for the instant, yet they are *not of longest continuance,* for they are not grounded in judgement but are rather fancies which follow the eye; and as beauty itself doth decay, so love and affection abate. . . . the chief delight which man hath is in change and variety. A man may be glutted with one favourite ... so truly I think the King was weary of an old favourite.

Now Sir George Villiers [the new favourite] had kept much company with the gentlemen waiters, who sometimes after supper did leap and exercise their bodies. But Buckingham of all others was most active; he had a very lovely complexion; he was the handsomest bodied man of England; ...[37]

When a man by virtue of his position controls access to important and much-sought-after posts in the State (whether he be a king or the chairman of a Welsh education committee) he is always open to the charge that he gives these posts to flatterers and favourites. Indeed it is the besetting vice of such a position quite regardless of whether unnatural vice is involved, as many heterosexual kings with a weakness for flattery have found to their cost. Offices have to be distributed by merit or in such a way as to placate the influential. If they are not, then those who are excluded are likely to rebel. The notables who are excluded may be powerful enough to do so anyway and if the king's councillors are not worthy occupants of their posts then the notables will gain widespread support for their rebellion. The problem of the king who is a homosexual and allows this to dictate his choice of councillors, officials and, most important of all, military commanders is simply a particularly serious example of the problem of personal power leading to favouritism. It is serious partly because of the intensity and yet uncertainty and changeability of sexual passions and partly because of the tendency of homosexuals to indulge in intrigue and flattery. Because of society's disapproval of his sexual tendencies the homosexual is forced to dissimulate and deceive in his everyday contact with the world. Within the homosexual sub-culture intrigue and jealousy seem to be rife and the individual acquires the skills that enable him to survive in such an environment. In this way a homosexual may well acquire the ability to manipulate the king-favourite relationship to his own ends, possibly in a way inimical to the interests of the State and certainly in a way guaranteed to generate resentment among the king's other subjects and advisers. Such manipulation and intrigue may occur even where the king himself is not a homosexual but surrounds himself with homosexual favourites simply because they are the most accomplished flatterers he can find. This seems to have been the case at the court of the German Kaiser Wilhelm II (Kaiser Bill of World War I). Commissioner von Tresckow of the Berlin C.I.D. wrote in his memoirs of *The Kaiser and the Court Camarilla:*[3] [8]

[The Kaiser's] impulsive nature led him into choosing men for something in their external manners which appealed to him. And thus it came about that he was soon surrounded by a group of homosexualists; because these people as I have already explained had cultivated a flair for sociability and subserviency . . . He allowed himself to be led by antipathies and sympathies and could not bring himself to entrust with official duties those who were personally unsympathetic to him; though in every point of view in ability as well as character they were eminently suited for these offices. The homosexualists clung to one another like burdocks and not one of them kept a secret from the other. Thus they formed a kind of force around the Kaiser, making a free outlook difficult for him. They sought to keep everything away which might spoil his humour and they took pains to see that only persons of their own ilk should be allowed into the intimate circle surrounding the monarch. When anyone is constantly surrounded by people who indiscriminately admire what he says and does and find everything faultless he will finally fall into the delusion of believing that he is an authority on all branches of human life and the end will be that he can no longer bear contradiction.

It must necessarily cause some surprise that the Kaiser did not see through the kind of people that surrounded him. In my opinion this failure was due on the one hand to the fact that he was woefully lacking in a knowledge of men and on the other hand to the fact that the homosexualists were supreme in the art of dissimulation. People who have to practise a technique of false pretences throughout their whole lives, so as not to arouse suspicion, naturally attain to a high pitch of perfection in hypocrisy. From this point of view one can honestly pity them because they practise dissimulation from necessity rather than pleasure . . . . The most outstanding member of the clique, indeed I may call him its leader, was Prince Eulenburg-Hertefeld, Count of Saudels, Knight of the High Order of the Black Eagle, and of ambassadorial rank in the diplomatic service. For many years he was the Kaiser's favourite and exercised an influence over the sovereign which in political and court circles was considered very strong. This status as the Kaiser's friend was so important that he refused many high offices of state so as not to lose the chance of being constantly in attendance on the Kaiser and in conversation with him. He was the most sociable companion I have ever known. . . . Unfortunately he was crafty and intriguing besides being jealous of and antagonistic to any person whom he looked upon as a possible rival as the Kaiser's favourite. He favoured and pushed his own creatures into positions where they could be of use to him. He did not hesitate to invent and circulate the most scandalous lies about decent men who were trusted by the Kaiser with a view to making it impossible for them to hold their positions. One of these was Count Dohna-Schlobitten who wrote a letter to Eulenburg: "You are such a liar that I am conscience-stricken at the thought of having introduced you into the company of our beloved and revered Kaiser, King and Lord . . ." Commenting on it [the letter] *Vorwaerts*[39] wrote "Eulenburg continued to enjoy the favour of the Kaiser and exercised a far-reaching influence on the policy of the German Empire."

The problem of the king's favourites becomes even more acute when his armed forces and imperial officials are organized in a modern bureaucratic manner. Bureaucratic organization, if it is to be efficient, requires that positions be filled according to merit and that each official should restrict his interests and actions to the duties and responsibilities of his own particular office. Royal favouritism can cut across these needs of the bureaucratic organization in a disruptive and damaging way. As von Tresckow notes of the Kaiser:

Every monarch has the social environment he deserves. When the old Kaiser [Wilhelm I, grandfather of Wilhelm II] reigned, those surrounding him at Court were men of honour who took a conscientious view of their duties and did not meddle in politics. They were quite content to be the loyal servants of their master and each confined his activities to his own particular office. The Emperor discussed political matters only with the responsible ministers; he did not listen to irresponsible advisers.[40]

Here we have a description of the ideal behaviour of a monarch acting as the head of a state bureaucracy. It is specifically contrasted by von Tresckow with the favouritism of the new Kaiser to the detriment of the latter. Favouritism, and in particular homosexuality which is a form of favouritism that is both intense and fickle, creates problems even for the primitive army. These are accentuated when a state's military power is organized in large bureaucratic mass armies. These have a distinctive organizational problem to solve. On the one hand they wish to function like all bureaucracies in a rational, impersonal, rule-governed way. On the other hand, they have to inspire considerable loyalty and commitment from their members to get them to fight. Unlike the tasks of most bureaucracies, fighting involves considerable direct emotional responses on the part of the participants—fear, anger, courage, loyalty, etc. In order to mobilize people to undertake these tasks their loyalty must be engaged. At a general level this may be achieved by appeals to patriotism or ideology, but when the army is actually fighting this must be reinforced by the strong loyalties of the small group—Tiger's so-called male bonds. The key problem for the modern army is how to integrate the organizational demands of the bureaucracy with these more primeval ties.

Tiger has noted that

> in certain groups such as of adolescents and for certain activities such as hunting, fishing or *warfare*, social process is charismatic rather than stratified. That is to say it tends towards equality, lack of systematized allocation of privilege, rank, etc., and towards a free-flowing camaraderie which—significantly from our point of view here—is seen to have a homosexual tinge. The other process of social stratification involves the unquestionable assertion of hierarchy, the recognition of social differences rather than similarities and strong control over the universe of potential mates among the youths of various social classes. Not only must stratification exist, it must also be seen to exist.[41]

The problem for the modern army is to reconcile these two kinds of social process. A large bureaucratic army is necessarily stratified, yet it also makes use of charismatic forms in a small group context—the free-flowing camaraderie with a homosexual tinge. The problem of control for the army is to use this free-flowing camaraderie but not to allow it to exist as an independent and possibly disruptive force. If the homosexual tinge becomes homoerotic reality then the small group may well become independent of the controlling military hierarchy and create a situation inimical to good order and military discipline.

The kind of male bonds seen as appropriate to the bureaucratically organized military group are characteristically (a) diffuse and (b) structured.

(a) Diffuse bonds are general ties of loyalty and comradeship which each group member feels for each other member. For any one member his bonds will link him in a diffuse way with all the rest of the group. He will not have bonds with particular individuals that are stronger and more intense than his bonds with the rest.

(b) Structured bonds are bonds whose nature, direction and strength are determined by the formal hierarchical structure of the military unit. Certain types of bond are appropriate between officer and NCO, between NCO and private, between private and private, NCO and NCO, officer and officer, etc. All male bonds in the unit must be congruent with the structure of rank and authority.

Homosexual bonds cannot easily fit into such a structure since they tend to be (a) specific and (b) independent of structure and hierarchy. If such relationships were permitted in such a group they would be destructive of morale and discipline since:

(a) By introducing strong bonds between specific individuals they would create dissension and jealousy within the group. Diffuse bonds are a source of solidarity but specific bonds create cliques and rivalry. Also the less promiscuous and the more affectionate the homosexual ties are the greater the danger there is of this happening. This, of course, may explain why society is more hostile to permanent homosexual relationships than to temporary liaisons and why homosexuals lead such promiscuous lives. By behaving in this way they are less destructive of the other type of male bonds on which society depends.

(b) Homosexual relationships may well cut across the military hierarchy as when such a relationship occurs between an officer and a private. It is easy to see how this could erode discipline and good order within the military unit

One reason then for society's hostility to male but not female homosexuality is that male homosexuality threatens certain key institutions, notably the military, that are characterized by male bonding. The superficial similarity of these male bonds to homosexual ones, the temptation and tendency for such male bonds to degenerate into homosexual ones, and the disastrous results when they do so, are probably the reason for the strong sanctions against male homosexuality. Since there are no comparable institutions where female bonding is vital there is no need for similar sanctions against lesbians.

Another reason for persecuting male but not female homosexuals and transvestites in a society where military institutions are important is to preserve the dominance of male over female essential to the functioning of the military. In militaristic societies male bonding and male dominance tend to get stressed because of the high status of the exclusively male institutions for aggression. Under these circumstances the homosexual or transvestite is punished essentially for failing to be fully male. His punishment is an expression of the pride in their own masculinity of the dominant males in that society.[42] Lesbians by contrast are merely failed women, i.e. failed failures (since in a militarist male-dominated society in a sense all women are failures), and there is no call to punish them. Paradoxically this produces a situation different from most other systems of stratification—the members of the lower class (the women) are allowed to pass themselves off as members of the high class (the men) but not vice versa. The more usual case is where the upper class (e.g. the aristocracy or the whites in the US) seeks to prevent infiltration upwards but where anyone can move down.

Evidence supporting the hypothesis that sanctions against male homosexuality are the result of the demands and needs of the military is available from many sources. In Britain, when homosexual behaviour between consenting adults was legalized in 1966, this did not apply within the armed forces. Any man can still be charged under the Army Act or Navy or Air Force Acts with disgraceful conduct of an indecent or unnatural kind. As David Owen, a member of the select committee on the Armed Forces Bill, said in Parliament:

we examined the question of homosexuality as it applies to the forces. The committee's unanimous recommendation was that it should remain subject to the Naval Discipline Act and the Acts affecting the other services. It was put to us forcibly that if this bill became applicable to the services it would undermine discipline.[43]

Furthermore much of the opposition to the Sexual Offences Bill came over the issue of whether it should apply to the Merchant Navy, and an amendment was put forward by Simon Mahon signed by eight Liverpool and Merseyside MPs (i.e. with strong connections with the Merchant Navy). Mahon's amendment stated:

> This house declines to give a second reading to a Bill which fails to afford the exemption and protection to the Merchant Navy now provided in the Bill to Her Majesty's Royal Navy, Army and R.A.F. and fails also to take into account that this omission will create circumstances which can lead to corruption of young seamen and the conditions which will be prejudicial to the best interests of the Merchant Navy and to the discipline and good order at sea which are vital to the best interests of our nation's merchant ships.[44]

Speaking to his own amendment Mahon declared "The presence of homosexuals could give rise to serious conflicts at sea and jealousies could even lead to violence."

Many MPs with previous careers in the armed forces also expressed fears that, even with these safeguards, the legalization of homosexuality among civilians would be bad for the forces. Captain Walter Elliot on two separate occasions raised this point in debate saying:

> I wanted to ask a question about subsection 5 in respect of the Naval Discipline Act. It is customary in the Navy when seamen are going ashore to warn them against various things. As I see it now and I shall be glad to have my Hon. Friend's confirmation—we will warn the man that if he goes ashore he can commit buggery but that if he comes back on board and does it he goes to prison if convicted. Is that the case? . . . . I will mention one side effect that may come from this. It is possible for an officer to go ashore and indulge in practices and when he returns on board he may be called on to serve on a court martial and send a man to prison for indulging in them. I believe that there are the seeds of corruption in this procedure . . . . [quoting Wolfenden Report] "We recognize that within services and establishments whose members are subject to a disciplinary code it may be necessary for the sake of

good management"—whatever he means by that—"and the preservation of discipline and for the protection of those of a subordinate rank."[45]

Field-Marshal Lord Montgomery commented

What is the greatest single factor making for success in battle or for efficient and well-trained armed forces in peace? It is morale. And what is the very foundation of morale? It is discipline. If these unnatural practices are made legal a blow is struck at the discipline of the British armed forces at a time when we need the very highest standards of morale and discipline with these forces *serving throughout the world.* Take an infantry batallion. Suppose the men know the officers are indulging in unnatural practices and it is legal and nothing can be done. Take a large aircraft carrier with two thousand men cooped up in a small area. Imagine, what would happen in a ship of that sort if these practices crept in.[46]

It is interesting that even the liberal Wolfenden Report made this exception and also that Mr Adair in his dissenting reservations on the proposal to legalize homosexual behaviour (among civilians only) stressed that "the effect on the morale of members of the services would be adverse and corrupting".[47]

The section of the Wolfenden Report from which Captain Elliot was quoting states in full

We recognize that with services and establishments whose members are subject to a disciplinary régime it may be necessary for the sake of good management and the preservation of discipline and for the protection of those of subordinate rank or position to regard homosexual behaviour even by consenting adults in private as an offence. For instance if our recommendations are accepted, a serving soldier over 21 who commits a homosexual act with a consenting adult partner in private will cease to be guilty of a civil offence or an offence against section 70(1) of the Army Act 1955 (which provides that any person subject to military law who commits a civil offence shall be guilty of an offence under that section and hence liable to be dealt with by court martial). The service authorities may nevertheless consider it necessary to retain section 66 of the Act (which provides for the punishment of, *inter alia,* disgraceful conduct of an indecent or unnatural kind) on the ground that it is essential in the services to treat as offences certain types of conduct which may not amount to offences under the civil code.[48]

The Wolfenden Report's solution of the problem created by homosexuality among the armed forces was to preserve sanctions against such behaviour within the forces but to cease applying such sanctions to civilians. The military are allowed to discipline their own members but not to impose similar rules on civilians even though they might wish to do so in the interests of military discipline. Some of the reasons why the military wished to see civilians also subject to restrictions on male homosexual behaviour are discussed in James Adair's dissenting view in the Wolfenden Report. Regarding the possibility of there being restrictions on military personnel that do not apply to civilians he observes:

> Such differentiations are always bound to provoke in service members a feeling of injustice. It would probably mean that if the acts were between a serviceman and an adult consenting civilian, the former would be guilty of an offence and the latter not—even though as past experience has demonstrated the original suggestion and even the payment of money as an inducement was by the civilian. Even as between members of the services it is difficult to see legislation that would not result in differentiation that would give rise to feelings of injustice.
>
> On the other hand if military law is to follow the course of the civil law amended as proposed, I cannot but express a fear shared by officers of all services and by all who gave evidence on behalf of the services that as between those under and over the prescribed age there would be feelings of grave injustice and as I assess the consequence an increase in the trend towards homosexual practices would be marked and intense while the effect on the morale of members of the services would be adverse and corrupting.[49]

Instances of the kinds of problems that Adair is referring to are given by Commissioner von Tresckow who notes:

> During my time as Commissioner at Police Headquarters the regiments quartered at Berlin and Potsdam were demoralized through and through by homosexualists who made a speciality of soldiers as the objects of their passion. This was particularly so in the cavalry regiments. They were being constantly enticed by homosexualists who found the gala uniform attractive and many fine young fellows from the country were physically and morally corrupted, during their period of service as military conscripts. Also among the officers, especially in the Guards regiments, there were several homosexualists.[50]

It seems very likely that this is a general problem and that von Tresckow's account of Berlin could be applied to London at the present day. It is interesting also that the Wolfenden Committee's regard for the "protection of those of subordinate rank" is found also in von Tresckow's account of the Hohenau scandal: ·

The worst feature of his [Hohenau's brother's] case was that he took advantage of his position in the regiment to make his subordinates the instruments of his passion. Feeling that one Hohenau scandal had been enough for me, I went to see him in his office at regimental headquarters and warned him. But he pretended to me not to know what I was talking about. He continued his unsavoury conduct until he was formally denounced, tried by a military court and sentenced to imprisonment.[51]

One cannot help feeling though that this concern for the person of subordinate rank is in fact the expression of another kind of fear altogether, viz. the fear that sexual relationships between persons of different rank could lead to the breakdown of the army hierarchy. It is not exploitation that is feared but disorder. If strong personal relationships are permitted between an officer and one of his men this reduces the social distance between officers and men, it puts the private in an ambiguous position *vis-à-vis* the officer and differentiates him from other privates in a way likely to cause resentment and dissension.

To return to the debates in the House of Commons in the 1960s, it is interesting to note that in both Houses of Parliament and on both occasions when a bill to legalize homosexual behaviour was introduced the opposition was dominated by former officers in the armed services. These men made a disproportionately large number of speeches against the bills and voted overwhelmingly against any relaxation of the law.[52]

The next question to be asked is why did these worthy gentlemen not succeed in stopping the bill to legalize homosexuality altogether and thereby save the day for the army. One answer to this question (though I would stress that it is not the only one) is to be found in the declining status and importance of the military in Britain. We have

never been a militaristic nation in the Continental mould but
so long as we had a large overseas empire, the military were
an important group. Imperial defence was a central, in some
ways *the* central problem, for any British government
Dreadnoughts and India were the important issues, not
inflation or the balance of payments. What the military said
and felt on any issue was important. When the Empire went
this was no longer so. The legalization of homosexual
practices occurred in the same era as the decline of the
British Empire, a period of declining military expenditure
which saw also the abolition of conscription.[53] The British
Empire had of course been in decline for some time, perhaps
since the end of World War I, but this was not apparent to
most people. In the 1940s and 1950s many British
possessions became independent but the loss of Empire was
concealed by the official pretence that it had merely been
metamorphosed into the British Commonwealth. Only in
the 1960s when the last major African possessions went
independent did the British finally lose their sense of
Empire. Only then did they lay down the white man's
burden.

We can find some support for this thesis in the fact that
the laws and social pressures against male homosexuality
were considerably strengthened in the last quarter of the
nineteenth century—not the *most* moralistic part of the
Victorian era but the period when an Empire was most
self-consciously and strenuously sought. It was a period when
reforms in the armed services had created a modern bureau
cratic army, a period when we became conscious of military
and imperial competition from other powers.

It is also the time of the Labouchère amendment and the
trial of Oscar Wilde. The Labouchère amendment to the
Criminal Law Amendment act of 1885 made the so-called
lesser homosexual acts offences for the first time. In the
words of the Wolfenden Report "it extended to homosexual
indecencies other than buggery the law which had previously
applied to buggery."[54] It is widely believed and this view
may be inferred from the Wolfenden Report, that this was a
spontaneous amendment suddenly put forward by the
eccentric radical Labouchère which was not discussed and

which nobody really intended. It is very doubtful whether this was in fact the case. The Bill was a Government measure moved by Sir Assheton Cross, the Secretary of State for the Home Department. The Government raised no objection to this sudden amendment nor to Sir Henry James's further amendment to double the proposed punishment for these new offences. Indeed, Labouchère declared that

> He did not think it necessary to discuss the proposal at any length, he understood Her Majesty's Government *were willing to accept it.* He, therefore, left it for the House and the Government to deal with as might be thought best.[55]

We do not know precisely what discussions Labouchère had with the Government beforehand but it looks very much as if he had their support and blessing. Indeed the whole business may have been a "put-up job" with the Government inducing the eccentric Labouchère to do the job for them. Labouchère was always jumping up tagging minor amendments to Bills, and in this way a major change could be made in the law without anyone noticing or seriously debating the issue. In this way the Empire and the new bureaucratic armed forces needed to safeguard it, and, even more important, the all-male quasi-military bureaucracies needed to run the Empire, could be made secure. The ways in which the Empire impinged on the morals of ordinary people were of course largely indirect. Few of them had ever worked in, or even visited our imperial possessions. Nevertheless the needs of the Empire exerted a dominant influence on the life of the nation. Britain was in many ways a very hierarchical society where the lower orders as a result of imitation or coercion came to adopt the *mores* and outlook of their betters, the national and imperial élite. The rulers of the Empire were chosen from this élite and their values and standards were those they felt necessary for the proper governing and administration of the Empire. Since they mixed socially with the home élite (on leave, on retirement, by marriage, by having their sons educated in England) who recognized the importance of their task and the moral qualities necessary to fulfil it, these became also the moral standards of the home élite.[56] They in turn imposed them on the rest of the nation.[57]

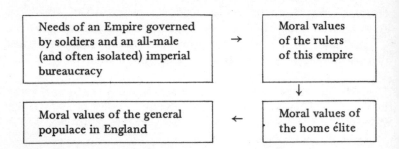

There is also in this period a tightening-up of the social pressures against homosexuality, notably in the public schools. In his book *Tom Brown's Universe*[58], a fascinating study of the development of the Victorian public school, J. R. de S. Honey has shown that throughout the Victorian period schoolmasters are obsessed with sin but their obsession varies markedly over time. In the early Victorian period sin in its most serious forms is seen by men such as Arnold of Rugby as drunkenness and indolence, indiscipline and disobedience, doubt and unbelief, rather than having anything to do with sex. Only later do Victorian headmasters become obsessed with sex. Only during the period around 1860 to 1880 does immorality begin to have a specifically sexual connotation. Furthermore, in the early part of this period the new drive for sexual morality is concerned *not* with homosexuality but with "solitary vice". Pulpit denunciations in the 1860s are concerned with masturbation rather than homosexuality. The great theologian Dr Pusey described the former as a new phenomenon, a new destructive vice introduced since the 1820s. The doctors also were concerned with its harmful effects and made special efforts to cure female masturbation, sometimes by drastic operations. The public schools responded to this new threat by planning their schools so as to eliminate privacy. Architecture and feeding arrangements were seen largely in terms of whether they fostered or discouraged it. It was a special concern of the Church of England Purity Society (led by public school headmasters), which issued tracts against it aimed at the public and preparatory schools.

But, as Professor Honey goes on to establish, during most of this period there is no concern about homosexuality. Up to the 1860s schoolboy friendships are glorified or seen as neutral. Unselfish love is exalted, especially between older and younger boys. The relationship between Tom and young Arthur in *Tom Brown's Schooldays* is portrayed as being permitted, indeed fostered, by Dr Arnold and the other masters.[59] Dean Farrar's novels, despite their preoccupation with pollution and vice, exalt friendship between boys and even the courtship of younger boys by older ones. This is not seen as leading necessarily to sexual sin. The Anglo-Catholic movement, too, is characterized by platonic, quasi-homosexual relationships especially involving Newman, but persisting after Newman left. There were some homosexual scandals in schools in this period which resulted in the sacking of masters or headmasters but these could the more easily be hushed up because of the lack of any widespread consciousness of homosexuality.

In late Victorian England, by contrast, and especially in the last quarter of the nineteenth century, we find a very different atmosphere—an atmosphere in which homosexual activities in the schools are now recognized, constantly suspected and regarded with horror. All associations between boys are seen as potentially vicious, and automatically so if the boys are from different age-groups. Friendship was seen as a mark of immorality and was therefore frowned on. In marked contrast to earlier Victorian England, in this later period spontaneous expressions of affection between males are regarded as taboo. We now have the growth of the stiff-upper-lip attitude which makes any personal emotion undesirable—an attitude eminently suited to the proconsuls of Empire being trained in the public schools.

It is possible then that the taboo against homosexuality reached its peak with the culmination of the British Empire and it is all the more plausible that it should disappear when the Empire declines and the need for it is over.

A similar pattern can be observed in German history. After

the formation of the German Empire in 1871 the German
Government sought to make that country the leading
military power in Europe and at a later stage to acquire a
colonial empire. Just as Britain was the leading imperial
power in Europe, so Germany became the leading military
power. In Germany as in England the period 1871—1918 saw
a strengthening of the prohibitions against homosexuality.
There had been laws against homosexual behaviour prior to
this period and the occasional scandal, but the laws were not
enforced very stringently and the scandals were not regarded
very seriously. After 1871 the military became increasingly
important in Germany, particularly in those German states
not previously dominated by Prussia, the home of militarism.
The army became the most central and almost the most
popular institution in the State and militarist doctrines were
influential at all levels in society.[60] The aim of German
society was summed up in the popular slogan "world-
domination or downfall."[61] In Spencer's terminology
Germany became a militant rather than an industrial
society.[62] It is not surprising that such a society should take
stern action against the homosexuals and that there should be
a series of scandals and trials involving men holding high
military and political posts. Prior to the period of military
dominance the existence of homosexuality among officials
was half-known and half-permitted. Now it was often fiercely
exposed and savagely punished.

Paragraph 175 of the German Penal Code, which made
homosexuality a criminal offence, was rigorously enforced
and the police began keeping a dossier on known homosexuals. Many army officers, notably Hohenau, Military
Aide-de-Camp to the Kaiser and Commander of a regiment of
the Cuirassier Guards and also of a regiment of the Gardes du
Corps, were tried by military courts and sentenced to
imprisonment. Hohenau's brother, Count Fritz Hohenau, was
blackmailed by a homosexual jockey called Assmann (*sic*)
and forced to resign from the diplomatic service when the
proceedings of the blackmailer's trial were described in detail
in a German newspaper.[63]

The press, and particularly the socialist papers, played a
leading part in exposing and attacking homosexuals in the

armed forces and in related areas such as the court and the armaments industry.

The newspaper *Vorwaerts* accused the head of the leading armaments firm, Krupp, of being a homosexual and of keeping a male harem in a Berlin hotel and another on the island of Capri. The charges made against Krupp were true and Krupp committed suicide.[64] Shortly after this Maximilian Harden attacked the homosexuals among the Kaiser's military and political advisers in his paper *Die Zukunft*. Samuel Igra describes Harden's motives thus:

> On December 8th 1906, Harden published his first article attacking the Camarilla. He mentioned the name of Prince Eulenburg and General Kuno von Moltke, a distant cousin of the Chief of the General Staff. Harden made it quite clear that he was not interested in their temperamental deviations as a matter of private and personal morals, but because men of Eulenburg's type in close and constant contact with the sovereign constituted a danger to the state and to the policy of the Emperor. Harden declared that as soon as these people gave open proof that they had ceased to interfere in matters of state policy no further revelations would be forthcoming on his part.[65]

Much of Harden's article was in fact based on evidence "supplied him not only by the Chancellor and the Foreign Office but also by some of the army chiefs."[66] Eulenburg sued Harden for libel and was eventually ruined by this action. The Crown Prosecutor broke off the case against Harden and brought proceedings against the homosexual members of the Camarilla.[67] Moltke was then put on trial for homosexual offences and Eulenburg was called as a witness. At Moltke's trial Eulenburg denied that he had indulged in "dirty practices" (mutual masturbation) but this denial led to his later being prosecuted for perjury. Eulenburg's health broke down and he was forced to retire from public life. His associate, General Kuno von Moltke, who had earlier been divorced by his wife on the grounds of supposed homosexuality, was dismissed from the army and Count Edgard Wedle, the Kaiser's chamberlain, was deprived of his offices and decorations and banished from the court. The sensational trials of 1907—8 were the beginning of a series of prosecutions brought against important military and political

figures and the period 1907—9 is filled with demands by the
public that homosexuality be stamped out and known
homosexuals expelled from their posts and punished. The
period is described by an individual who wrote under the
pseudonym of Count Axel von Achwering:

It is not easy to give details of this terrible affair; it can only be
sketched superficially. It had been an open secret for some time that
certain practices had gained ground in the smartest regiments of the
Gardes du Corps; the eldest son and heir of a former favourite of the
old emperor had to leave Berlin hurriedly owing to some revelations
made by a soldier of his squadron. Thanks to the high position of his
father the officer was allowed to take refuge in Russia. Later on a
member of one of the embassies was discovered during a police raid in a
most suspicious situation, together with some officers in a small
apartment hired for the purpose. There again the story was hushed up
and the individual left the German capital within a few hours of the
catastrophe. At last, however, it became impossible for the *military
authorities* to shut their eyes to the doings of certain high officials and
finally the *Minister of War* had to present a report on the matter to the
Emperor and to ask the latter for orders. Wilhelm II became furious
after the first moments of consternation that followed upon the cruel
revelations. He instantly gave orders that the matter should be sifted to
its very depths. Regardless of the consequences he declared his intention
of allowing the law of the land to mete out to the culprits such
punishment as it considered necessary. . . . Fearful things came to light
and facts were revealed which destroyed the honour of more than one
noble family. Some of the most intimate friends of the Emperor found
themselves involved in these revelations. The scandal reached unheard-
of proportions. Men with high titles were ignominiously *dismissed from
the service* and had to go and hide their shame abroad . . . . [68]

The Chancellor, von Bülow, noted in his memoirs that

while the Emperor was staying at Highcliffe, Spahn, the Centre Party
leader, put several questions in the Reichstag on the revelations in the
Moltke-Harden libel action which had brought to light offences against
morality reminiscent of heathen Rome. He was highly indignant that
two especially guilty officers, Count Lynar and Count Hohenau, should
have been pensioned off and put on the retired list. Nevertheless he
thanked the Emperor and the Crown Prince for having intervened so
swiftly. I answered that the offences against morality revealed by the
Moltke-Harden case had filled me with disgust and shame, but that I

must protest against any suggestion that the *German army—the German people*—were rotten at heart.[69]

For all these observers the danger of homosexuality is its effect on the army and on imperial policy. It is the military authorities and the Minister of War who take action against the homosexuals and the men proceeded against are those who hold important positions in the army or in related sections such as the court or the armament industry. For Chancellor Bülow, who himself had been accused (falsely) of homosexual relations with his secretary, it is the state of the German army that is all important. Indeed the army is so important that he explicitly links and equates the German army and the German people.

In the first world war Germany was defeated, lost her colonial empire and was prohibited from maintaining large armed forces by the victorious powers. The military lost their central position in the State and were deprived of direct political power in the new republic. In the 1920s the Weimar republic was characterized by the lack of armed forces and by a high degree of toleration of homosexual behaviour. Because the army was no longer as important, society no longer needed to persecute the homosexual. Berlin in the 1920s was one of the most permissive cities in Europe. Christopher Isherwood's novels, *Goodbye to Berlin*[70] and *Mr Norris Changes Trains*[71] give an interesting picture of the free and at times extravagantly open life that homosexuals were able to lead in Berlin at this time. A more sinister side to this freedom was the prevalence of homosexuality among the various Nazi organizations that developed in opposition to the Weimar republic, notably the S.A. (Sturm-Abteilung) led by Captain Ernst Röhm. Konrad Heiden wrote of the S.A.:

The perversion was widespread in the secret murderers' army of the post-war period and its devotees denied that it was a perversion. They were proud, regarded themselves as "different from the others", meaning better . . . he [Hitler] unscrupulously used the forces of perversion just as he used murder and lies. A heart-broken father from the little town of Uffenheim in Franconia whose son had been perverted by Heines in the S.A. complained to him; he replied that the young men must take care of themselves, the S.A. was no kinder-garten.[72]

Samuel Igra has noted that homosexuals were equally prominent in other Nazi organizations besides the S.A.:

The vices of Captain Röhm, commander of the storm troops with three million men under his control, were a matter of world-wide knowledge and comment. Baldur von Schirach, Reich leader of the youth from the time of Hitler's accession to power until 1939, was arrested by the police for perverse sexual practices and liberated on the intervention of Hitler, who soon afterwards made him leader of the Hitler Youth. Among the S.S. and S.A. groupleaders and gauleiters, the more outstanding criminals in this matter, were Edmond Heines, S.A. group leader at Breslau, Julius Streicher, gauleiter of the Nuremburg district and Kube of the Frankfurt-on-Oder district. It was not merely that these men practised their vices in private and among their own clique but they made a system, almost a cult, of their moral corruption and used their positions of power to molest with impunity innocent boys and girls whose features and physique they fancied . . . . Julius Streicher, the notorious Jew baiter, was originally a school teacher but was dismissed by the Nuremburg school authorities following numerous charges of pederasty against him . . . . Heines not only indulged in homosexual orgies himself—he was often Röhm's consort in this—but he promoted the vice as a lucrative business.[73]

The presence of so many homosexuals in the Nazi movement created problems for Hitler in his relationship with the regular army and with German politicians who had held high rank in the Kaiser's army. Heiden wrote of one incident in the 1920s:

A delegation led by Count Ernst zu Reventlow, an elderly party comrade, brought him [Hitler] a message from Ludendorff: the General viewed the activities of the homosexuals in the S.A. with great misgivings. Hitler told Reventlow to tell General Ludendorff that all this was a matter of total indifference to him, Hitler. His actual words were unprintable.[74]

When Hitler came to power in 1933 he needed the support of the regular army, the Reichswehr, more than ever. The army was hostile to the S.A. and alarmed by Röhm's demand that the S.A. and the Reichswehr be merged. The army was opposed to the S.A. on political and organizational grounds. The S.A. was in the eyes of the army simply a mass of uniformed toughs whose experience of fighting was limited to brawls in the streets with rival political factions. Also the S.A. was the left wing of the Nazi party and the party itself was a revolutionary national socialist party whose rise to power had alarmed some of the traditional elements in German society. The army was willing to support Hitler but reluctantly, and only provided he agreed to curb its rival for the control of the state's armed power, the S.A. They also expressed strong distaste for the homosexual activities of the S.A. leaders and members. The army's complex hostility to the S.A. is revealed in Heiden's account of their response to Röhm's demand that the S.A. be made part of the regular army:

Röhm as a member of the Reich Cabinet now raised his voice and demanded that the S.A. be made a part of the Reichswehr. Even if only a fraction of the three million S.A. men most of whom were engaged in civilian activities could become soldiers as many S.A. leaders as possible were obviously to become soldiers and this with a rank corresponding to their S.A. rank. Thus one fine morning these armed poultry farmers or department store porters would wake up with the rank of general or at least colonel, just because they had won the titles of S.A. group or brigade leaders as a result of various scuffles in beer cellars or back alleys. Blomberg (General Werner von Blomberg, the Reichswehr minister) sharply rejected Röhm's demands.

By his aggressive move, Röhm gave the enemies of the S.A. their long desired occasion to blame and deride what almost everyone in Germany knew about the S.A. and their degenerate leaders; they particularly attacked Röhm's newly organized Berlin headquarters as the scene of extravagant and obscene orgies.[75]

Hitler was in effect now forced to choose between the regular army and the S.A. He realized that the army was the stronger and more efficient body and an essential feature of his plans to attack Germany's neighbours and seize their territory. In June and July 1934 Röhm and the other leaders of the S.A. were murdered and many other S.A. men murdered or imprisoned on Hitler's orders. Hitler publicly

denounced the S.A. leaders as homosexuals and used this as
an excuse for his purge of the S.A. Goebbels and Dietrich,
Hitler's press agent, enlarged on this in their descriptions of
the purge and made it a central feature of their propaganda
against the S.A. leaders. Heiden notes that

> Heines's room directly adjoining Röhm's, says Dietrich's account,
> presented a disgraceful picture. Heines lay in bed with a homosexual
> boy. The disgusting scene which took place during the arrest of Heines
> and his friend defies description. Hitler ordered Major Buch to
> ruthlessly exterminate this pestilential tumour. Heines and his com-
> panions were dragged out and shot in a car by Maurice and Weber: they
> were the first dead. They were literally buried in mud. A storm of
> public defamation descended upon these dead men, which described
> their unnatural tendencies with the most loathsome details; Goebbels'
> propaganda made it almost their principal crime that they had defiled
> the Führer's pure movement with their dirty practices—which only four
> days earlier Hess had termed "little weaknesses".... As Hess later
> suggested these arrests [of S.A. leaders] were fairly arbitrary, made
> chiefly on the basis of feeling—and Hitler's feeling seems frequently to
> have been based on a suspicion that the person concerned had
> homosexual tendencies .... In the speech which Hitler made before
> the non-arrested party leaders on June 30th, he chiefly accused Röhm
> and his men for their loose or depraved conduct and declared that for
> this alone they deserved to die. To Futze, whom he had appointed
> Röhm's successor, he sent an order comprising twelve points which
> dealt almost exclusively with parties, drinking bouts, automobile trips,
> squandering and unnatural lewdness indulged in by Röhm and his
> gang—and stressed the necessity of putting an end to all that.[76]

At one level we can analyse these events simply in political
terms. Hitler purged the left wing of his party in order to gain
the support of the army and used the fact of its leaders being
homosexuals as a convenient propaganda weapon. It is
doubtful whether such an account fully explains the ferocity
with which the S.A. leaders' homosexuality was denounced,
and the singling out of homosexuals among the leadership for
execution. Rather we must supplement such an account by
explaining the differing attitudes to homosexuality in the
S.A. and in the regular army.
    The S.A. under Röhm was never a highly co-ordinated

bureaucratic army. Although large in size the S.A. was based "on a tiny unit, the so-called 'Schar' (squad); such a squad was formed when somewhere a leader arose of his own accord 'and set up the squad' ".[77] Such a force was similar to the fighting units of earlier pre-industrial cultures. In such a context there is a choice of methods of solving the problems created by homosexuality for a military unit. Either it can be totally forbidden as in the Old Testament it was forbidden to the warriors and people of Israel, or it can be institutionalized and made a controlled and focused aspect of military and social organization. This was the solution adopted by the Spartans and by the Pathans of the North West Frontier district, by the Japanese Samurai, by the Teutonic Knights and the Knights Templars. Here the strong ties of comradeship between the (all-male) members of a warrior band are allowed to take on an erotic component. These erotic relationships are regulated and controlled by the group in such a way as to ensure that they do not disrupt the group but rather contribute to its solidarity. The members of such a group see themselves as a homosexual warrior élite and reject and despise women. Women are seen as totally inferior because they are unable to participate in the activities and relationships of the warriors.

In the nineteenth century enormous bureaucratic armies were developed which for the reasons discussed earlier were unable to institutionalize homosexuality and were forced to suppress it. However, in the twentieth century many fascist thinkers, reacting against the rational and impersonal qualities of bureaucratic organization, urged that the old homosexual warrior bands should be revived and used as the basis of military organization. Such a view was put forward by some of the early Italian fascists and much later by the Japanese writer Yukio Mishima.[78] Mishima's novels are full of violence and homosexuality and a nostalgia for the military traditions of the Samurai. In 1970 Mishima tried to organize a fascist revolt in the Japanese army and when this failed he commited *hara-kiri* (ritual suicide by disembowelment) in the traditional Samurai manner. Ideas of this kind were also common among the Nazis. Heiden says of the homosexuals in the Nazi movement:

They boasted about their superiority in more or less the same terms which Plato had coined in his *Banquet*: "They [the homosexuals] are the best among the boys and young men because they are the most valiant among them. This is strikingly demonstrated by the fact that after growing up they—and they alone—are fit for ruling the State." Röhm said that the misfortune of the present age was domination by women; he praised the epochs that had been dominated by figures like Alexander the Great, Caesar, Charles XII of Sweden, Prince Eugène of Savoy and Frederick the Great. Alfred Bäumler, the National Socialist philosopher, whom his comrades in 1933 at once made a professor at the University of Berlin, wrote a whole book about the "heroic young man": Everywhere the relation between man and man is degenerating he lamented, . . . with the pervert's arrogance he went on "The contest for a woman has the peculiarity that both contestants are always defeated, for the victor like the vanquished loses his time . . . . Because the German has essentially a warlike nature, because he is a man, because he is born for friendship—democracy which in its ultimate consequence leads to the right of women to judge over men, can never thrive in Germany".[79]

Bäumler derived his ideology of militarism, homosexuality and anti-feminism from Professor Hans Blüher, whose study *Die Rolle der Erotik in der Männlichen Gesellschaft* [The Part played by Sexual Attraction in Male Companionship] had a great deal of influence on the Nazis. Blüher urged that men should avoid all association with women except for the physical purpose of procreation. Blüher's view that "woman is man's deadly enemy"[80] became a popular slogan. By this he meant that contact with women involves a loss of the military virtues and therefore must be avoided. Blüher attacked family life and urged that a military élite should be housed and trained in segregated all-male communities. He declared that "If there were only the family as the basis of the human social system, nothing more would be achieved beyond the maintenance of the species. The founding of the state begins with the introduction of a second pole and that pole is the male community".[81] Samuel Igra comments on Blüher's work:

[for Blüher] there is no eros except man-to-man love. It is a degradation of true love to direct it towards woman as the object. As all such emotional or spiritual association with women brings a deterioration of the manly and soldierlike virtues it must be ruthlessly avoided. ... Love is a creative force not in the vulgar sense of merely propagating one's kind but in the higher sense of cultural creativeness and especially as the sole and unique force that is capable of creating the state and assuring its leadership. This creative eros is debased and loses its pristine quality if it be allowed to enter into the relations between men and women or in family life. On the other hand it is preserved and strengthened in segregated male communities, who practice a certain well-regulated ritual of homosexualism among themselves and mingle with womenfolk only when they wish to beget their offspring. Thus Blüher and his disciples would revive the Teutonic Knights in a modern form. ... Describing the nature of the segregated male communities he says they are based on a unique principle of companionship which differs essentially from the traditional forms of association such as the family and the clan, the contractual kind represented in democratic citizenship, trades unions and vocational or scientific societies, etc. The reactions of the male community show a solidly collective and alert vitality, totally unlike the sluggishness, indifference and laxity of institutions such as the civil service. ... Blüher declares that the life of the *Bund* (male community) is sustained by a psychological fluid which pervades it. This fluid is of an erotic or more exactly a homoerotic nature. ... The perfectly developed *Bund* requires a certain amount of homoerotic practice in the mutual relationship of its members; but this must not be carried to undue excess. This purely physical practice must submit to a regulated restraint, so that part of the energy may be sublimated into a sociologically creative force.[82]

Blüher provided a militarist ideology which appealed to many in the Nazi party and in the S.A. It had an atavistic anti-bureaucratic quality about it which appealed to the bands of impulsive brawling thugs that constituted the S.A. It did not, however, achieve any popularity with the leaders of the army. They continued to abhor homosexuality and were opposed to the introduction of such practices into the armed forces. They recognized that homosexuality was incompatible with the kind of army they wanted, viz. a large, highly disciplined and co-ordinated army organized along bureaucratic lines. They insisted that Hitler purge the S.A. of its homosexual leaders and that the military and civilian regulations against homosexuality be rigorously enforced. During the 1930s, when Germany was re-arming and the military gained in power and importance, homosexuality was once again prohibited and punished as it had been in the years leading up to World War I. Indeed, homosexuals were even sent to concentration camps.

A similar relationship between militarism and persecution of homosexuals can be seen in the Soviet Union.[83] In the 1920s there had been little or no harassment of this group and after the end of the civil wars little emphasis on military preparedness either for defence or attack. In the early 1930s the Russians began to re-arm on a large scale, partly because they feared the growing military strength of Nazi Germany and partly because they coveted the territory of neighbouring countries in Eastern Europe. In March 1934 they prohibited male homosexuality by law and allowed the courts to sentence men found guilty of homosexual acts to between three and eight years in prison. There were many arrests and a vicious campaign of persecution of known homosexuals. The law only applied to male homosexuality; lesbianism remained unnoticed and unpunished.

It is curious to note that the only important countries in Europe to retain laws against homosexuality right up to the 1960s were Britain, Germany and the Soviet Union.[84] These are also the only three European countries to create bureaucratic mass armies that were able to fight a protracted war under twentieth-century conditions and whose morale did not crack up in the process. Of these countries Britain and the Soviet Union were imperial powers with large empires to defend and Germany sought to become such a power. Germany and the Soviet Union are countries with strong militarist traditions, large conscript armies during most of this century and a tendency to invade their neighbours.

By contrast we can look at a country like Denmark where the taboos against male homosexuality are almost absent and where the dominance of male over female and the persecution of failed males are much less in evidence. The Danish sociologist Manniche writes of his own country:

> We are not puritans in this country. Our life has been too easy since we stopped going on raids all over Europe in the Viking days. Denmark has not been involved in any major war for the last two centuries.

World War II brought a rapid occupation that in itself prevented much show of martial spirit. This has given the military tradition very unfavourable conditions for many years: a rather important point since a military society generally has a high degree of (sexual) stratification, men being normally considered superior to women.[85]

Denmark is perhaps an extreme case, but Britain is also curiously lacking in militarism. Unlike most other countries we no longer have conscription in peacetime, and army officers do not usually wear uniforms off duty. We are also one of the few countries where historically it has been respectable to be a pacifist.[86] While we had an Empire we needed taboos against homosexuality. With the loss of the Empire the taboos became redundant. The military and other groups concerned with imperial power have declined in status and importance during the last twenty years. Buggery may not have rotted the British Empire but the decay of empire did create a situation where society became morally indifferent to the existence of male homosexuality. It is perhaps of interest at this point to quote a British army general as described by Simon Raven:

Normally politics and religion are eschewed in officers' conversation but grounds for controversy still remain and I have never forgotten the trouble I got into for contradicting a general who announced that sodomy had rotted the Roman Empire. The fact that this officer scarcely knew a word of Latin and by his own confession had never read a line of Gibbon was held to be irrelevant. The general had spoken and so sodomy for this occasion at least had indeed rotted the Roman Empire, however Tacitus or Professor Adcock might opine.[87]

Intuitively the general is right in seeing a relationship between sodomy and the rot of empires. However, he seems to have got his argument the wrong way round—it is the rot of empires that leads to a permissive attitude towards sodomy.

6 Drugs and Permissiveness

. . We stood talking for some time together of Bishop Berkeley's ingenious sophistry to prove the non-existence of matter and that every thing in the universe is merely ideal. I observed that though we are satisfied his doctrine is not true, it is impossible to refute it. I shall never forget the alacrity with which Johnson answered, striking his foot with mighty force against a large stone till he rebounded from it,—'I refute it thus'.

JAMES BOSWELL, *The Life of Samuel Johnson*

Until the 1960s Britain appeared to be a permissive utopia as far as heroin addiction was concerned. American social scientists, appalled at the results of punitive legislation against such addiction in their own country, repeatedly pointed to Britain as an example of how superior our permissive methods of handling the problem were.[1] By not punishing the addict (but only illegal suppliers)[2] and by providing him free on the NHS with large quantities of pure heroin, we seemed to have avoided the major social problems of addiction. By contrast, in the United States it was and is illegal even for a doctor to supply the addict with drugs; addiction is a crime in itself punishable by jail and more or less compulsory attempts at cure.[3] We on our part responded to this deserved praise from our inferiors (the Americans) with that characteristic smug complacency which is one of the many pleasing aspects of our national character, and it never occurred to us that anything could go wrong. Thus as late as 1959 the United Kingdom Government reported to the United Nations in reply to a request for information about addiction in Britain "As drug addiction is not a serious

140

problem in the United Kingdom there has been no justification for seeking powers to obtain detailed information about the small number of known addicts".[4] As Dr Norman Imlah puts it "The British system of providing known narcotic addicts with their drugs on prescription under medical supervision arose out of the complacent belief that nobody would abuse the system".[5] The medical profession as usual were supremely confident that the system they had evolved and which they alone controlled must be superior to any other and certainly to the American system where the doctors had been ignored and pushed into the background by rival agents of social control, the lawyers, the politicians and the police, and notably the Federal Bureau of Narcotics. The British Home Office was more cautious and vigilant and, although accepting the findings of a series of medical reports on the subject, does not seem to have ever subscribed to the simple dichotomy: Britain = permissive = good *versus* America = punitive = bad.[6]

In 1960 there was indeed a good deal of support for this simple view that British permissiveness worked. The number of known heroin addicts was very low and only rising very slowly, mainly as a result of greater recognition and detection. From 1944—54 only 44 new cases or five a year occurred and between 1954 and 1959 there were only 49 new cases or ten a year.[7] The *real* number of addicts was probably not much in excess of the number of *known* addicts, for there was no sizeable black market in heroin.

The numbers of addicts were very small both in absolute terms and in comparison with other countries such as the United States where there are about 60,000 addicts (a fairly stable figure since the mid-1950s) and about one in every 2,000 to 4,000 people is an addict.[8] At no time had addiction in Britain spread rapidly in epidemic fashion and as Rufus King put it (ironically in view of what has happened since) "The possibility of some epidemic-like change in the pattern is recognized; but the situation has remained stable for many years and there are no present indications to suggest any significant growth in the addict population."[9] Indeed there seemed no way in which it could change. Since addicts could get all the drugs they needed legally and free

from their doctor there was no possibility of profit for the
drug pedlar, who therefore stayed in countries like America
where his activities paid better. Because British addicts were
assured of regular supplies and freedom from harassment
they had less need of one another for supplies and solidarity
and so they never met or interacted in any way. There was no
such thing as an addict sub-culture into which young
neophytes might be drawn.[10] In any case, studies in America
seemed to show that ordinary addicts possessed a "strong
moral code that acts as a barrier against initiating novices".[11]
Although this code is often broken under conditions of stress
such as impending withdrawal, there seemed to be no reason
in England why the addict with his guaranteed regular
supplies should experience such stress and break the moral
rule. One may doubt the existence and strength of such a
code in America where clearly the addict has strong
economic and psychological motives to spread heroin addiction, thereby creating a bigger, safer market, a larger addicted
community in which he can feel more normal. However, in
England these motives did not seem to apply. Schur sent a
questionnaire to 13 British medical specialists with 434
patients to see how likely British addicts were to spread the
habit.[12] The replies to his question "How many of the
addicts you've observed would be likely to induce friends to
take up narcotic drugs" were:

All			A few	6	(211)
Many	}	2 (34)	None	4	(186)
About half			Don't know	1	(3)

The first number is the number of doctors Schur questioned, the
second is the number of addicted patients those doctors had.

In 1961 this looked reassuring. But in retrospect one can
see that a large enough number of addicts were potentially
willing to spread the habit, to create an epidemic under
slightly changed conditions. Far from being secure the British
system was balanced precariously on a knife edge, though at
the time it seemed so very safe and stable. After all, backing

up the system were the honest and reliable members of the British medical profession who could be trusted not to abuse it themselves and to quickly detect and prevent any abuse by others.

The main benefit from Britain's permissive policy towards addiction was that the addicts never needed to resort to illegal methods to get their drugs. There were no openings for drug pedlars and gangsters to set up a black market in heroin, selling it to the desperate addict at an exorbitant price. There was no need for the addict to commit further crimes to raise the money to pay the drug pusher. We had (and possibly still have) avoided the full vicious circle of deviance and repression that characterizes the United States.

Addiction (primary deviance)	→	Repression by Law. No legal supplies	→	Addict (whose earning power is reduced by his habit) has a desperate need for money because of the high price of his drugs on the black market
		↑		↓
		Further repression of addiction because of the severity of these secondary consequences	←	Resorts to crime to get the money (secondary deviance)

The British addict by contrast rarely got on the wrong side of the law because of a fear of being cut off from his legal source of supplies by police pursuit or imprisonment. As Schur puts it "by refusing to treat the addict as a criminal Britain may have kept him from becoming one".[13]

The central feature of the British system was that authority and control lay with the medical profession rather than with the agencies of law enforcement as in America. The addict was seen "as a sick person in need of medical care rather than a criminal to be hounded by the police".[14] Further, the system was not merely permissive towards

addicts, it was also permissive towards the doctors who ran
and administered it. The control of doctors supplying heroin
to addicts was placed in the hands of other doctors, the
medical inspectors of the Ministry of Health, and not with
the police. The rules governing the doctors' behaviour were
loose, they were not enforced very rigorously and the
penalties for infringing them were relatively light. From time
to time the Home Office tried to persuade doctors to take
greater care over prescribing to new patients and to inform
the Home Office about the occurrence of new addicts, but
they had no power to enforce this and it was only in April
1968 that a statutory obligation to register addicts was
placed on the doctors. Similarly the Home Office tried to
discourage "maintenance therapy" whereby an addict was
simply kept on a stable dose of heroin indefinitely with no
attempt being made to cure him, and laid down conditions
under which this procedure was and was not permissible. In
practice the conditions were so loose and the loopholes so
great that each individual doctor could and did prescribe
exactly what he thought fit for a particular patient. The
doctor's right to prescribe what he thought best for the
patient was not seriously curtailed in any way and at this
time no one thought to challenge it.

A striking indication of the strength of the doctors'
position was shown by their defeat of the Government's
proposal to ban the manufacture and importation of heroin
in 1955. Despite the strong pressures from other countries
(notably America) and from the World Health Organization
to institute such a ban, the doctors through their strong
pressure groups such as the BMA were able to force the
Government not to take any action. One of their main
motives in fighting the ban was to preserve the existing
situation in which the presenting of drugs was controlled by
the doctors rather than by legislation.[15] It was also thought
that such a ban could lead to a black market in heroin and a
rise in the number of addicts. Now, many years later, it is
possible to argue that if we had adopted the WHO ban on the
use of heroin when it was suggested we could have avoided
the rapid rise in the number of heroin addicts that occurred
in the 1960s.[16]

One justification for placing so much uncontrolled power in the hands of individual doctors was seen in the situation that had arisen in the United States, where the stringent legal regulations governing the prescribing of addictive drugs to addicts had caused most reputable doctors to opt out and to refuse to treat addicts at all. Doctors were totally forbidden by law to prescribe enough heroin or morphine to the patient to keep him "comfortable by maintaining his customary use" but forced to attempt to get him off narcotics as quickly as possible.[17] Several doctors acting in good faith were prosecuted for prescribing narcotics in an illegal way and the Government-sponsored narcotics clinics were closed down following a scandal. As the gangsters moved in to supply the addicts' needs and the addicts turned to crime to pay them, respectable doctors became less and less willing to involve themselves with the addicts' problems. Once again a vicious circle had been set up.

Doctors forbidden to prescribe freely by law	→	Doctors cease prescribing narcotics	→	Addict forced to get his drugs on the black market. Becomes involved in criminal activities.
		↑		↓
		Doctors do not wish to be involved with such people.		

Paradoxically one result of the British policy of placing addiction in the hands of the doctors was that very few addicts ever got cured. This was not simply because the available methods of treating drug addiction were ineffective and cured only a small proportion of those trying them. Many addicts and their doctors were not interested in achieving a cure. There were no real legal or professional pressures on an individual doctor to make him want to put his patient through the tricky and unpleasant process involved in withdrawing him from drugs. Even if the doctor wished to withdraw the patient from drugs it was almost impossible for him to get a poorly motivated addict to agree to this. As Imlah puts it "In Britain where the addict knows that the doctor is allowed to prescribe drugs until the addict can be persuaded to accept withdrawal and treatment, the doctor is at an obvious disadvantage in bringing the addict to this point if they both know that the addict can step outside and obtain the drug without undue difficulty."[18] As a result many addicts soon became regarded as incurable and were prescribed an amount of heroin sufficient to suit their needs over an indefinite period of time. The aim became not to cure the addict but to make a "stabilized addict" of the patient, able to lead "a useful and relatively normal life" provided he received a regular minimum dose of the drug and with the dose showing no signs of escalating upwards. This procedure was justified by terming it "maintenance therapy".[19]

Maintenance therapy worked fairly well before 1960, largely because at that time the British addicts, far from being inadequate people with severe personality problems who had drifted into drug-taking, were largely either normal people who had become addicted following the routine use of narcotic drugs in medical treatment or doctors and nurses who had been tempted by their easy access to such drugs. People of this type were able to live fairly normal lives despite their addiction and were able and willing to take care of their general health and to submit to the advice and demands of the doctor treating them. Even so, as a result of their addiction they experienced considerable difficulties in holding down a job and failed to achieve satisfactory sexual or family relationships with their spouses. Schur's survey of British medical specialists brings this out clearly. [20]

Question 1:
Have you found that addict patients (in other than withdrawal-treatment situations) seem able to function satisfactorily in an occupation or job when given a regular supply of drugs.

Proportion of patients for whom answer "yes" given by doctor	Number of doctors	Corresponding number of patients
Practically all	—	—
Many	1	6
About half	4	106
A few	4	253
None	1	6
Don't know or not applicable	3	63
	13	434

Question 2:
Do addicts when regularly administered drugs (as previous question) seem able to function satisfactorily in sexual or family relationships?

Proportion of patients for whom answer "yes" given by doctor	Number of doctors	Corresponding number of patients
Practically all	—	—
Many	—	—
About half	1	28
A few	4	266
None	5	88
No answer	2	7
Does not apply	1	45
	13	434

On both the key tests of social adequacy, the ability (*a*) to work and (*b*) to lead a normal family life, the addicts are certainly failures even though on the surface they appear to be coping with life reasonably well. Their disabilities stem very largely from the debilitating effects of the drugs they take which tend to destroy the addict's sexual drive and his energy and enthusiasm for his work. When he has just taken a fix he may be enervated by the soporific euphoria induced by the drug; as it begins to wear off he feels the incipient pains of withdrawal. At neither stage is he (or she) fit to meet the occupational, sexual and interpersonal demands that society makes on him (or her).[21]

The relatively mild nature of the disabilities suffered by British addicts compared with the appalling secondary consequences of police harassment of addicts in America led some American sociologists to postulate

(a) that heroin was a relatively harmless drug which did not produce any major organic deterioration and less harmful than other commonly used addictive drugs such as barbiturates or alcohol;[22]

(b) that drug addicts were not, as many psychological studies had shown, weak and inadequate personalities;[23]

(c) that the addict's problems were neither the result of the physical effects of drug addiction nor of a deficient personality but stemmed entirely from the way he was regarded and treated by other people.

In other words his secondary deviant behaviour, his observed psychological problems and his poor physical condition were the result not of drug taking but of being labelled and harassed by a society that disapproved of his addiction.

This view of addiction was based partly on observation of more permissive societies such as Britain and partly on historical data which seemed to show that prior to the passing of laws against the consumption of narcotics in America between the years 1914 and 1920, large numbers of respectable Americans had regularly taken narcotics, notably morphine, without visible harmful effects. In this argument great stress was laid on the fact that "it is known that if the addict is getting his supply of heroin he can cope with the world in such a way that the observer regards him as normal".[24] Indeed it is so difficult to tell if an individual is an addict that the American law-enforcement agencies have spent a great deal of money and effort in designing chemical tests to distinguish the addict from the non-addict.[25]

Views of this kind have been put forward in a moderate and responsible fashion by sociologists of the high calibre of Schur and Duster. Unfortunately they are also often set out in an extreme and misleading way as in the following quotation from an American sociologist:

> Nor is it possible to defend the notion that the use of addicting drugs necessarily transforms even the healthy personality so that it becomes "character disordered". Again this is a matter of social circumstance . . . when addicts have easy access to the drugs they need . . . they usually do not manifest so-called character disaster traits . . . where the laws are tolerant as in England the large majority of addicts get along quite well in their jobs, in raising families and otherwise being respectable members of the community . . . if US addicts could get their drugs without having to steal or go to jail, etc., most of the so-called character defects would disappear overnight . . .[26]

In many ways there is a great deal of sense in these arguments when applied to America where a tough punitive policy against drug addiction has created more problems than it has solved, but like most of the arguments put forward by proponents of labelling theories they become absurd when taken too far. In a British context they are not simply absurd but dangerous for they are often used by British trendies to justify an ultra-permissive policy towards drugs or at least to return to the position as it was before the reforms and restrictions imposed in the 1960s. If the problems associated with drug addiction are not physiological or even psychological in origin but rather stem from the social pressures and restrictions on the addict, they argue, then we should abolish the restrictions, give up trying to cure the addict and maintain him on whatever dosage enables him to function normally. These arguments are unlikely to carry much weight politically in Britain after our experience of a spiralling drug problem in the last decade, but it is as well to stress that the arguments are false even when judged in terms of the evidence and criteria employed by those putting them forward. In the first place, even under the most favourable of social circumstances such as England in the 1950s, the addicts were unable to lead a normal family life or hold down a job even though many appeared normal on the surface. The concern that doctors showed in America well before World War I at the effects of morphine addiction indicates that addicts had similar problems there too. The fact that these addicts appear normal to the casual observer is irrelevant. Many serious illnesses do not manifest themselves in obvious symptoms (some cancers for example) while other trivial ailments (such as certain allergies) may give the sufferer an appearance of being dangerously ill. This is also true for many character disorders. Certain psychopaths are not easily distinguishable from other people and only reveal themselves when they commit some inexplicable bizarre and sadistic crime. It may subsequently be discovered that they had previously suffered some form of brain damage. Again it is very difficult to assess whether or not a driver has consumed too much alcohol to be able to drive his car safely. He may appear to the casual observer or even the experienced doctor or police officer perfectly sober and in control of all his faculties and yet be a menace if allowed to take the wheel. For this reason it was necessary to introduce the breathalyser, a chemical means of testing how much alcohol he has consumed and hence the probability of his being fit to drive. In each case nothing appears to be wrong and yet further investigation reveals an underlying problem. These are not necessarily mere instances of arbitrary labelling, simply because they are not reinforced by appearances. Indeed, it is extraordinary that so much weight should be placed on superficial appearance though it certainly fits in with the views of men who see the world entirely in terms of labels and counter-labels and are unwilling to admit any sort of objective testing of reality.

THE PERMISSIVE SYSTEM BREAKS DOWN

This was permissive England at the beginning of the 1960s. What happened next was so disastrous as to sweep away many of the old permissive institutions and relationships and to discredit entirely the view that totally permissive methods were the best ones for dealing with drug addiction. The first sign that the system was collapsing was that the number of addicts rose at an ever-increasing rate. Indeed during most of the 1960s Britain had the fastest-growing rate of heroin addiction in the world, with the numbers of new addicts doubling every two years at one stage.[27]

As the Brain committee (so complacent before!) now admitted in their second report, the British system of control had totally broken down. As Imlah stresses, this was *not* due to organized illicit traffic in heroin but entirely due to excessive prescribing by doctors acting "within the law and according to their professional judgement".[28] The recipients of these legal prescriptions kept what they needed for their own use and sold the surplus to potential addicts. These would, after a time, become fully-fledged addicts themselves, register with a doctor, get their heroin on prescription, use some of it and sell the rest on the black market, creating yet more addicts. The British system had cracked apart at what were supposedly its strong points—the reliability and honesty of the individual doctor, the addict's unwillingness to sell his drugs,[29] the lack of a buyer for such a sale in a country where heroin was freely prescribed—all of which were now seen to be a sham and a delusion. Despite the absence of a punitive policy and despite large-scale organized drug-pushing, a black market in drugs appeared and an addict sub-culture formed. Although initially the spiral began with a few addicts selling prescriptions (their own and other people's that they had bought as a kind of middle man) for cash, it soon gathered momentum for another reason—the strong desire of many of these new addicts, particularly those with underlying personality defects, to proselytize drug-taking, to push as many other people as possible into taking addicting drugs.[30] Also the rapid rise in numbers of addicts brought Britain closer to the critical level at which it becomes profitable for criminals to operate. A key factor preventing the manufacture or smuggling of heroin in Britain in the past has been not so much the fact that it is freely prescribed to addicts by the NHS but the small size of the market. The production and distribution of illegal heroin is subject to very rapidly increasing returns to scale once the market reaches a certain size, and any further rapid rise in the number of British addicts would almost certainly bring in the gangsters.[31]

Nor was it only in Britain that the permissive system broke

down in the 1960s. In Sweden too the attempt to control addiction (to intravenously administered amphetamine rather than heroin) by permissive methods broke down completely, with a rapid rise in the number of people addicted.[32] In 1965 the Swedes decided to use the maintenance-therapy approach with this drug in order to eliminate the criminal behaviour of addicts and the black market in drugs that supposedly stemmed from a punitive approach to drug addiction. The result was two years of total chaos with a vast rise in the number of addicts, a flood of new supplies on to the black market as a result of over-prescribing and an enormous increase in the number of crimes committed by addicts. In Sweden at one stage a third of those being legally supplied with drugs were arrested for criminal activity (during the two permissive years) and a rising percentage of criminals was found to be on these kinds of stimulants. Eventually 70 per cent of people arrested for all offences were found to be taking amphetamine. There was a high death rate among those taking this and other addictive drugs. Indeed, an advertising firm in Stockholm, alarmed at the fatal consequences of narcotic addiction, erected four hundred placards in the form of death notices in the streets of the city, stating that narcotics had caused the death of the person named. After two years of this disastrous experiment it became evident, even to the Swedish liberal establishment that the permissive approach had failed and maintenance therapy for amphetamine addicts was abandoned in 1967.

The new British heroin addicts differ markedly from those studied by Schur. They are younger and less likely to be in medical or allied occupations. These changes are shown in the Table below (see footnotes 7 and 27).

These new young heroin addicts under the permissive and non-punitive British system seem to show many of the physical and psychological deficiencies found in American addicts, deficiencies which sociologists had previously ascribed to harassment by the law-enforcement agencies or the stringencies of having to obtain the money to pay for their next fix. In the latter part of the 1960s, as the authorities tightened up on prescribing drugs for addicts, hostile social pressures probably were an important factor in

Numbers of Addicts known to the Home Office taking Heroin and Allied Drugs

YEAR	1951	'57	'59	'62	'63	'64	'65	'66	'67	'68	'69	'70	'71	'72
Age * Under 20			0	3	17	40	145	329	395	764	637	405	338	279
20–34			50	132	184	257	347	558	906	1530	1789	1813	2010	2262
35–49			92	107	128	138	134	162	142	146	174	158	156	178
50 and over			278	274	298	311	291	286	279	260	241	253	226	204
Total in Medical or Allied Occupations	77	88	68	57	56	58	45	54	56	43	43	38	44	33
Total number of Addicts Known	310	359	454	532	632	753	927	1349	1729	2782 **	2881 ***	2661	2769	2944

*   (some cases where the age is not known)

**   (statutory notification introduced in 1968)

***   (new stricter controls start to bite)

moulding the addicts' behaviour, but this was not true of the early 1960s when attitudes to addiction were still based on our earlier experience with the stable addicts. However, the problems associated with the new addicts can be observed even in this earlier period.

Unlike the American addicts, British addicts receive their heroin on prescription under controlled circumstances from medically or pharmaceutically qualified suppliers who take care over the dosage and purity of the drug and who supply them free with sterile needles and syringes. Nevertheless they have a mortality rate that is between twenty and thirty times the rate expected for a British population of the same demographic characteristics and over twice that of the heroin addicts in New York. One survey of heroin addicts known to the Home Office stated that

Heroin addiction in Britain at present carries a high mortality risk. Sixty-nine non-therapeutic heroin addicts known to the Home Office have died, sixty-five between 1960 and the end of 1966. . . . There has been an increase in the number of deaths and a decrease in the mean age of death with the greater number of younger addicts at risk. Among British-born non-therapeutic addicts the deaths before 1965 occurred at a mean age of 30·3 years compated with a mean age of 24·8 years for the deaths during 1965—6. Fifty per cent of all deaths occurred before the age of 28 years. . . Most deaths could be attributed to self-administration of drugs or to the direct consequence of chronic drug intoxication on personality or psychological function.[33]

These young addicts die from overdoses of their drugs, from septicaemia and tetanus as a result of using contaminated needles and by committing suicide. Even those who do not die from such complications are progressively enfeebled by their drug habit and have a low life expectancy. The infections due to dirty needles, physical weakness due to loss of appetite and progressive nutritional deficiency and the loss of vital adrenal hormones from the body as a direct result of taking heroin cause such addicts to have a very low resistance to disease.[34]

Most of them die not from the direct effects of the drug but from second-order effects. As a result of taking heroin the new addicts become indifferent as to whether they live or die, whether they are sick or healthy. They tend to be unhappy, anxious people who took to heroin originally because they thought it would relieve their anxiety and detach them from the world which rendered them unhappy. The drug had the desired effect but at a cost—they were no longer able to control that world, they no longer cared what happened in it or what happened to them. As a result they eventually committed suicide either suddenly and directly (the suicide rate among addicts is fifty times the expected rate for the same age group)[35] or by a neglect of their health over a period of time. The addict needs even more than a non-addicted person to regulate his life carefully—he needs to be careful over the dose of the drug, over the cleanliness of the needle—but the impact of the drug on a weak person is such as to render him unable to take these precautions. In a survey of addicts who were prescribed heroin at London clinics[36] it was found that 84 per cent had in the month prior to the interview used drugs other than those prescribed for them by the clinic and that 89 per cent regularly used unsterile injection techniques. As a result most of them had suffered from complications such as septicaemia (18 per cent) hepatitis (44 per cent) abscesses (51 per cent) and an overdose of the drug (44 per cent). Over a third of these addicts had at some time been given hospital treatment for physical complications associated with drug use.

We are still left with the problem of why the new British addicts have a higher mortality rate than the earlier addicts and perhaps more surprisingly why this rate is higher in Britain than in America. In part the lower American rate is probably due to the fact that some American addicts who die from complications as a result of the drug habit are not known as addicts to the authorities. The cause of death is recorded as hepatitis or suicide but this is not linked to addiction. The high death rate of addicts in Britain simply reflects better knowledge of the true causes of their death.

In addition, the British addict receives a much larger dose of the drug on prescription than his American counterpart can raise on the black market. It seems possible that this large controlled dose is even more harmful than a small irregular one.[37]

dosage higher in Brit.

It has also been suggested that the British addict is more likely to die than the American precisely because he is regarded as a sick person rather than a criminal. Sick people are expected to die and therefore they do—it is simply part of the sick role that society expects them to play.[38]

The flaw in this argument is that it fails to explain why the mortality rate is higher among the new addicts than among the pre-1960 addicts. In both cases doctors and public alike regarded the addict as sick and possibly as incurable. But the doctors did not expect their addicted patients to die nor did they want them to. A good patient either recovers or learns to live with his illness. Prior to 1960 most addicts were good patients in one or other of these ways. There is no reason why doctors' attitudes should have changed except *as a result* of a rise in the mortality rate of the addicts. The increased mortality must have preceded and caused any change of attitudes in a pessimistic direction and not the other way round. After a time-lag the doctors probably did become aware that the addicts were dying off at a faster rate, but this need not necessarily have affected their behaviour to the detriment of their treatment of the addict. It is also unlikely that they would communicate their pessimism to the addict for fear of producing the very effect here described.

The increased mortality of the "new" British addicts over the "old" probably reflects the weakness of will and character of the new addict and his isolation from society. The "old" addict was surrounded by people who were not addicted and who would put pressure on him to take care of his health, to take the drugs under sterile conditions. There would also be indirect pressures put on him to keep in good health in order to fulfil standard social obligations. He would not be allowed to retire from the world into a sub-culture whose only interest was drugs. By contrast an addict of the new type who has few contacts with non-addicts and lives surrounded by other addicts is under no such pressures and expectations. If he uses a dirty needle, he is only doing what most of his associates are doing. There is no one to warn him, for all live in a world where nothing matters any more. There are no stable people to provide a boundary to his indifference, only a merging of one addict's indifference with another's. This would explain the lower mortality rate in America, for there the addict is forced into contact with the outside world to acquire the money with which to buy his drugs. He has to have legitimate or criminal employment. He has to have dealings with non-addicts that force him to organize his life to some extent, to exhibit some degree of rational foresight. The secondary delinquencies of addicts that cause so much havoc in America may well be the factor that keeps American addicts alive longer than their British counterparts.

The personality disorders and behaviour problems noted among addicts in the United States which were allegedly the result simply of the addict's difficulties in obtaining a supply of his drugs seem to be equally common among the new British addicts who have not experienced these pressures. A survey of addicts treated at clinics in London revealed[39] that only 14 out of 111 addicts interviewed reported no illicit use of drugs in the previous month and no form of criminal involvement in the previous three months. Over a third of the addicts reported criminal activities other than those covered by the Drugs Act during the three months before the interview. Of the sample interviewed only 39 per cent were in full-time work and only 24 per cent had worked a full week in the week prior to the interview. As Cockett notes in his study of drug abuse and personality in young offenders in Britain

... addiction results in a greatly reduced capacity for work, a deterioration in physical condition and hence a reduced ability of the individual to play his part in community activity, particularly perhaps during the more recent eras of industrial development and economic complexity.[40]

Cockett's study is interesting because he compares the personality traits of these drug-users with those both of other young delinquents not taking drugs and with a matched sample from the general population. He is able to show that the drug-users have personality problems and tend to be weak characters, and the criteria he uses to demonstrate this do not depend in any way on the fact of their being drug-takers. It is sometimes alleged that studies of this kind involve the

Hedonist = Someone who believes that having
Pleasure is most important thing in life.

circular argument: "Drug-takers are weak. How do we know
they are weak? They must be weak. They take drugs." But
this is in no way true of Cockett's research. He uses
personality tests that do not involve attitudes to drugs or
behaviour with drugs and which were designed for general use
in a variety of contexts. He concludes that:

> Abnormal psychiatric states are commonly encountered among drug
> addicts. These states are not usually regarded as a cause of the addiction
> nor is addiction itself normally regarded as an abnormal psychiatric
> condition. More often the addiction is recognized along with the
> psychiatric abnormality as an accompaniment or consequence of
> underlying mental illness. . . . we established an association for drug
> abuse with neurotic and other psychotic symptoms on the one hand,
> and psychopathic traits (that is emotional disposition character
> features) on the other. In particular we found a higher proportion of
> neurotic and other psychiatric symptoms among drug-takers than
> among controls* . . . (all the drug-takers combined show a neuroticism
> score significantly higher than that of the non drug-taking delinquent
> controls) . . . we were able to differentiate further and show by means
> of a diagnostic test that these conditions which especially distinguished
> the drug-takers were anxiety, depression and hypochondriachal states.
> Our results thus indicate that what has elsewhere been found about
> drug addicts is also true of drug-takers of less than addicted degree and
> applies progressively up the drug-abuse scale.[41]

Perhaps the most typical finding of this study is that the
addicts are weak, inadequate people:

> We are able to identify certain elements of personality forming a
> component, albeit a fairly small one, which specifically constitutes
> vulnerability to drug abuse. . . The relevant elements of personality
> imply what is popularly understood by "inadequacy" and "weakness of
> character".[42]

Descriptions such as these of the addict as weak or
inadequate are often attacked as being biased or meaningless.[43] Those who mount such attacks prefer to regard the

---

*Controls are individuals who are not addicts but who are selected for purposes of
comparison with addicts. (Author's note)

addict as someone who disagrees with society's values and is attached to a hedonistic philosophy. According to this view the addict is not inadequate but simply does not wish to do the things that are regarded as criteria of adequacy. It isn't that he can't work or can't screw but simply that he chooses not to. He has chosen a way of life that does not involve such activities and which instead is centred around his drugs.

This argument quickly runs into a number of difficulties. While it may be true that many addicts hold to a hedonistic philosophy, so do many people who do not take to drugs, even though they may have the opportunity to do so. What differentiates this latter group from the addicts is that they do not share their personality problems—they are more likely to be "adequate" people. As a result they are able to attain the happiness which a hedonist seeks without becoming addicts. Indeed, if the happy hedonist *is* given morphine or heroin he does not find the effect of these opiates pleasurable. Experimental studies indicate that when subjects were given doses of these drugs the effects in many cases were indifferent and even unpleasant (this was in marked contrast to the effect of a true euphoriant such as amphetamine sulphate, which all of the subjects found pleasant).[44] The "new" heroin addicts are typically disturbed and unhappy people even before they become addicts, and in a way that is not a result of their hedonistic philosophy. What distinguishes them from non-addicts is not their hedonism but their unhappiness. A hedonistic philosophy may make unhappiness harder to bear and indirectly lead to their addiction, but the main reason for the addict's plight lies in himself and not in his philosophy.

The taking of heroin or similar drugs is not likely to take these people any nearer to the goal of happiness which is at the centre of any hedonistic philosophy. The drug may relieve anxiety at first but in the long run it will simply make them even more unhappy than they would have been had they not taken it. The result of such drug-taking is not ecstasy but horror. The heroin addict is unlikely to experience sexual pleasure for the drug robs him of both desire and capacity. If addicts are hedonists, they are extremely irrational hedonists, for their actions are those least likely to bring them lasting pleasure. The pain of impending withdrawal, the ill-health induced by addiction and neglect, the suicide of the desperate are hardly indices of pleasure successfully achieved.

It is precisely because he is unable to obtain goals he sets for himself (let alone those which society reasonably seeks to impose) that the addict is described as weak or inadequate. Addicts themselves (without prompting by those treating them) say that they would in the first instance like to live without drugs and secondly like to be able to form lasting personal relationships. The fact that they are unable to do so indicates weakness that exists prior to their becoming addicts and which is accentuated by their addiction. The range of things they are able to do is more restricted than for the adequate person and is further limited by their dependence on drugs. Those addicts who became addicted accidentally as a result of medical treatment recognize this and perceive that their lives are impoverished as a result. For those who chose to become addicts this is more difficult to accept, for it involves admitting that there are forces within themselves that they do not like and which they cannot control.

Similarly some sociologists cannot accept that such forces exist and bitterly attack the psychologist for speaking of "personality" or "heredity" or "early conditioning". Yet the psychologist is not imposing on us some new scientific cage which robs us utterly of our freewill. The man in the street who robustly asserts that he is free to choose nevertheless accepts that his choice is influenced by factors within himself he would prefer to do without. Often, though, he will regard such factors (although definitely within himself) as not being part of his true self. He may say that "I do not feel myself today" or of another that "he is his own worst enemy". Winston Churchill, who was subject to long fits of depression, always referred to them as his "black dog".[45] In this way we are able to distance ourselves from those causes of unhappiness which lie within ourselves. Whether or not we recognize directly or indirectly that such melancholy is part of us, we nevertheless do not deceive ourselves to the extent of ascribing it entirely to the outside world. Rather we either accept it as part of ourselves we would sooner be without or we regard it as an illness of which we wish to be cured. Depression has more of the characteristics of a disease than of a philosophy and so in a different way does addiction. It spreads like an epidemic disease and the quasi-mathematical models of the epidemiologists fit the spread of addiction reasonably well.

The moral and philosophical objections to regarding the addict's problems as stemming from his weakness of character seem here to have little substance. Nor can it be agreed that this view leads the person who holds it to take a tough punitive line towards addicts. Cockett, whose study of personality weakness in addicts was quoted above, concluded that

> . . . it seems clear that the individuals most in need of safeguarding are the young, the immature, and the inadequate or weak. On the whole our society does aim to safeguard the young and the weak by legal and other means. In view of our general results it would appear appropriate for it to do so where drugs and their possible abuse are concerned.[46]

Islam

This may be paternalistic in tone but it is hardly the language of strong moral condemnation. Since the view that the defining characteristic of the addict is weakness is supported by much empirical evidence and is not open to ethical or logical objections, I propose to make it the central aspect of the analysis that follows.

This finding that the addict is weak or inadequate is repeated in many other studies.[47] It would seem both that people with deficient personalities are attracted to heroin and that their personalities deteriorate further under the effect of the drug. The addict is typically an immature, emotionally shallow person unable to tolerate frustration and with no fixed goals in life. In his family background he may well have lacked a strong father figure and may have had an over-protective mother but has typically lost all contact with his family by the time he becomes an addict. A history of poor achievement at school relative to his ability is followed by a poor work record. He may well suffer from character disorders of a psychopathic kind and his weakness and disorder are characteristic of the permissive society that produced him. He is perhaps its logical conclusion and certainly its most typical failure at present. Under the influence of drugs his character deteriorates even more. He loses such skills and abilities, such pride in his person and his achievements as he once had. He becomes totally unreliable and mendacious and loses all his associates except for other addicts. He ceases to care for his health and lives only for his drugs. All this happens as inevitably in permissive England as in punitive America, though even in England social pressures must play a part in the later stages. As the addict's habits and attitudes deteriorate, he becomes progressively less acceptable to the rest of society and is rejected by everyone except other addicts. As he comes to associate solely with other addicts so his behaviour and attitudes come to resemble theirs rather than those of the wider society; so once again a vicious circle of rejection and deterioration is set up in the later stages.

The important thing to stress though is not how the vicious circle operates but how the addict got into it in the first place. The British experience shows clearly that a deficient personality and the effect of a dangerous drug are sufficient to start up the spiral even in the absence of punitive sanctions and a criminally operated black market. Even the social sanctions have not been operative for many addicts. Schur did a survey of attitudes to drug addicts and other deviants in that most characteristic of British communities, Willesden.[48] Although the respondents were punitive to a man (or woman) to the extent of enthusiastically supporting the public flogging of sex deviants they did not respond in this way to the drug addict.[49]

Attitudes towards addicts may or may not have hardened since this survey (1958?). Nevertheless, the absence of tough attitudes at the beginning of the period of escalation of addict numbers shows that social sanctions were no more a cause than legal ones. Further, it is exceedingly doubtful whether a sufficiently large and widespread change in attitudes could have occurred sufficiently rapidly for social sanctions to have become established, and even before he becomes addicted the addict has generally mixed exclusively with people whose attitude to addiction is uniformly permissive. We can, therefore, rule out hostile social pressures as a major cause of the personality deterioration of British addicts.

STRICTER CONTROLS INTRODUCED

For once the permissive society is entirely to blame. That so many people in such a society should want to take addictive drugs in the first place is bad enough, but in addition permissive policies allowed potential addicts easy access to drugs and later failed to put sufficient pressure on them to get cured. Fortunately society now seems to have realized how foolish the permissive approach towards addiction was, and several important reforms have resulted in much stricter control of this problem. Nor have we in Britain made the mistake of going to the opposite extreme by treating the addict as a criminal to be pursued and harassed by the police and punished by the courts. In America just such a policy has been successful in reducing the number of addicts from 3 per cent of the population in 1895 and 2·5 per cent in the period 1900—20 to between 0·025 and 0·05 per cent today, but this success has been achieved at an enormous cost in terms of the crime and rackets it created and the suffering it caused the residual addict population.[50] The American cure is probably worse than the disease. So far the British reforms have not followed this pattern. Britain continues to treat addiction as primarily a medical problem but has introduced much stricter controls over the relationship between the addict and his doctor. Doctors are no longer allowed to prescribe drugs to addicts but must send them to special treatment centres whose staff alone have the right to provide them with their drugs. Also there is now (since April 1968) a statutory obligation to register addicts with the authorities. In this way it has been possible to cut down on over-prescribing by individual doctors and to prevent the addict from going to several doctors and obtaining separate quantities of drugs from each of them without revealing that he has an existing legitimate source of supply. Closer liaison between doctors at the centres, police and pharmacists has made it possible to clamp down on addicts selling off surplus drugs obtained on prescription and to limit the scope and scale of the black market in heroin.[51] On the whole the new restrictions seem to be having some effect and the number of addicts is no longer rising as rapidly as in the 1960s.

The answer to the problem of addiction would seem, then, to be to retain a system of controls based on the doctors rather than the police but to alter considerably the medical ethics relating to the relationship between the doctor and this particular class of patient. There has to be a considerable shift in the balance between a doctor's devotion to his patient's welfare and his duty to society. Normally the former is crucial, but in the case of the addict the latter must prevail.

It is for this reason that the doctor's right to prescribe what he thinks fit for the patient has, in effect, been set aside in this area. Further, even if his patient objects it is a doctor's clear duty to register him as an addict if appropriate and to send him to a special treatment centre. He must do so even if in his professional judgement this is not the best course of action to take for this particular individual patient. He can no longer freely prescribe heroin to him as and when he thinks fit.

The most urgent problem is to cure those who are already addicted. There is no question of maintaining them indefinitely on heroin (though maintenance on methadone *may* prove to be more effective), for even if great care is taken over prescribing it is exceedingly difficult to provide them consistently with exactly the dose they need. If you give them too much, they sell off the surplus, thus creating new addicts; if you give them too little a black market is called into existence to make up the deficit. So long as a reservoir of addicts exists (particularly of the new, younger, unstable and amoral kind) there is always a threat that the problem could escalate again. Besides, the events of the past ten to twelve years have killed for ever the myth of the stabilized addict. Addicts do *not* live a normal working or family life and their health rapidly worsens with time. As a result of their weak personalities and the moral deterioration induced by their drugs they are constantly drawn into other forms of deviant activity, often of a serious nature. The "stable" addict hardly exists, for almost all addicts in Britain would now seem to have illegal supplies of various drugs in addition to their regular legal prescription and many are deviant in ways not relating to drugs.[52] It is kinder to the addict and better for society if, instead of maintaining them in this unpleasant and precarious state, a determined effort is made to cure them or to switch them to some safer drug.

Society has also tightened up control on other drugs commonly prescribed by doctors (but also taken extensively in other contexts) notably amphetamines and barbiturates. Control has been left in the hands of the doctors but the framework within which they operate has been changed and pressure is put on the individual practitioner to conform to certain rules.

In addition to the drugs considered so far, which have in various ways involved control by the medical profession, it is necessary to discuss three other widely used drugs that are not prescribed by doctors, viz. tobacco, alcohol and marijuana. In the last ten years there has been growing concern about the effects of all three.

TOBACCO

Over the last twenty years it has become increasingly clear that tobacco smoking can cause lung cancer. During the 1960s the Government at last began to take some action to try and reduce the consumption of tobacco. In 1965 advertisements for cigarettes on television were banned and later the tobacco companies were forced to inscribe a warning on each packet of cigarettes that cigarettes can damage the smoker's health. Indeed all cigarette advertisements now contain the proud boast that "each packet contains a Government health warning". The Government has also allocated funds for anti-smoking propaganda and for the setting up of anti-smoking clinics where smokers can be cured of their addiction. What probably had far more effect in cutting down smoking was the very heavy increases in tobacco tax during the 1960s which doubled the price of a packet of cigarettes in ten years. As a result there was a drop of 8 per cent in total tobacco consumption during this period although prior to 1960 it had been rising rapidly.[53] It would seem that classical economics was right and that price has more effect on consumption than persuasion, a consideration that may also apply to alcohol consumption and may have implications for the question of whether society should legalize marijuana. (Other things being equal lung-cancer rates seem to be higher in countries with low taxes on tobacco, e.g. Jersey.)

ALCOHOL

In the 1960s there was also a growing awareness that the major drug problem in Britain was that of alcohol abuse. A report by the medical council on alcoholism (1970) estimated that there were at least 300,000 alcoholics in Britain and that the cost of alcoholism to industry could be as much as £250 million per year.[54] It also noted that the number of alcoholics had steadily increased since the late 1940s and that in recent years there had been an alarming increase in the number of teenage alcoholics. The problem would have been even more serious had it not been for the salutary effect of heavy taxation and severely restricted drinking hours. Indeed, during the period 1900–45 these factors, together with better social conditions, had actually lead to a steady fall in alcohol abuse. International comparisons also seem to show that rates of alcoholism are strongly related to the price and accessibility of alcohol in a country. Certainly this would seem to be a contributing factor to the high rates of alcoholism found in France or the United States.[55]

One interesting result of the high taxation of spirits in Britain is that cirrhosis of the liver (due to alcohol) is a rich man's disease whereas in America it is a disease of the poor (who drink more heavily as a relatively cheap means of escaping from reality in a country designed for the rich).[56]

In addition it became increasingly clear in the 1960s that alcohol was a major factor in causing road accidents. Some 40 per cent of all road accidents and 50 per cent of all arrests are associated with alcohol, and studies in the United States indicated that alcohol was responsible for more than half of their traffic fatalities.[57]

In Britain it was estimated that, if all drivers ceased to drink while driving, the number of traffic accidents would be cut substantially and that there would be an even bigger drop in the more serious accidents. Accordingly the Government introduced the breathalyser test in 1967 in order to make it easier to detect and punish drunken drivers. The supporters of this measure justified it on causalist grounds—it would deter motorists from driving after drinking and cut the number of road accidents. Opponents of the breathalyser by contrast relied on moralist arguments—they saw it as an infringement of personal freedom and, in particular, as breaking the ancient legal principle that no man could be compelled to provide the evidence that would be used to convict him. The causalists, as might be expected, won the day and the breathalyser was introduced, but the moralists did succeed in preventing random tests from being made. The police were only allowed to apply the breathalyser test where they already had reasonable cause to suspect a motorist of having drunk enough alcohol to impair his driving. Even so, the breathalyser test had a remarkable effect in the subsequent two years and can be cited as a triumph for causalist legislation.[58]

Breathalyser introduced
↓

Prosecutions for driving while under the influence of alcohol	1966—67	1967—68	1968—69
	13,656	20,957	26,392
Deaths	7,898	6,746	7,084
Fatal and Serious *Casualties*	26,640	17,805	19,890
Serious Injuries	98,413	87,236	89,372
Total Casualties	386,452	345,993	348,942

To produce a decrease of this magnitude on the rising trend of road accidents is a remarkable achievement, for which the breathalyser was certainly responsible—as is indicated by the fact that the number of fatal and serious accidents between 10 p.m. and 4 a.m. (i.e. after people have been drinking) fell by a third in the first year after the breathalyser test was introduced.

MARIJUANA

With regard to both tobacco and alcohol society's response to the problem created by these drugs has been to introduce new cautious causalist restrictions. However, in the 1960s another drug, marijuana, whose harmful effects may be compared with those of alcohol and tobacco, became increasingly popular, though it remained illegal to consume it. The question of whether this drug should be legalized came to excite a great deal of controversy. Both moralists and causalists took part in this debate. Those moralists in favour of legalization argued (in the words of an advertisement they placed in *The Times*) that the law prohibiting the sale and consumption of marijuana was "immoral in principle and unworkable in practice".[59] By this they presumably meant that the law infringed the right of the individual to take the drug if he wished and made criminals out of a large number of otherwise law-abiding individuals. This strident declaration of moral principle provoked a reply from the moralists on the other side, and the Home Secretary, Mr Callaghan, in refusing to amend the law declared his intention to "call a halt to the advancing tide of permissiveness".[60]

Already, however, it seems that causalist arguments are beginning to prevail and that the issue will eventually be decided on this basis. Those in favour of legalization argue, first, that the costs of enforcing the law in terms of police time and effort and the damage done to the lives of those convicted may well exceed the harm done if the drug were on free sale. Secondly, they argue that the drug is no more harmful than alcohol or tobacco, which are legal, and that therefore if we are to apply consistent and equitable criteria to the question of which drugs we permit and which we ban we must legalize marijuana. Those against legalization admit that the first argument has some validity but quite rightly dismiss the second argument as irrelevant. We already suffer the casualties of two harmful drugs, alcohol and tobacco, and it is now too late to attempt to suppress them. Why should we add to our problems by introducing a third harmful commodity?

This last line of thought seems valid in principle but it does omit one important point, namely that if a new substance, marijuana, were introduced and if it were used as a partial substitute for alcohol and tobacco, this would probably result in a fall in consumption of these substances and a commensurate drop in the harmful consequences that are associated with them. How big this drop would be would, of course, depend on the extent to which marijuana became a substitute for tobacco and alcohol and on the relative prices of the three substances. If marijuana were legalized the Government would presumably entrust its growth and manufacture to the breweries and tobacco companies who provide the existing legal drugs. They have the experience in quality control and in collecting the tax on such items and the licensed retail outlets necessary for the controlled sale of the new drug. By manipulating the level of taxation on these three drugs and by adjusting the terms and conditions of sale, the Government could exert a great deal of control over the amounts sold and hence over the amount of damage caused to those taking the drugs. Let us assume that the Government was thus able to choose a set of optimal prices, determined by tax, that minimized the social and individual havoc caused by the drugs. If we call the total harmful consequences of marijuana use under these circumstances M and the fall in the harmful consequences of tobacco and alcohol (resulting from people switching to marijuana) T and A respectively, then the causalist conditions for legalizing marijuana are given in the following relationship:

$$M - T - A < m + C$$

Here m is the harm done by the present level of (illegal) marijuana consumption and C is the total cost to the community of enforcing the present law. It might be objected that this does not take into account the possible pleasure that people derive from alcohol, tobacco or marijuana. However, as was stated in Chapter 1, this is not a factor that causalists normally take into account *per se*. It will, however, be reflected in the size of C, that is the cost of enforcing the law. The more people take marijuana and the more pleasure that is derived from it, the greater the cost will be of enforcing the law, both in terms of policing and of the harm done to those convicted. It is always dangerous to prophesy what the authorities will do next. However, it would not be surprising to learn that our causalist rulers are already making calculations of this kind.

7 Drugs, Total Institutions and the Permissive Society

> The 'eathen in 'is blindness bows down to wood and stone
> 'E don't obey no orders unless they is 'is own
> 'E keeps 'is side-arms awful, 'e leaves 'em all about
> An' then comes the regiment and pokes the 'eathen out. . . .
> The 'eathen in 'is blindness must end where 'e began
> But the backbone of the army is the non-commissioned man!
>
> RUDYARD KIPLING—'The 'Eathen'

One organization that claims to have a high success rate with certain types of addict is the Synanon Community in California.[1] Synanon claims that it cures about half the people who come to it and that about 90 per cent of those who stick with Synanon for over three months do stay off drugs permanently.[2] Furthermore its success rate is rising, although it is taking in an increasing proportion of younger, less mature addicts, and at all times it has taken in a larger proportion of those addicts who are totally down and out and who most need help.

The secret of Synanon's success is that it is a total institution with a difference. It is certainly a total institution, but one that differs in certain significant respects from the classic total institutions analysed by Goffman[3] and one that combines aspects of other total institutions in a unique way. For the addicts who go to stay in the Synanon Community it is (at any rate at first) very much a total institution in that they work, sleep, eat and play in the same place (the Synanon house) under a single authority.[4] Their entire life is conducted within the community and governed in each and every way by the rules of the community. One

important aspect of the inmate's life that is strictly controlled is the amount and nature of his contact with the
outside world.[5] The amount of contact with the world the
inmate is permitted depends on his status in the hierarchy
which in turn depends on how successfully he conforms to
the rules of the community. He is forced to abjure the
company of his addict friends outside and in some cases that
of his family. Further, like the "asylums" that Goffman
studied, its main purpose is to process people and to change
them, in this case to turn addicts into law-abiding and
productive non-addicts. Synanon is hierarchical and moralistic, with an elaborate system of rewards and punishments,
rather than egalitarian or permissive. In this sense too it is
very like the classic total institutions. Where it differs
strongly from, say, the jail or the mental hospital is that there
are no supervisory staff and hence no split between staff and
inmates as there is between attendants and patients, or
warders and prisoners or, come to that, teachers and pupils,
officers and men or keepers and monkeys. All the inmates in
Synanon are ex-addicts who have been through exactly the
same mill. This is true from the newest arrival right up to the
head of the organization. Furthermore each "novice" is
expected to aspire to higher positions within the Synanon
organization. There are no restrictions on mobility and good
and productive behaviour is rewarded with promotion.
Prisoners cannot in this simple sense aspire to become
warders, or patients nurses or psychiatrists, or pupils teachers,
nor generally do the other ranks stand much chance of
becoming officers.[6]

Unlike many other total institutions Synanon is an open
institution in three senses:

(*a*) Mobility is possible throughout the hierarchy.
Privilege is the reward of virtue and a cohesive factor,
rather than the attribute of a status division fixed by
outside fiat;

(*b*) Entry into Synanon is voluntary. The members are
not forced to join by outside compulsion. Nor has
Synanon any real sanctions to prevent an inmate walking
out altogether save his own loyalty to and need for the
Synanon community. There are no bars or walls or

security guards, nor contractual ties nor vows to God nor oaths of loyalty;

(c) The aim of the organization is to bring its members back into the world whether they choose to continue living in Synanon or not. Synanon's "graduates" are expected either to return to the wider community and have a full family and occupational life while retaining only friendly ties with Synanon, or to occupy senior posts in the Synanon hierarchy. Those who stay either live there and take responsibility for running its internal affairs or conduct Synanon's own relationship as an organization with the rest of the world.

Perhaps the nearest total institutions to Synanon are the British public schools. They are both processing institutions whose aim is to take a person who is asocial by reason of his youth or his addiction and to mould him into a particular pattern, but a pattern congruent with the demands of the outside society. Until the mid-nineteenth century the British public schools were unstable, rebellious institutions often on the verge of insurrection. During the period 1780—1830 there were disorders in all the main schools and the country was far nearer a student revolution than it has been since. On several occasions uprisings in the schools were only put down when the military were called in. They were characterized (even when not revolting) by a general sullen collective hostility to authority, by disobedience, and combinations against the staff, by indolence and indiscipline. They were ineffective institutions that could neither control the boys nor inculcate in them society's values and attitudes.[7] In many ways their failure of organization and failure to achieve their purpose can be compared with the failure of such institutions as asylums and prisons today.

Despite this unpromising start, by the 1860s the public schools had transformed themselves. They were models of discipline and sobriety, within their small communities law and order prevailed and the school's authority went unchallenged by the pupils. The schools came to produce a standard, recognizable public-school product, properly socialized in the values and attitudes of his school. This disciplined, unemotional stiff-upper-lip product, well trained for both loyalty and leadership, proved invaluable in governing the vast empire that Britain acquired during this period. What then was the secret of this remarkable success story? How did the change occur? There seem to be three main factors involved: (i) the introduction of the prefect system, "the system which hands over the life of a school to an oligarchy of a dozen youths of seventeen"[8] (ii) the high moral tone introduced into many of the schools by headmasters such as Arnold, and (iii) the congruence between the values and beliefs inculcated in the schools and those of the outside world, or at any rate that section of British society from which the pupils were drawn. The introduction of the prefect system broke down the division of the school into masters and pupils. By creating an elaborate open hierarchy among the pupils with the prefects at the apex holding almost total power, the Victorian innovators created a stable and durable social system within the school. In many ways the prefects were more influential than the staff—indeed they were the school's leadership. Since any junior boy could hope in time to be a prefect and to enjoy their rank and privileges, there was no motive for the juniors to combine against the prefects. The schools at the same time developed a strong corporate ethos and strict moral standards.

The way in which Arnold introduced the prefect system and altered the moral tone of his school is well described by Lytton Strachey in his essay on Dr Arnold in *Eminent Victorians*:

He consulted the Old Testament and could doubt no longer. He would apply to his scholars as he explained to them in one of his sermons, the principle which seemed to him to have been adopted in the training of the human race itself. He would treat the boys at Rugby as Jehovah had treated the Chosen People: he would found a theocracy and there should be Judges in Israel. For this purpose the system prevalent in most of the public schools of the day by which the elder boys were deputed to keep order in the class-rooms, lay ready to Dr Arnold's hand. He found the "Praeposter" a mere disciplinary convenience and he converted him into an organ of government. Every boy in the sixth form became *ipso facto* a Praeposter with powers extending over every department of school life and the sixth form as a body was erected into an authority responsible to the headmaster and to the headmaster alone for the internal management of the school.⁹

Charismatic headmasters like Arnold were able to impose such an ethos on their schools partly by force of personality and partly by exploiting the pervasive religious beliefs of mid-Victorian England. (Arnold was of course himself a clergyman.)

The force of Arnold's charisma and the importance of religion in his school are amusingly described by Strachey:

> He himself [Arnold] involved in awful grandeur ruled remotely through his chosen instruments (the prefects) from an inaccessible heaven. Remotely—yet with an omnipotent force. As the Israelite of old knew that his almighty Law-giver might at any moment thunder to him from the whirlwind or appear before his very eyes, the visible embodiment of power or wrath, so the Rugby schoolboy walked in a holy dread of some sudden manifestation of the sweeping gown, the majestic tone, the piercing glance of Dr Arnold . . . the effect which he produced upon the great mass of his pupils was remarkable. The prestige of his presence and the elevation of his sentiments were things which it was impossible to forget. In class every line of his countenance, every shade of his manner imprinted themselves indelibly on the minds of the boys who sat under him . . . To be rebuked however mildly by Dr Arnold was a notable experience. One boy would never forget how he drew a distinction between "mere amusement" and "such as encroached on the next day's duties" nor the tone of voice with which the Doctor added "and then it immediately becomes what St Paul calls revelling". Another remembered to his dying day his reproof of some boys who had behaved badly during prayers. "Nowhere", said Dr Arnold, "nowhere is Satan's work more evidently manifest than in turning holy things to ridicule". On such occasions, as another of his pupils described it, it was impossible to avoid "a consciousness almost amounting to solemnity" that "when his eye was upon you he looked into your inmost heart".¹⁰

In the latter half of the century these reforms were accepted and consolidated. There was a marked rise in the proportion of ordained headmasters. Charisma became routinized and religious intensity gave way to muscular Christianity. Athleticism now became the other moral prop of the public school. All these changes in the public schools were reinforced by parallel changes in the wider society. The debauchery of Regency England gave way to the propriety of Victorian England, the rakish aristocrats lost power to the earnest middle classes with their earnest middle-class Queen and her earnest middle-class consort. Though many intellectuals came to doubt and even to lose their faith later in the century, the moral impact of religion was immense and continued to be so until World War I. An individual immersed in a public school could find no escape from it because the moral values the school forced on him meshed so neatly with those of the wider society, of his family, his peers and his social class. Society reinforced the school—it did not in any way challenge it—and the school reinforced society.

The relationship between Synanon and other similar and disparate total institutions such as asylums and public schools is summed up in the diagram below.

Purpose of the → institution	Institution as an end in it- self	Processing institution	Goal-oriented institution
Closed	Concentration camp P.O.W. camp	Borstals Asylums Jails	Compulsory labour camp Slavery
Inter- mediate	Orphanages Homes for aged or incurable or blind Monasteries	Public schools	Domestic service Army Merchant Navy
Open	Kibbutzim	Synanon	Lumber camp

Here I have categorized total institutions according to (a) the nature of their purpose, (b) whether they are open or closed institutions. I have defined purpose in terms of the *main* avowed aim of the institution concerned. The first category I term "end in itself", i.e. the main aim is to provide a particular kind of life for the inmates either with or without their consent. It may be that the purpose is to lock them away from society, or it may be that they have withdrawn from society to lead a particular kind of life that is qualitatively different from that of the wider society. Either way the aim is isolation from society in a total institution as an end in itself. The second category I have termed "processing institutions" because their main aim is to take individuals from the wider society, process them into a different kind of person and then return them to society. Finally we have goal-oriented institutions whose main purpose lies in some task outside the institution. They are organized that way simply because it appears the most efficient way to get that task done. Labour camps exist to develop Siberia, slaves to pick cotton, armies to kill people and maintain peace, lumber camps to fell trees, etc. There are of course some ambiguities in all this. The army, it may be argued, is not just for killing people and maintaining security—it is also a way of life. Nevertheless the Houses of Parliament do not vote vast sums of money to provide soldiers with a way of life, not even the cavalry. Money is allocated to the armed forces in order that they may defend us from our enemies and kill them. By contrast the kibbutzim are not there to grow oranges or fight Arabs. Although they do both these things, so do all the other Israelis. They were founded primarily to provide a distinctive way of life and they have succeeded only too well. Similarly, monasteries have many practical functions. They may well run schools or hospitals, or brew noxious and addictive alcoholic drinks, but all these things can be done without having a monastery, without creating a total institution, without religious intensity. The monastery is an end in itself and the good works and bad works are simply manifestations of this end.

I have differentiated on this basis between concentration camps and prisoner of war camps on the one hand and labour camps on the other. I have assumed that the main aim of the former is to keep the inmates locked up or even to destroy them. They may be used to perform useful tasks, but this is not the main intention of the men who set them up. Labour camps are more difficult to categorize since clearly the men who set them up—notably in Russia—are as much interested in putting political and other prisoners out of the way as in achieving some practical end. However, I have charitably assumed that the main function of such camps was to provide a slave labour force to perform such difficult tasks as opening up Siberia, mining uranium in Czechoslovakia, building the Moscow underground, etc. Their inmates are thus marginally closer to the negro slaves of America and the West Indies than to the victims of the concentration camps.

Two institutions that do defy these simple categories are jails and orphanages. This is because of the necessary ambiguity in the purposes of such institutions. We are not clear whether we send people to jail to punish them or to reform them. If it is the former then jails are an end in themselves. If it is the latter then they are processing institutions. In practice, jails attempt to do both—hence the ambiguity. Similarly there is a problem with orphanages. These are, first, a dumping-ground for children who, like the aged, the blind or the incurable, need looking after but have no one willing to look after them, and, secondly, processing institutions like the public schools whose aim it is to turn the orphans into good citizens who can be safely let loose in and on society.

The criteria to be used and the questions to be asked to decide whether total institutions are open, closed or intermediate are twofold: (i) Do the inmates enter them voluntarily or are they compelled to do so? Can they leave at will or are they kept there by force? (ii) Is the internal hierarchy an open one which all can aspire to ascend or is there a marked status division which it is difficult or impossible to cross?

In the closed institutions the inmates are placed and kept there against their will. From this basic fact stems the rigidly divided hierarchy that is characteristic of them. The inmates need guards. They can hardly be expected to guard themselves. The old question *"quis custodiet?"* has a specific meaning and unambiguous answer for such institutions. There are of course some apparent exceptions—voluntary mental patients and the Italian prisoners of the last war can be said to have chosen to enter their institution though admittedly under great pressure from others. Open prisons and open asylums lack walls and guards, though of course anyone who tries to leave will be pursued and returned to a more overtly closed institution. Also even in this class of total institution there is some scope for promotion. A convict can become a "trusty" who has privileges and freedoms denied to other prisoners, a negro slave could become an indoor domestic servant and gain status and power over the other slaves by virtue of his personal contact with the master and his family. A surprising number of ex-mental patients return to work as nurses and other staff in mental hospitals after they have been discharged. But all these are minor exceptions. By and large these institutions in the top row are closed institutions both in terms of movement in and out of them and in the nature of their organizational hierarchy.

By contrast the kibbutzim, Synanon and the ordinary lumber camp based on free wage labour are open institutions. The inmates are free to come and go and all positions in the hierarchy are open to everyone. In the "intermediate" category there is, as the name suggests, an intermediate degree of openness. In some cases it is the entry into the institution that is not entirely free, in others the inmates' freedom to leave it is curtailed. In these institutions there are varying degrees of access to the top positions in the hierarchy but in none of them is there the total freedom of mobility of Synanon nor the absolute divide into staff and inmates that characterizes the closed institutions. We can see this more clearly if we take a particular institution such as the army. Entry into the army may be voluntary—as in the present British army which is entirely a volunteer army whose members have joined either from loyalty to their country, or for the money—or compulsory, as in a conscript army. A conscript army in peace-time though is in some aspects a processing institution. The regular soldiers who are volunteers in effect process civilians into something approaching soldiers. After this period of basic training in military skills and military attitudes they are returned to civilian life. The conscripts are normally only in the army for a short, fixed period of time. The regular soldiers join up for a period of years. It is difficult to leave before one's time is up, but, unlike the prisoner, the soldier decides himself how long his "sentence" will be. Also even though it is difficult to leave it is not impossible. If he can raise the money a soldier can buy himself out. Thus the soldier's position is intermediate between that of the lumberjack who can easily quit his job and take another and that of the slave or camp inmate who cannot alter his status at all. Between the soldier and the lumberjack comes the merchant seaman. He is bound to his ship and can be punished by law if he deserts it but he is free to sign off at the end of a voyage and need never go to sea again. Unlike the soldiers, the seamen can organize themselves in a trades union and (as we have seen to our cost) take strike action if they choose.

The army hierarchy is not a continuous open one. There is a sharp break between the officers and the NCOs which it is difficult to cross. A private can reasonably aspire to become a corporal or a sergeant, but he is unlikely to cross the sharp divide to lieutenant. Nevertheless some privates do rise to become first NCOs and then officers. The army is not a closed hierarchy. Below and above the officer/NCO divide there is free promotion, and some promotion does occur across this divide.

The monasteries likewise are intermediate institutions. Entry into a monastery or convent is nowadays generally a matter of free choice and monks and nuns who wish to leave are not physically prevented from doing so. Nevertheless they are bound to the institution by their vows. These are lifetime vows which it is difficult to renounce and bind the man or woman who takes them much more strongly than any ordinary contractual obligation, even though they are not legally enforceable and no coercion is involved. The monastic hierarchy is freely open to all and each and every novice can dream of becoming the abbot. Novices are at the bottom of the hierarchy and have in a sense to prove themselves—to demonstrate that they have a "vocation". Nevertheless in most particulars the rules to which they are subject apply equally to those higher up the scale. Each novice can expect to become a professed monk and the most worthy among them can aspire to even higher positions in the hierarchy. The hierarchy is, however, not entirely an open one for some monastic orders are decisively divided into the choir monks and the lay brothers. It is from the former group that the key posts in the monastery are filled. The later group rank below them and are restricted to the more menial tasks of the monastery. The monastery, rather like the army, recruits at two separate levels and there is little subsequent movement between the two. However, in these days of egalitarian democracy monasteries and convents are finding it increasingly difficult both to recruit lay brothers and lay sisters and to keep the existing ones in their traditionally "lower place".

The public schools are on the whole open institutions rather like Synanon but with certain important restrictions. The pupils at these schools can aspire to become prefects, but cannot directly aspire to become masters or the headmaster. The masters are often old boys of the school but there is a gap between their leaving the school as boys to enter college and their return to the school as masters. The public schoolboy or girl can in theory enter and leave the institution freely, but in practice it is difficult to do so unless he or she has sympathetic parents. An orphan having no parents is even more dependent on the institution in which he lives and even less free to move. Orphans, the blind, the aged, the incurably ill, the sanatorium patient all enter institutions because they have to. They cannot leave—they have nowhere else to go since they are incapable of looking after themselves. They are not compelled to stay in the manner of a prisoner, but their freedom to come and go is a very limited one. Their ability to play a large part in the running of the institution where they live is similarly restricted by the handicap that forced them to reside there in the first place.

Domestic servants provide a final example of the intermediate categories. Those who "live in" the household of the family they serve are part of a total institution, albeit a small and personal one. They are free to enter and leave service as they choose, though there will be strong informal pressures on a domestic servant to stick with the family. The domestic servant operates within a very limited part of the household hierarchy. A maid can aspire to become a housekeeper, a footman can become a butler but they are separated from the members of the family that employs them by a status gap that cannot be bridged. The master or the sons of the household may occasionally sleep with the servants but in the better class of family they do not marry them. There always remains the division between the family and the servants, a division which is, however, softened by the large amount of personal contact between members of the two groups.

As a result of the diverse purposes and degree of openness of the total institutions they differ very widely in the nature of their communal life. One obvious way in which they differ is in the degree to which sub-cultures occur within the institution over which the hierarchy has no control and the degree to which these express opposition to the official purposes and organization of the institution. In the asylums described by Goffman and in other "closed" total institutions there is a flourishing underlife of this kind[11] but in Synanon it is not permitted to exist. In the intermediate institutions there is more of an underlife than in Synanon but less than in an asylum or a jail. In an army or a monastery or a public school there is ambivalence and hostility to the hierarchy, but this is normally less important than loyalty and voluntary conformity. Prisoners see the warders as out there, as part of a separate world with which they have few ties and little loyalty. The Synanon member is totally committed to his institution. The attitude of the private soldier to his officers and to the NCOs is a mixture of the two. Perhaps for this reason we have in the sergeant or the sergeant-major a butt for endless jokes and humour. These are not directed at the prison-camp guard for whom the inmates can feel simple unambiguous hostility or the Synanon hierarchy who demand and receive total loyalty.[12] The sergeant, like the foreman or the mother-in-law, is mocked because only in this way can hostility to them be safely expressed. It is not just the threat of reprisal that prevents direct hostility, but also the joker's own loyalty to and respect for the persons he is mocking. These figures are also ambiguous in another sense—no one is quite sure to what group they belong. Is an NCO an officer—he gives and transmits orders, he is called a non-commissioned *officer,* he has status and power over and above that of the men—or is he one of the men—he is promoted from the ranks, he is unlikely to gain a commission, he has more in common with the men in life style and social background than with the officers? Is a foreman one of the management or a worker? Is a mother-in-law part of the family or is she just a relative?[13] As a result of this dual ambiguity all these essential and valuable people who are vital to the proper functioning of the army or the factory or the traditional working-class family are made figures of fun.

We can widen our comparison between these different types of total institutions by asking the fundamental question "What is the nature of compliance in these institutions?", i.e. why do people do what the hierarchy tells them? The American sociologist Etzioni has described three basic types of compliance, normative, remunerative and coercive,[14] i.e. people do what they are told either because they feel they ought to do so (normative), or because they are paid to do so and need the money (remunerative), or because they are forced to do so (coercive). If we apply his types to the various total institutions we get the pattern shown below.

In the first row there are those same institutions categorized earlier as closed. Since the inmates are forced to go there and are held there by force the nature of compliance is clearly coercive. There is no simple correspondence between remunerative compliance and intermediate institutions or

Type of compliance	Institution as an end in it self	Processing institution	Goal-oriented institutions
Coercive	Concentration camp Jail P.O.W. Camp	Borstals Asylums	Slavery Labour camp
Remunerative	Homes for blind, aged, Orphanage incurable		Lumber camp Domestic service Merchant Navy ─Army ───
Normative	Monastery Kibbutz	Public schools Synanon	

normative compliance and open institutions though these categories do correlate to some extent. Those who work in the goal-oriented institutions do so because they are paid to, but the degree to which remunerative and normative compliance predominates differs between different institutions.

For the institutions that exist as an end in themselves or as processing institutions there are differences between those institutions whose members are there because they are indigent and have no choice—the blind, the old, the orphaned, etc.—and those whose members have freely chosen to enter them. Where Synanon is exceptional is that the addicts who go there are initially as helpless as those in the remunerative categories and like them have nowhere else to go, yet the form of compliance is normative. It is difficult to formulate a decisive test of whether normative compliance is the key form in a particular institution, but one test could be the existence of an "old boys" organization or of some link between the institution and ex-members now living outside. By this test the public schools with their old boy network and their old boys' clubs, the army with the British Legion, and regimental associations and other veterans' groups clearly exhibit normative compliance. They have called forth a loyalty from their inmates that persists after they leave. Men are proud to wear a regimental tie or an old school tie. They do not wear a tie to show they have been at Wormwood Scrubs or Broadmoor or Colney Hatch or even a lumber camp or a home for the blind or their local workhouse. Ex-kibbutzniks, Synanon members and even ex-monks also keep in touch with their old organization unless they were forced to leave it in disgrace.

All this, of course, has major implications for the stability of the organization. Those depending on coercion are always faced with potential conflict between the two sides within them—the coerced and the coercers. The "normative" institutions are more stable and not liable to conflict between the different strata in the hierarchy in this way. However, conflict could break out if there was a vertical split—a split at the top of the hierarchy among the leaders over the issue of how the institution should be run. Monasteries, armies and perhaps even Synanon in the long run are liable to potential schisms of this kind. The institutions whose inmates are there because they are helpless and dependent on charity are stable because the inmates are for this reason apathetic. Goal-oriented institutions employing and paying men to carry out tasks may be conflict-ridden or free of conflict depending on the nature of the work and the degree of personal contact between employer and employee. Lumber camps are characteristically strife-ridden while domestic servants are noted for their loyalty to their employers.

Now that we have seen something of the similarities and differences between Synanon and other total institutions and discovered what its distinctive features are, it is perhaps as well to look at its functioning in detail. In this way we can try to see exactly what is meant by terms such as "total institution", "hierarchy", "authority" and "mobility" in the context of Synanon's day-to-day working.

Synanon is a total institution yet it is also an open institution. It is total both in the objective sense defined above and also in the subjective perceptions of those who live there—for them it is their whole world. Daniel Casriel quotes one of their members as saying:

> You begin to realize that everything here at Synanon is important. On the contrary nothing is important on the outside since you can't do anything about it anyway. Synanon is a tribe-like organization and the tribal rites of Synanon take on all-important meanings.[15]

For the addicts who go there it is necessary that they cut themselves off in this way. Many of them have few ties with the wider society and are in a desperate and totally alienated state when they come to Synanon. This makes it easier to organize them into the "paternalistic tribe-like family" that is Synanon.[16] They accept their new autocracy because it is all they have. Yet at the same time Synanon is an open institution. Its members join it voluntarily and are free to leave at any time. This openness is an important part of Synanon's treatment of the addicts. The addict is taught to live without drugs and without alternative or additional forms of anti-social behaviour in an open environment. He learns these things not behind bars and merely because of the compulsion captivity imposes on him but in a house where he is ultimately free to come and go.

Synanon is a total, open and autocratic institution. It is not a democracy but a corporation where the rules are fixed and the important decisions are taken at the top. Furthermore, there is no toleration of opposition within Synanon. Potentially hostile cliques are attacked and broken down by the members to prevent such opposition forming. There is no underlife to the institution, no alternative focus of loyalty for the member—these are stifled at birth. The code of the streets that the addict should never co-operate with or inform to the authorities is ruthlessly attacked and eliminated at an early stage in his career at Synanon. It is constantly emphasized that his only loyalty must be to Synanon and to its rules. Each member has the responsibility of spotting and attacking such bad behaviour in others at an early stage. This provides a totally effective policing system and also constantly reinforces the solidarity of the group. The periodic common detection and punishment of any deviant individual holds the whole group together and boosts its morale and its confidence in the common norms.

When it began, Synanon had a charismatic leader, Chuck Dederich, whose word was law. He made policy for Synanon without reference to precedent, tradition or law, simply on the basis of his "immediate inner urges and personal conclusions".[17] Something of his style and of his total authority is conveyed in a harangue by him to a recalcitrant novice quoted by Lewis Yablonsky:

> You'll join us 100 per cent, you know, with everything you've got . . . . Don't waste your time trying to fight the authority. You will not win. I guarantee it. I know the kind of guy you are because I was one once myself. You will want to fight all the authority symbols in here. There is only one top authority symbol and that's me. You're not going to whip me. I guarantee that. Tougher guys than you have tried.[18]

Later as Synanon grew larger and older there was, as in the English public schools, a routinization of charisma and a shift to bureaucratic authority. Nevertheless Synanon remained a hierarchical body, not an egalitarian one. But all the ex-addicts and would-be ex-addicts are part of the hierarchy—no one is outside it, there are no staff and no inmates. Everyone has had the same life in the past, the same experiences, the same problems. They are all in it together. There is a definite status hierarchy but no single divisive status gap. Because of this a member of Synanon has no qualms about mounting a moral attack on another member guilty of some deviant act. Yablonsky describes the advantage he has over an outside therapist dealing with addicts or criminals,[19] "The resocialised honest ex-criminal is the best man to resocialize other criminals. Reid has paid the dues of having 'been there' himself. He feels fully entitled to view negatively criminal addict behaviour. Professionals and others who 'work with' the criminal in some respects have less of a right to attack the behaviour in the same way . . . . . . Many professional therapists admonish each other to be non-judgemental and withhold value judgements on deviant behaviour. The Synanist on the other hand feels entitled to express a complete emotional and ethical response.

"The objects of a Synanon attack accept the right to attack them because it comes from one of their own—hence they are more receptive. They would probably not sit through the same kind of attack if it were to take place in a professional establishment and was administered by professionals."

Synanon members have all had similar experiences as addicts. A fellow Synanist is thus acceptable as therapist and authority and is all the more so because the roles of patient and therapist are interchangeable. All are therapists and all are patients and the recovery and emotional growth of any one person is of concern to all the others.[20] Each member can help each other member by self-revelation, a possibility not open to the ordinary professional therapist who has never been an addict. At the same time the members are not equal. New junior members are expected to model themselves on the senior Synanists and not vice versa. Synanon socializes the new member by "role emulation" in this way, much in the same manner as children are turned into adults.[21]

Because of the power the community has over its
members, it is able to destroy the values and attitudes the
addicts had before they joined the community and replace
them with Synanon's own values. This brainwashing process
is explicitly recognized as such and approved by the
leadership. Dederich is quoted by Yablonsky as saying of
brainwashing: "Great stuff. When you clean a brain you wash
it. If you have a dirty brain you wash it and make it clean".[22]
The aim of this process is to "indoctrinate" each member
with clear moral standards, with clear fixed boundaries as to
what is and what is not tolerated by the community and thus
by the member himself. Everything about the addict is
changed, his values, his behaviour, his concept of himself,
even the language he uses. At Synanon language is seen as the
vehicle of culture and behaviour. In order to destroy the
addict sub-culture and alter the addict's behaviour patterns
he must be forced to give up the jargon, the slang, the very
language of the criminal and the addict. He must be given a
new vocabulary and a new set of social and emotional
responses to words and the old ones must be eliminated.
Yablonsky notes that initially the addict is taught the
vocabulary of the social sciences as a bridge back to normal
language. He quotes Dederich as saying to his graduate class
in social welfare at the University of California:

> The next big thing you do is to attack the language. Eliminating their
> criminal language is very important. We get them off drugs by telling
> them, "Live here without drugs and you can have all this". We get them
> off negative language by initially giving them another. Since there is
> some vague connection between their personality problem and the
> social sciences, we encourage them to use this language. The language of
> psychology and sociology is great stuff. Whether or not the recovering
> addict knows what he is talking about is exquisitely unimportant at this
> time. Very quickly, in a matter of about ninety days, they turn into
> junior psychiatrists and sociologists. They become familiar with the use
> of a dozen or twenty words and misuse them. Who cares! It doesn't
> make any difference. Now they are talking about "hidden super-ego",
> "transference", "displacement", "primary and secondary groups". This
> is all coming out, and they are not saying "fix, fix, fix" all the time. "I
> used twenty a day". "I used thirty a day". "Joe went to jail". "I went
> to jail behind this broad". "Where did you do time?" and all that. They

get off that and they talk about ids, superegos and group structure. They make another set of noises. Eventually when they learn the meanings of these words they stop using them.[23]

(This is curiously similar to the role of sociology in the rest of society as seen by some of its practitioners. Sociologists are potentially deviant persons who talk elaborate nonsense in an involved jargon. It doesn't mean anything and they don't understand each other, but it enables them to avoid overt criminal or other deviant behaviour. Some of them in time learn the meanings of the jargon they use, stop using it and return to normal society cured of their anti-social tendencies. This kind of sociology is not a science nor even a form of learning. It is simply a form of harmless therapy for middle-class deviants.)

Having eliminated the bad old values, Synanon inculcates into the addict its own values—these are the values of the wider society, only more so. Thus the wider society's values of honesty and sobriety are enforced in Synanon even more emphatically. Complete, total and absolute honesty is demanded. Even the kinds of minor pilfering and fiddling that the outside world winks at are utterly denounced and destroyed. Sobriety similarly is emphasized—not merely are addictive drugs banned but even less-addicting drugs including alcohol that are widely tolerated in the society outside. Thus Synanon makes demands on its ex-addicts that are greater than those society makes on its ordinary members. They are expected to behave *even better* than the man in the street. There is also inculcated into them an ethic of work and self-help. In Synanon everyone works and all jobs are essential. There are the domestic chores of the house to be done and Synanon's business with the outside world to be transacted. Synanon runs warehouses, garages and factories and takes on industrial contracts at competitive prices. Synanon is not run like a traditional charity and there is no need for simulated artificial duties—making pots, basket-weaving therapy and other such nonsense. Everyone works for the simple reason that Synanon has to keep running and keep paying for itself. The survival of the community depends on the efforts of its members. Self-help and the value of work are not abstract concepts to be learned, but basic necessities of life.

What are the techniques Synanon uses to achieve this transformation of its members? We can conveniently divide consideration of these into psychological and sociological aspects, looking in turn at the mode of interaction between individual members and then at the social structure of Synanon itself and the way this facilitates these modes of interaction. Many of Synanon's leaders consciously guide the institution along lines suggested by social scientists with whose work they are familiar and copy socialization processes used in the wider society and described by psychologists or sociologists. The addict who has newly arrived at Synanon is regarded by those already there as a child who has to be turned into an adult. For a model of how to do this they turn to the social scientists' description of how this is done most effectively in the everyday world.

When the addict arrives at Synanon he is given a brief period of unconditional love and affection by the senior members while he escapes from his physiological need for heroin. The model for this is the mother's unconditional affection for a small helpless baby who cannot be held responsible for its actions. During the initial and unpleasant period when he is coming off the drug, he is given full emotional support in this way and is not saddled with responsibilities. Later their affection becomes conditional on good behaviour. If he behaves badly the regard and affection of all the people around him is abruptly withdrawn. Since he is by now very dependent on the feelings of the community towards him, this has a decisive influence on his behaviour. For many addicts this is the first time in their lives that they have been confronted with such firm, consistent and universal reactions to their behaviour. Good behaviour is rewarded and reinforced. Bad behaviour is met with emotional withdrawal or even hostility. And there is no escape from these total and universal reactions. He cannot take refuge in the sympathies of other newcomers for there is often a ban on newcomers even talking to each other and no resistance on their part to the moral demands of the community would be tolerated.

These general and diffuse communal pressures are re-inforced by the unique forms of group therapy that Synanon has pioneered, notably the "Synanon" itself from which the organization takes its name.[24] This is a "leaderless group encounter for the creation of aggressive and provocative interchange".[25] Such encounters involve seven or eight members at a time and are held about three times a week for an hour and a half on each occasion. Each member of the group is a therapist, each therapist a member of the group—there are no divisions. Such a session can be called at any time by any two members if there is some problem or argument they have been unable to settle privately. The members of the group subject one another to ridicule, cross-examination and hostile attack and there are no restrictions on what they can say to one another. It is a destructive and cathartic experience in which anti-social tendencies on the part of any member are described and attacked. No excuses, no defences, no rationalizations are permitted. The erring person is harassed and provoked to admit his faults. His only counter-weapon is to attack and denounce the same faults if and when he can detect them in his accusers. It is a traumatic experience but a positive one—one which leads to modifications in behaviour and attitudes. It is the complete opposite of non-directive therapy. It deliberately focuses an attack on particular aspects of an individual's character and behaviour and attempts to destroy and alter them. The individual is verbally knocked down but then carefully set up again by the more senior members of the group who try to end all such sessions on a constructive note.

Yablonsky quotes a psychologist as saying that such attacks intuitively use the basic principles of conditioning theory to achieve their effects,[26] viz. (i) constant repetition; (ii) "analogy", i.e. repeating the same things in different ways to avoid monotony; (iii) a "relay system" with several people taking up the argument in relays, each imposing on it his own personality and technique. This gives an opportunity for the group to use the method known expressively to the British police as "hard and soft", i.e. a rapid alternation between a hostile attack by one person and a sympathetic appeal by another. Great emphasis is placed by Synanon on altering men's behaviour rather than their feelings or internal states. Instead of attempting to alter the patient's internal problems in the hope that he will stop acting out these problems in anti-social behaviour, Synanon attacks the behaviour first. Good behaviour is enforced now, and in time the acquisition of good habits alters the addict's internal feelings and mental processes. Long before the addicts have fully abandoned the impulses and feelings that characterize an addict they are expected to behave as if they had totally ceased to be addicts. Behaviour is controlled and directed, and feelings and personality follow later. The approach of the Synanon authorities is thus much more like that of the behaviour therapists than that of the psychoanalysts which concentrates on the understanding of the unconscious rather than directly altering overt behaviour.

This emphasis on behaviour rather than feelings, thoughts or even words is carried over even into the way in which the community hierarchy exerts (and chooses not to exert) its authority over the individual member. Casriel quotes Dederich the Synanon leader as saying:

> Permissiveness in the area of verbal resistance or rebellion to authority is encouraged rather than discouraged. The insistence is on performance. For example, if it is suggested that one of the boys or girls help in the kitchen he is free to gripe or beef as loudly as he wishes but it is required that he comply in the area of action.[27]

The theory behind this is that verbal rebellion towards authority means nothing and relieves inner tension whilst compliance in behaviour creates habits of obedience to authority.

All these techniques are used in the context of an institution strongly geared to the efficient provision of rewards and penalties for its members. We have already laid great stress on the open nature of the Synanon hierarchy. It is now time to look in detail at what this entails. There are essentially two sources of status in Synanon. The first is the length of time an inmate has been off drugs. He gets no kudos for giving up his drugs in the first place—this is deliberately treated in a very matter of fact manner—but he does gain approval and status for staying off drugs continuously for a long period of time. The length of time an inmate has stayed off drugs is celebrated in a series of birthday parties when he has been off them for one year, two years, three years, etc. These are very emotional celebrations (cf. Alcoholics Anonymous) in which all the community participates. Simply accumulating a series of "birthdays" gives an inmate status by seniority. This is clearly open to all who succeed in abandoning addiction however inept they may be in other ways. The second source of status is the position a man holds in the organizational hierarchy. This is an open hierarchy in which anyone can rise as far as his ability will permit. It is a "realistic step-by-step achievable status system that is socially approved and similar to status-oriented goals in the outside world".[28] The stages in the hierarchy are as shown below.[29]

STAGE I
Lives and works in the main Synanon building. Does domestic work or routine office work. Under close surveillance and closely regulated in his degree of contact with the world outside.

↓

STAGE II
(Normally attained after 6 months to 2 years)

   Lives in Synanon but works outside or promoted to supervisory level and becomes an internal administrative "coordinator". Has more freedom to mix with the community outside.

↓

STAGE III
(Attained after 18 months to 2½ years)

   Works and lives outside or promoted to the higher managerial level within the organization ("assistant to the directors"). They may live outside and work within Synanon. Free to come and to go when they please but maintain strong links with Synanon.

↓

STAGE IV
Directors of Synanon.

The Synanon member who obeys the organization's rules and works hard and effectively can ascend this hierarchy stage by stage and gains in power, status and freedom accordingly. But any serious infringement of the rules is met with instant demotion. Casriel quotes the case of one stage II member who broke an important rule and was forced to quit his job and revert to stage I. This was deliberately done in an autocratic and humiliating way. He was told to

take somebody with you to your boss who will explain to him that you're in a serious situation that could lead to your going back to using drugs again and that you're going to pull out of the work situation for a while to come back to the club.[30]

Tremendous emphasis is placed in Synanon on techniques of humiliation and degradation. A member who breaks one of the more important rules of the house is verbally "taken apart" by several of the more senior members acting in concert. His entire career since he came to Synanon is critically reviewed, often with considerable verbal brutality. This is an unpleasant experience for the victim, but the members seem to accept it as a valid procedure and it does result in rapid improvements in the behaviour and attitudes of the person subjected to it, and also in those of the other members. Casriel quotes one member as saying "When the word gets around that haircuts are being given people seem to get in line."[31] As well as verbal "haircuts" an erring member may receive a real physical haircut. As a punishment for bad behaviour a member may be given the choice of leaving or having all the hair shaved off his head. If he accepts this humiliating punishment, this of course intensifies his involvement with the community that has imposed it.[32] Community solidarity is reinforced by the public ritual at which the offender loses his hair. The offender remains bald or in a state of near baldness for some weeks afterwards and this is a reminder to him and to others of his offence, of the community's collective reaction to it and of the nature and importance of the rule that was broken. In Phoenix House, a British institution for addicts similar in some ways to Synanon, an even greater emphasis seems to have been placed on such techniques of humiliation.[33] An offender against the rules of the house may be subjected to a haircut, may be forced to wear a stocking on her head, or a placard on his or her back giving details of the offence or of the offender's moral weakness or may be forced to sit on a child's stool as a public penance. The rules are upheld and reinforced by making a public spectacle of the offender, by a public humiliation that emphasizes the supremacy of the community and its codes.

The ultimate in public humiliation in Synanon is the so-called "fireplace ritual" which is applied to those who have broken one of Synanon's two fundamental prohibitions—(i) No drugs or alcohol to be consumed, (ii) No physical violence. It is also applied to anyone who has seen others break these rules but has not reported the matter. The transgressor is placed at the fireplace in the main room of the house before all the other members. He is then attacked verbally by the others, ridiculed and abused, forced to confess his heinous offence in detail and to accept the blame for it of the whole community. The community then collectively decides either to expel the malefactor or to give him one last chance and keep him with them.

"Keeping him with them" is in part the secret of the success of the Synanon rituals. A member who has been attacked and taken apart by the others is carefully put together again at the end. He is cast down but also raised up. He is isolated and expelled, but also brought back and accepted. He is humiliated and condemned but also restored and allowed to atone. The rituals do not result in a frightened, isolated and depressed member who might leave or commit suicide. He is carefully reintegrated into the group by the guidance of the senior members and made to feel wanted and cared for. He is made to feel wicked and foolish but also made to understand that it is in his power to become wise and good. The degradation is not permanent. It is not expulsion from the ranks of the community or even from the ranks of the virtuous but an opportunity to reform and reaffirm one's membership.

I have chosen to describe Synanon at length for three reasons. First it is the very antithesis of the permissive society. It is curious that such an institution should exist at all. It is even more curious that it should have grown up during the 1950s and 1960s, the years when the wider society grew rapidly more permissive. Yet in many ways the two things are closely connected. Synanon fulfils a need of the permissive society. It caters for those people who are unable to survive in such a society and who succumb to temptations such as heroin addiction. It gives them a genuine "alternative society" in which there are clear goals and moral rules from which they must not deviate. Secondly Synanon is an institution with a wider future. In America it is spreading to other casualties of the permissive society—petty criminals and dropouts as well as addicts. For people of this kind it may well offer opportunities for reform and self-respect that neither prison nor psychiatrist can provide. But one must emphasize that it only works for certain kinds of people with certain kinds of problems. It works for the down and out rather than those who are merely slipping. It works for the man or woman whose problems stem from an inadequate personality and not for those who suffer from neurotic disorders of a different kind. It is those plagued by too little guilt rather than too much for whom Synanon is effective. To apply Synanon techniques to the wrong people would not just be ineffective, it would be cruel. Thirdly, although Synanon is an American institution it has implications for Britain. I have chosen to describe Synanon in detail rather than its British imitators simply because it has been going longer and has been studied in depth by such distinguished American observers as Casriel, Endore and Yablonsky. In time our own distinctively British institutions will be studied by British sociologists in the same way. Until studies are available of the quality of the American ones we must look to the effect of Synanon on permissive America for the cure for permissive England.

Not surprisingly Synanon is a very unpopular institution in many quarters in America. There are after all many groups who have a financial or moral stake in the existence of heroin addiction—and I don't simply mean the pushers. First there are all those who make a living by treating or studying addicts—therapists, psycho-analysts, probation officers, social workers etc. A self-help organization like Synanon threatens their vested interests in the addict-curing industry. Synanon uses techniques which they regard as invalid or even wicked and the techniques work whereas their own methods fail miserably. One psychologist who visited Synanon described their attack therapy as "the most destructive approach to human behaviour I have ever witnessed".[34] It must have been very embarrasssing for him to see it succeed. Secondly, there are those who like to think of the addict as unredeemable and incurable since it boosts their sense of their own goodness. It is comforting to listen to the howls of the damned and upsetting to see the damned entering the company of the elect. When Synanon has set up a house in a new area it has often had to face incredible opposition from the local residents. Because they believe addicts are incurably ill and incurably wicked they see the establishment of a Synanon house in their area as leading inevitably to the spread of crime, addiction and moral degeneracy throughout the neighbourhood. They are almost equally upset when this doesn't happen and the former addicts turn out to be model citizens. Thirdly, there are the trendy, radical social scientists who are half in sympathy with the values and attitudes of the addicts and criminals they study and who find them a useful stick to beat society with. Many of those who work in the field of what they call the sociology of deviance are fascinated by, and get vicarious satisfaction from, the anti-social behaviour of the people they study. They would like to have been criminals themselves but came from the wrong sort of background and lacked the opportunities to acquire the skills and habits necessary for success in this field. They would like to be wicked but haven't got the guts for it so instead they study or treat those whom society has singled out as being wicked. They would like to be addicts but fear the consequences so they experiment with soft drugs and live on the fringes of the addict culture. Synanon's clear moral stand against all drugs including alcohol, abhorrence of criminal behaviour and intolerance of hip talk is anathema to the trendies. Also many of the trendies see drug addiction either as something the law and society should permit or as a symptom of something deeper that is wrong with society.

The problems of the addict can be used both as a causalist argument for amending the law and society's attitudes (thereby easing his problems) and as a reason for altering aspects of society that they dislike, which they can allege are the "real" cause of addiction. The motives and arguments of such people are revealed in the comments one American sociologist and editor made on an early version of Yablonsky's manuscript:

> But everyone does in any society known to man have to escape occasionally and if the drugs are useful in this regard and otherwise not harmful—why not? Why should the non-addict forgo use of non-addicting drugs? In claiming that they should, Synanon goes beyond the point it needs to make *vis-à-vis* the proper therapy for addicts. In this respect Synanon seems too square, needlessly moralistic, indeed puritanical . . . . Nor is it possible to defend the notion that the use of addicting drugs necessarily transforms even the healthy personality so that it becomes "character disordered". Again this is a matter of social circumstance. It is too bad for Synanon's thesis—but unfortunately true—that when addicts have easy access to the drugs they need (as is the case in the US with many upper class people and many people in the medical profession) they usually do not manifest so-called "character disorder" traits, are not the little punk failures that Synanon would like to believe all addicts are. Where the laws are tolerant as in England, the large majority of addicts get along quite well in their jobs, in raising families and otherwise being respectable members of the community, etc . . . . perhaps the weakest part of Synanon's anti-criminal stance is the refusal to see any difference between law and justice, i.e. its easy assumption that because the individual conflicts with the law of his society regarding drugs it's the individual who needs changing, not the law that should be changed.[35]

All the standard conventional arguments of the American sociologist are raised here and they are all wrong. The sentence "but everyone does in any society known to man have to escape occasionally" admits of two meanings, a weak one and a strong one in connection with drugs. The weak meaning is that we need to escape by some method or other. This may be true, but it is a trivial statement. There are open to Synanon members all manner of forms of escape excluding only drugs. The strong meaning is that drugs are "useful in this regard" and by implication necessary. This version is false. The continued existence and success of Synanon demonstrates it to be so. The question "Why not?" can equally well be asked about abstinence. What is wrong with *refraining* from using drugs such as heroin or even "non-addicting" drugs such as alcohol?

The argument about the English addicts has already been refuted in an earlier chapter. One can also have doubts regarding the stability of upper-class addicts in America. Such people do not allow themselves to be studied very easily, but impressionistic evidence such as the dramatist O'Neill's portrait of his mother in *Long Day's Journey into Night* indicates that they have severe problems.

Finally the argument about law and justice reveals the writer's desire to use the addict as part of an attack on society. If Synanon cures the addicts this removes a source of conflict, a source of moral indignation, a rallying point for the libertarian moralist. Moral indignation at the faults of society is a very satisfying emotion—it is pleasant to feel virtuously superior to society, disinterestedly to inflict blame on the establishment and ordinary decent people alike. To see addicts being transmogrified into identikit versions of the ordinary decent people you hate and despise is a moral outrage. What is particularly upsetting for the trendies is that Synanon's "square", "moralistic", "puritanical", "anti-addict", "anti-criminal" stance is an essential part of its success. Whatever we feel about Synanon from a moralist standpoint, it is certainly justified in causalist terms. It works. Whether one sees Synanon as upholding moral standards or as an attack on human dignity and freedom, it works. Those who enter it suffer less pain and create less social problems than if they had been left to rot. Synanon is a moralist institution that can be justified in terms of the causalist arguments of the age.

8 Conclusions

The ultimate result of shielding men from the effects of folly is to fill the world with fools.

HERBERT SPENCER, *Prison Ethics*

At this stage of the book the reader is perhaps entitled to demand whether or not I am in favour of the changes I have described in the individual chapters of this book. Am I in favour of increased permissiveness? Do I think that the shift from moralism to causalism is a good thing? I find these questions very difficult to answer. On any one issue I find myself inclined to take a permissive line. I find I am in favour of most of the individual changes that have taken place. Whether we analyse them in terms of the shift from moralism to causalism or in terms of increasing permissiveness I think that the new more permissive laws on divorce, abortion, and homosexuality are an improvement on the old. If capital punishment has no deterrent effect, I can see no point in hanging murderers. "Permissiveness with affection" is a better attitude to pre-marital sex than the old insistence on chastity. Nor am I perturbed at the further moves in the direction of permissiveness that are likely to take place in the next few years. Abortion on demand, the legalization of cannabis, the final withering away of the censor—none of these changes evokes any fear or hostility in me. Yet nevertheless, I am profoundly uneasy at the package deal that has been termed "the permissive society". I am in favour of allowing abortion, abolishing hanging, tolerating homosexuals, but I do not wish to live in the kind of society that is willing to allow changes of this kind. I accept the social and legal manifestations of the permissive society but I reject the general ethos of the society. I feel that the permissive society has done the right things, but for the wrong reasons. We have gained in tolerance, in compassion and in freedom, but not because of our belief in these values. We are tolerant not as a matter of principle but as an expression of moral indifference. We refrain from punishing others not because we are merciful but because we no longer make strong moral demands on the individual. We do not forgive neglect of duty, rather we have ceased to believe in the concept of duty and so there is nothing to forgive. We are freer but we no longer know how we should use this freedom. It may be that these gains in tolerance, freedom and compassion (which are very real benefits) are more secure in a permissive society because no one will ever feel strongly enough about any issue to wish to reverse them. Even so I feel that we may have paid too great a price for this security. We now live in a society which makes few moral demands on the individual, yet these same individuals feel entitled to make moral demands on society.[1] There is a good side to this, best seen in the welfare state, which is the institutional expression of the individual's moral claims on society. But the "morality of welfare" is only one part of a nation's morality—the other part, what might be termed the "morality of excellence", is now lacking.[2] The morality of welfare is securely established in the permissive society and it is unlikely that it will be severely challenged. The morality of excellence by contrast is severely undermined. We know what are the individual's rights in society but we do not know what his duties are. We know what each individual is entitled to, simply by virtue of membership of the society but we do not know how to reward virtue or excellence—indeed it is doubtful if we can any longer say which activities or persons are meritorious in this sense. If, as the Whiteleys argue, "The best indication of the moral standards of a community is the way that community distributes punishment and reward, praise and censure"[3] then we are gradually ceasing to have any moral standards. Does this matter, it may be asked. Perhaps after all people are happier without moral standards. There are fewer individuals subject to punishment, blame or censure and all are freer to follow their own personal inclinations. There is some truth in this argument but there are also important drawbacks to a totally permissive society. For the individual the problems of striving to live up to a moral code and the fear of censure or punishment for failure are replaced by the anxieties of uncertainty and disillusionment. Life has ceased to be as difficult as it used to be but it has become pointless. Again this is not a new phenomenon. In Allen's book about the 1920s *Only Yesterday* (quoted in Chapter 1) he notes that

The new code had been born in disillusionment and beneath all the bravado of its exponents and the talk about entering upon a new era the disillusionment persisted. . . . the decade . . . was . . . unhappy. With the old order of things had gone a set of values which had given richness and meaning to life and substitute values were not easily found. If morality was dethroned what was to take its place? Honour, said some of the prophets of the new day: "It doesn't matter much what you do so long as you're honest about it". A brave ideal—yet it did not wholly satisfy; it was too vague, too austere, too difficult to apply . . . there were millions to whom in some degree came for a time the same unhappiness. They could not endure a life without values and the only values they had been trained to understand were being undermined. Everything seemed meaningless and unimportant.[4]

The Americans of the 1920s never did resolve their moral crisis. In the years that followed their society was hit in turn by a slump and a war. They then had something to live for, if it was only to battle with adversity. Such a cure is worse than the disease and not one ever to be wished on even the most lax of permissive societies. So we are left with the sad situation where people are unhappy precisely because the only goal left to them is happiness (even if this takes the unselfish form of a desire for other people's happiness in addition to one's own). Hedonism has its anxieties as well as duty, particularly if, as today, it takes the form of a demand for happiness now and happiness unlimited, which is a far cry from the more subtle hedonism of the Epicureans or the later utilitarians. The desire for happiness now, coupled with an unwillingness to defer pleasure until later, means that the range of pleasures available to the individual is even more limited than in the most puritanical of societies. The puritan is deficient because he is forbidden to enjoy certain simple and immediate pleasures. Yet in many ways the things he was forbidden are trivial and unimportant. Did it matter that much for the Welsh nonconformist that he never drank or gambled, that his Sundays were restricted and his life was often ruled by caution rather than spontaneity? By contrast the true child of the permissive society is liable to miss out on solid joys and lasting pleasures. He is less likely to know the pleasures of lasting relationships, of hard-won achievement, of trained appreciation, because he is less able to surmount the initial difficulties that these present. On the whole, all that is left to him is immediate sensation. Perhaps for this reason the permissive society is also the sensate society in which sensory and physical experiences alone are valued and sought after.[5] Such delights are inferior to the more lasting pleasures described above in the sense that anyone who has known both in their fullness would always choose the latter.[6] Also in the long run such pleasures have discontent built into them. The sensations we now pursue seem potentially limitless and for this reason we will always be disappointed. There is no point at which one can stop and declare "this is what I want" or "now I have had enough". Where happiness is defined as sensation, the pursuit of happiness becomes never-ending and increasingly futile. As a rather macabre joke physiologists have shown that, if an electrode is placed in the pleasure centre of a monkey's brain and the monkey is trained to press a button to get a synthetic thrill, the monkey will abandon all else and kill himself in an orgy of pleasure. It is macabre not just because the unfortunate monkey dies in this way but because it is a reflection of the way society could go. Perhaps already we are seeing the beginning of this in the sad fate of heroin addicts who in effect kill themselves at a young age in pursuit of an elusive and disappointing pleasure.

What is needed in society is a morality that achieves a better balance between jam today and jam tomorrow. The puritanical ethic that is now losing its hold on our society prevented people from enjoying jam today. Either you did not get it, or else, if you did get it, you felt guilty about it. Perhaps its worst feature was the way in which it prevented men and women fron experiencing and enjoying sexual relationships—though this has always seemed to be more characteristic of Catholic countries than of our own. Despite national propaganda to the contrary it is the Irish, the French and the Italians who are the frustrated peoples of Europe rather than the British. The Irish, in particular, must be frustrated, for they are deprived both of many normal sexual outlets and also of additions or substitutes such as pornography. A celibate priesthood, laws against contraception and an institutionalized denial of female sexuality are far more likely to lead to guilt and frustration than our English hypocrisy. At least in the Protestant countries the maxim "Better to marry than to burn" soon became shortened to "Better to marry".[7]

The permissive ethic that has replaced that of the puritans has its own distinctive drawbacks. Jam today, too much jam today and no concept of jam tomorrow is apt to make the taker sick. Promiscuity is an advance on chastity but it is not much of an advance. It is to be hoped that the kind of balance described by Wright and Cox as "permissiveness with affection" is the point at which our sexual morality will in fact come to a rest. Here a concern for present pleasures is in balanced harmony with a desire for a more lasting relationship. It is just such a balance that we need to seek in other areas of our lives if we are to survive the permissive society.

Such a balance is necessary not just for the well-being of the individual but also for the survival and progress of our society. We live in a highly organized and inter-dependent industrial society where the comfort and indeed the survival of any individual depends on the continued efforts of many other individuals. Simply in order to keep going it is essential that the work ethic and the ethic of duty do not disappear in a welter of permissiveness. It is essential therefore that we continue to imbue our children with those values. As society becomes richer there is less need of the rigid severity of the Protestant ethic. It may well be that it is better to relax and enjoy life than to strive to grow even faster. Nevertheless, it is necessary for most people to go on working diligently at their calling if we are to continue to enjoy the basic material underpinning of the permissive society. The most idle and permissive of layabouts will have toothache and will need a dentist, he will have appendicitis and need a surgeon, he will want sex without children and must call on the services of an army of pharmacists and chemists. If any of these shirk their duty because they are imbued with a permissive morality and cannot be bothered to work then we all suffer. What is true of these immediate services is equally true of more distant ones. We are equally dependent on the electrical engineer, the accountant or the policeman, and we will go on being so for the foreseeable future. We have created industrial society and we must live with it. We cannot retreat into total permissiveness unless we are prepared to do without penicillin and the contraceptive pill, without railway trains and tape recorders, without electric light and perhaps without half the population of our overcrowded island. There is no such thing as a post-industrial society. There is only industrial society and we must live with it. Nor is there any prospect that life in such a society will get markedly easier. The long burst of peace and prosperity that Britain has known in the last twenty years—the prosperous years that created the permissive society—may well be coming to an end. I do not subscribe to the view that we will soon be facing social and economic collapse brought on by an exhaustion of the world's raw materials and the uncontrollable release of noxious waste products. These are real and severe, but solvable problems—solvable, that is, if we have the cohesion and discipline to tackle them. To retreat from the problems of industrial society into a mindless permissiveness would be the most disastrous response we could make. These problems are created by industrial society but they can only be solved by the use of the material techniques and social organizations peculiar to industrial societies. They are industrial problems demanding an industrial solution. Even before the world gets to such a point, external demands may be made on our society which we can only meet if we remain a disciplined and coherent society. The demands will be moral, economic and military. The poorer countries will require assistance from us to provide their populations with a more tolerable standard of living. Our harder-working and better organized international competitors such as Germany or Japan will force us out of world markets if we are not able to match them in the cost and quality of our exports. Finally there is the ever-present military threat from eastern Europe. Recent years have seen a thaw in the cold war and accordingly we have considerably reduced the strength of our armed forces and accepted social changes that have rendered our citizens much less willing and able to act as soldiers. All this is welcome—provided we are not attacked by a society such as the Soviet Union which is far more heavily armed than we are and whose unpermissive morality makes for good soldiers.

It is premature then to assume that we can allow the permissive society to take its course on the grounds that our society's external and internal problems are about to be solved. They are not solved and they probably never will be. Perhaps we can relax a little but we certainly cannot afford to relax much.

Although I dislike the permissive society and would prefer to see many of its trends halted or even reversed this does not mean that I would want to see this done by drastic repressive social or legal action. Having supported the main legal changes in a permissive direction, I do not want to see these changes reversed. Such a reversal would create needless suffering and provoke severe and divisive conflicts in society. I have in this chapter suggested that we need to remain in a state of military preparedness and in an earlier one that societies with a strong military tradition and powerful military institutions tend to persecute male homosexuals. It does not, therefore, follow that I would support the restoration of legal sanctions against homosexuals or even that I agree with the general social disapproval of such men and their activities. The advantage of being aware of the link between the military and disapproval of homosexuality is that we should be able to use this knowledge to find a means of attaining a state of military preparedness without persecuting homosexuals. In the first place we can see that the persecution of the homosexuals is the dependent variable. You cannot achieve military preparedness by persecuting homosexuals. Rather can see that the attainment of military preparedness is likely to result in pressures on society to supress homosexuality. The reaction of society to this should be to recognize the pressure and to resist it. Similarly I can find little merit in the neo-Freudian notion that sexual repression and the sublimation of sexual drives is necessary for the creation of an advanced and complicated civilization.[8] Rather those societies which, for religious or economic reasons, had cultures that stressed the deferment of pleasure of all kinds tended to be both hard-working and achievement-oriented on the one hand and puritanical about sex on the other. To regard our restrictive attitudes to sexuality as a cause of our cultural achievements is to put the cart before the horse. Again it should be possible once we understand something of the relationships between different aspects of our culture to win both ways, i.e. both to have a society remarkable for its cultural achievements *and* to allow freer sexual relationships. This may produce a certain degree of cultural strain, but we ought to be able to produce social mechanisms to absorb this strain.

The shift in the thinking of society's rulers from a moralist to a causalist mode may also produce difficult social problems as has been indicated in earlier chapters. The causalist mode of tackling moral questions is one that developed because it was the best method of governing the relationships between large bureaucratic organizations. The moralist way of looking at the world which had evolved in small communities and which sought to regulate the relationships of individuals living in such communities proved unsuitable in this new context. One cannot describe ICI or Distillers or the Department of the Environment or the Prudential Assurance Company or the Transport and General Workers Union as "good" or "bad", "praiseworthy" or "blameworthy" in exactly the same sense as one can apply these terms to particular individuals. They are not persons and the relationships between them are more usefully seen in terms of cause and effect than in terms of reward and punishment. In Lord Thurlow's words "They have neither a soul to save nor a body to kick". The attempt by the lawyers to retain the fiction that such vast institutions are persons and can be treated as such has not been a successful one and the law and lawyers have been forced to adapt themselves to these new circumstances. The legal relations between such institutions are increasingly causalist ones. Devlin's category of quasi-criminal laws is a good example of this which he describes thus:

> The distinction between the real criminal law and the quasi-criminal in their relationship to morals is that in the former a moral idea shapes the content of the law and in the latter it provides a base upon which a legal structure can be erected. In the former the law adopts a particular moral idea usually taken from a divine commandment. In the latter no more is required of the law than that it should maintain contact more or less remote with the general moral idea that a man, if he cannot reach the perfection of loving his neighbours, should at least take care not to injure them and should not unfairly snatch an advantage for himself at their expense . . . The distinguishing mark between the criminal and the quasi-criminal lies not in the use of a special statutory provision but in the presence or absence of moral content in the statutory provision containing the offence . . . The first distinguishing mark of the quasi-criminal law then is that a breach of it does not mean that the offender has done anything morally wrong. The second distinguishing mark is that the law frequently does not care whether it catches the actual offender or not. Owners of goods are frequently made absolutely liable for what happens to the goods while they are under their control even if they are in no way responsible for the interference; an example is when food is contaminated or adulterated. Likewise, they may be made liable for the acts of their agents even if they have expressly forbidden the acts which caused the offence. This sort of measure can be justified by the argument that it induces persons *in charge of an organization* to take steps to see that the law is enforced in respect of things under their control . . . The majority of quasi-criminal offences are committed in the course of trade or commerce and the fines imposed in respect of them fall upon the shareholders of a limited company or the proprietors of the business.[9]

Devlin also underlines the fact that the law of tort is based on causalist rather than moralist principles and draws a distinction between the nature and functions of different aspects of the law very similar to Durkheim's distinction between repressive and restitutive law.[10] Devlin writes:

> But that is not the way in which the law of tort has grown up nor is it the function which it now performs. Normally the relevant question in this branch of the law is not "who is to blame?", but "who is to pay if things go wrong?"; and the judgement is expressed as a sum fixed not as punishment for blameworthiness but as compensation for damage

done. I do not think that a branch of the law whose object is to provide compensation for damage can be used directly to serve a moral purpose. The reason put shortly is that while liability can be made to depend upon moral guilt, full compensation for injury done cannot be made to depend on the degree of moral guilt; guilt depends upon a state of mind but damage done does not.[11]

These features have been part of the law for a long time but the tendency, as time passes, is for quasi-criminal laws to multiply and for the number of "absolute" liability offences to increase as large impersonal institutions become more important and their relationships more complex. In itself this does not matter, for the relationships between big institutions are best regulated in this way. To try to apply moralist criteria would at best create chaos and at worst produce a blind and irrational application of moral principles in areas where they cannot apply. Rather, the problem is as follows: first, we need to regulate the relationships between the large institutions and the individual. The responsibilities of the institution to the individual fit easily into a causalist framework but the converse is not true. Secondly there is a tendency (as outlined in Chapter 2) for the State and other institutions to seek to place the morality of relationships between individuals on a causalist basis. Thirdly, because causalist morality and modes of thinking have prevailed in large areas of social activity, the moralist mode of regulating social relationships is undermined even in areas where it is appropriate. The difficulty with causalist rules is that they are perceived by individuals as *external* regulations, to be obeyed for reasons of prudence only. They cannot be *internalized*; they cannot become part of the individual's conscience. An individual acquires a conscience at an early age as a result of being a member of a small group and being exposed to rewards, punishments and persuasion. He learns that certain activities are disapproved of and in general these are activities which have a simple and visible harmful effect on someone else. You do not steal from another individual because you know what it feels like to suffer loss. You do not assault other people because you know what it feels like to be assaulted. Sympathy and empathy are essential aspects of conscience-formation, but they cannot operate in the case of one's relationship to a large institution. There is no point in trying to imagine what the Post Office feels like if it is swindled, or how British Rail feels if a carriage window is smashed. Further we do not come into contact with impersonal institutions until fairly late in life. Our early experiences and our early moral learning occur in small groups—in the family or in peer groups. The rules of the large institutions which we encounter later in life are not easily seen as extensions of the moral impulses we have acquired; hence they are seen as alien and external. (Some children are brought up in institutions, but the result is often that they are lacking in the skills and moral responses most of us acquire through small groups. It does not help them to cope with large institutions, although they may become dependent on them.) Many of the rules of such institutions are felt to be arbitrary in another sense, namely that there is no clear boundary between good and bad activities. Among individuals in a small group it is easy to distinguish *meum* from *tuum*. It is clear which bicycle belongs to which child and that to appropriate someone else's is wrong. By contrast it is difficult to tell which are justified expenses claimed by an executive from his firm and which are not, and even more difficult to tell when tax avoidance becomes tax evasion.[12]

Driving a car is a legitimate activity and only becomes morally wrong if the driver is deliberately reckless. But in between the two extremes of the "good" driver and the reckless driver comes the careless driver or the driver who makes a mistake. No clear line can be drawn between the good driver and the careless one. However careful we may try to be, we all make mistakes and we all have moments of inattention.

To some extent we are aware of these problems: thus the ordinary man often distinguishes between the morally culpable act and the act that simply breaks a rule. We do not regard theft from a company or the Government as severely as theft from an individual or theft involving violence.[13] We have devised terms like "fiddles" or "pilfering" to distinguish such peccadilloes from more serious thefts. In some cases the distinction even gets institutionalized. Thus when American dockers were negotiating a new labour agreement following the introduction of containers, they demanded and got "compensation for loss of pilfering rights" (i.e. when containers were introduced, the dockers were physically prevented from pilfering the cargo as they had done before and they were only willing to agree to containerization if they were compensated for this interference with legitimate theft). The problem remains that behaviour of this kind can be a serious nuisance. Also, and more important, the very existence of this grey area tempts many people into the black area beyond. A man in the habit of pilfering at work—a nuisance but not important nor subject to strong moral censure—may find it a short step to stealing from an individual whom he does not know or even to stealing from one of his workmates. A burglar who robs a bank which he regards as a "thing" to which he has no moral responsibility may come to regard the night watchman as a "thing" and kill him accordingly simply because he got in the way. In this way a moral rot sets in which erodes the whole basis of the moralist order. If it should continue the result will be disastrous.

Responses to this tendency have been very varied. Some people have argued that the answer is to extend our "moralist" sense of moral responsibility to all institutional relationships. This is surely unworkable and also wrong in principle. It is hardly possible to make people feel the same way about impersonal institutions as they do about other individuals—nor is it right that they should be expected to do so. Again it is not reasonable to expect people to feel moral indignation or guilt about actions whose harmful consequences are not immediately apparent. There is no simple solution, for example, to the moral conundrum that runs:

First philosopher: "This action is wrong, not because it is harmful on its own, but because if everyone did it there would be chaos."

Second philosopher: "But everybody is *not* going to do it. Therefore the action is not wrong."

To some extent the problem arises because the term *wrong* implies moral turpitude whereas the action being discussed is clearly one that is best tackled within a causalist framework of rules. But when we have done that it is still very unlikely that people will have a bad conscience about such an action. (An example would be the parking of a car on a single yellow line. One car may not matter but many such cars would create an obstruction or even a traffic hazard.)

Other people have argued that there should be no moralist offences, that all actions should be treated in a causalist manner. Devlin writes of Lady Wootton's argument in this respect:

> Lady Wootton considers that the criminal law should not be used punitively but only preventively. There should be a number of forbidden acts and any person who commits one will break the criminal law; but his state of mind when doing the acts should be irrelevant to the question of whether or not it is criminal, because he is not going to be punished for it but only prevented from doing it again. On this theory there is of course no room for any distinction between criminal and quasi-criminal law.[14]

It would probably be more accurate to say that "any person who commits one will break the quasi-criminal law." In effect the concept of crime would be abolished and only quasi-crimes would be left. *Mens rea* is at the heart of moralist morality. To remove any consideration of state of mind, of intention, of motivation from the criminal law is to undermine moralism even more. I do not believe that this should be done since, for activities that *can* be regulated by moralist rules (both in the sense that it is practicable and in the sense that it is not inequitable), this is a more effective means of social control than causalism and also one that most people prefer.

The danger for a legal system (and indeed a society) that tries to become completely causalist in its moral outlook is that first, in the short run, the citizens of such a society come to see the society's "official" causalist morality as unfair or meaningless because it fails to correspond to their moralist outlook; secondly, in the long run, the citizens lose their moralist outlook but fail to show any enthusiasm for the new causalist code. Instead of the rational ordered society that was the intention of the causalist reformers we would simply have an anomic world devoid of any moral force at all.

I have indicated earlier in the book (see p.44) that despite the causalist arguments mustered by Parliament and by other moral leaders and decision-makers, the ordinary citizen remains moralist in his outlook. Decisions that appear to the causalist planner as rational utilitarian choices appear to the victims as grossly unfair. To take a simple example from another field—that of State welfare: I was recently told of the case of a woman who had applied to her local authority to be rehoused on the grounds that her present accommodation was inadequate. The council sent round an official to inspect her home and after looking round carefully he told her that he thought it unlikely that her request would be granted. "Why?" asked the poor woman looking round the tiny apartment. "Well" said the official "I'm afraid you keep it much too clean and comfortable." Now from his point of view this was a rational and justifiable criterion to use. If you are an official with limited resources for rehousing people in your area it makes sense to give priority to those who indicate by the squalor of their homes their inability to deal with the problems posed by cramped and difficult lodgings. On the other hand, from the woman's point of view, his decision was totally unjust. She had been penalized for being virtuous. Her efforts to keep her family's home clean and liveable-in had been rewarded by a lengthening of the time for which she would have to endure the discomforts of overcrowding and inadequate housing.

A similar sense of unfairness is felt by ordinary people at attempts by the authorities to use causalist methods of social control that try to eliminate crimes or conflicts by penalizing a person other than the one seen by public opinion to be truly culpable. A favourite example of this is the case of *Beatty* v *Gillbanks* (1882).[15] In that year the Salvation Army (not the most provocative of organizations) wished to march through the streets of Weston-Super-Mare (not the most violent of towns). The local magistrates refused to allow this because they feared that they would be attacked by their rivals "the skeleton army", a mob of hooligans hostile to the Salvationists. The Salvation Army ignored the bar, marched and were arrested. The Salvationists refused to be bound over and were sentenced to three months in prison. The magistrates were acting as true causalists for, although there was nothing wrong in the Salvation Army's behaviour, it could have led to public strife and hence on the causalist argument it was reasonable to prevent them from doing so and to punish them for it. However, the year was 1882 when moralism was still the dominant mode of looking at such matters. The Salvation Army appealed successfully to the High Court where the judges ruled that "there was no authority that a man may be convicted for doing a lawful act [i.e. marching in procession] if he knows that by doing it he may cause another to do an unlawful act" (vis. create disorder).

Even today most people would agree with the judges' ruling, though it has been superseded by causalist measures such as the Public Order Act. It is quite likely that, if there were to be a similar test-case today, the causalist view would prevail and an innocent group or individuals (in the eyes of the public) would be punished for provoking the guilty.

Common sense tells people that good actions should be rewarded and bad ones penalized. Causalism in its present form tends to undermine this point of view. Attention is concentrated on the harmful side-effects of penalizing the wicked. Such penalties are held to divide them from the virtuous and to create a conflict between the two groups which tends to drive the wicked ones into even greater wickedness (for some reason, less stress is placed on the corollary that rewarding the good should make them even more virtuous; rather it is held that they become smug and exclusive). Consequently the causalist is keen to avoid the penalizing of the wicked and to put stress on other causal factors in the situation. We see this in the suggestion that drivers should be penalized for not locking their cars (rather than car thieves for stealing them), or that supermarkets should be prevented from displaying their wares quite so temptingly. There is some sense in this, but the causalist in concentrating his attention on the labelling effect of penalizing the wicked neglects the fact that such penalties (and rewards) also have an instructive side to them. We learn to adjust our actions to the rewards and penalties society offers and in this way society's values are upheld and enforced and harmful actions prevented. It is not necessary to evoke moralist criteria to justify systems of rewards and penalties. We have an alternative causalist justification to hand.

Indeed it seems quite likely that our present moralist procedure could in large measure be justified in causalist terms, i.e. moralism works and causalism often does not. Only when the causalists come to put emphasis on learning as well as labelling will we have a causalist system that is truly effective. If they do not, then we will rapidly approach the thick end of the wedge as existing moral attitudes are ever eroded and never reinforced.

Rather what we must do is to preserve the distinction between acts that are best regulated in a moralist way and those best regulated in a causalist manner. We must if anything sharpen the distinction between the criminal and the quasi-criminal, between *mala in se* and *mala prohibita*. However we must also be prepared to rationalize the application of this distinction and transfer activities from one category to the other as the needs of society and the state of the collective conscience change with the times. Moralism seen as a method of social control has the merit that it is powerful and effective, but its disadvantage is that it is inaccurate and inflexible. Causalism has the merit of being precise and rational but it is weak because it can never command intense popular support. Both these modes of social control are necessary and what is needed is the rational division of our actions between the two modes. It is not necessary to argue that the allocation of rules into the two categories should follow the present pattern. Some actions (e.g. indecent exposure) that arouse great moralist hostility to the wrong-doer are relatively harmless. Other actions such as drunken driving that are known to cause great harm are often generally regarded as not being morally culpable. The test of whether an action should be forbidden in a moralist fashion by the law is, first, that it should be harmful and, secondly, that it should generally be regarded as morally wrong. If an action should fail to conform to the first test then it is best left unprohibited and unpunished or at most treated as a nuisance. If an action meets the requirement of the first test but not of the second then it is probably best regulated within a causalist framework. To try to apply moralist criteria to such an action and to punish it accordingly is self-defeating. A good example is given by Devlin:

> It is an offence to have carnal knowledge of a girl under sixteen years. Consent on her part is no defence; if she did not consent it would of course be rape. The law makes special provision for the situation when a boy and girl are near in age. If a man under twenty-four can prove that he had reasonable cause to believe that the girl was over the age of sixteen years, he has a good defence. The law regards the offence as sufficiently serious to make it one that is triable only by a judge at assizes. "Reasonable cause" means not merely that the boy honestly believed that the girl was over sixteen, but also that he had reasonable grounds for his belief. In theory it ought not to be an easy defence to make out but in fact it is extremely rare for anyone who advances it to be convicted. The fact is that the girl is often as much to blame as the boy. The object of the law, as judges repeatedly tell juries, is to protect young girls against themselves, but juries are not impressed.[16]

Juries are not impressed because they have their own view of what is, and what is not, morally wrong and of who is, and who is not, to blame. When this differs from that of the law, the law is ignored. Conviction by a jury carries with it a moral stigma and juries will not apply this where they feel it is not justified. Under these circumstances the wisest thing to do would be to treat this offence as a breach of causalist rules only and deal with it as a nuisance and not as a crime.

By rationalizing the boundary between causalist and moralist rules in this way many of the disputes about the "enforcement of morals" would disappear. However, we would still be left with some difficult cases of crimes without victims that would cause disagreement. The problem of whether we determine the moral character of our people by an aggregate of individual decisions or by a collective decision is not one we are ever likely to resolve finally and a good case can be made out on either side. Basil Mitchell gives as an interesting analogy the problem of the survival of the cultural identity of the Welsh people. It is an analogy which highlights the problems but does not help us to resolve them. He writes:

In point of fact it sometimes happens that an effort is made by law to safeguard institutions less because they are thought to be good than because they are thought to be characteristic. No doubt in all such cases motives are mixed but it is reasonable to suspect that some of those who want to preserve the Welsh language and the Welsh Sunday do so not because they believe that these institutions have peculiar merits but because they are characteristically Welsh. They want to preserve the Welshness of Wales even if it means that the majority have to learn a minority language and those who want to drink on Sundays are frustrated . . . Without the Welsh language and the Welsh Sunday, Wales would suffer no greater injury than that of becoming largely indistinguishable from England. One would have to say something like that the survival of the Welsh way of life was at stake, not what makes Wales viable or what makes it civilized but what makes it Welsh.[17]

This is a very real dilemma for Welsh people. As individuals most of us choose to speak only English and to become largely anglicized. We do not speak Welsh, we have no intention of learning it and we resented having to learn it at school. Yet at the same time many English-speaking Welsh people feel sorry for the Welsh speakers whose language and culture are dying out. We are trapped in a moral dilemma which it is not easy to resolve. It is exactly the same dilemma that Britain as a whole faces when the issue of individual morality and the character of our people is being discussed. Should we accept entirely the logic of our open and plural society and allow moral changes to occur autonomously or should we attempt some kind of collective regulation of these changes?

I do not know the answer to this question but I will suggest one or two criteria that I think can be used to justify the social and legal enforcement of morals even within the context of a wholly open society. The first is a simple welfare criterion. As a result of the creation of the welfare State we are all protected from extreme deprivation and suffering where possible and we enjoy the right to make certain claims on the State. This necessarily means that the State can make corresponding claims on us as individuals. As Spencer predicted[18] we have chosen to sacrifice our liberty in this way. If there is no welfare State then an individual is entitled to live a life of total dissipation and idleness. If as a result he starves or suffers that is his own look out. However, the welfare State with more or less efficiency aims to prevent people suffering from whatever cause—whether it be their own fault or, as is more usual, circumstances beyond their control. Under these circumstances if a man is to avail himself of the resources of State welfare then he must accept a degree of paternalistic regulation by the State.

There are those who deny this and argue that there are no reciprocal obligations involved. In the past the State or society has attempted to make moral claims on individuals without granting them any rights or assistance. Such claims were rightly derided as *humbug*. Today we are faced with the opposite fallacy, viz. that individuals have moral claims on society regardless of how they behave. A new concept is needed to describe this foolish point of view. I suggest we reverse an existing term and call it *bumhug*.

There are of course many other common varieties of "bumhug" in Britain today which are in each case the reverse of an earlier humbug. In the past a pretence was kept up that the reality of social life and of the working of our institutions was always in accordance with the ideal. Civil servants were models of rectitude, our soldiers were brave and humane, our wives virtuous and contented and our policemen wonderful. Utter humbug of course. But today it is bumhug that we must beware of. The bumhug (like humbug this noun applies to both the quality and the person exhibiting the quality) sees clearly the gap between ideal and reality and concludes from it that society is totally corrupt. He fails to see that institutions need both the ideal and the reality and that, were the gap to be closed completely, it would be fatal for society. If we were to abandon the ideals and to institutionalize the reality as recognized and approved brutality the result would be a combination of totalitarian authority and general disillusionment. For some few people in England the world seems like that already but that is no reason for extending such conditions (and hence such opportunities for perception) to all. Totalitarian societies are more egalitarian than democratic ones in the sense that everyone is liable to be treated in a harsh fashion (not just a few malefactors) but that is not an argument in their favour.

Similarly if we were to abandon the reality and enforce the ideals rigidly we would create unworkable chaos. No rules would be enforced for fear of infringing the rights of the people for whom the rules were enacted. No rewards, no penalties would be issued for fear of selecting the wrong recipients. Nothing could be or would be forbidden—at any rate until people tired of their democratic ideals so rigidly enforced and called for a return to comfortable workable reality.

A further aspect of past humbug was that we allowed society's representatives a degree of power and licence that was forbidden to others. This was carefully controlled but nevertheless it existed. If a policeman pursued a burglar and in the fight that followed the burglar was injured—well that was too bad. He had, after all, been breaking the law. If the burglar injured the policeman he was of course liable to have to face a further charge in court. If the burglar killed the policeman then he would of course be charged with murder and he would probably also be severely beaten up by the dead policeman's colleagues. Most people quite rightly sympathized with the police on such an occasion but they felt uneasy about doing so. Their uneasiness expressed itself in a denial that such incidents could occur in England or in a species of special pleading on behalf of the police. More humbug. However, such humbug is rapidly being replaced by bumhug. The bumhugs judge the actions of officials or institutions or of law-abiding citizens more harshly than those of lawless deviants. If a demonstrator attacks a policeman, that is fun. If the policeman retaliates, that is fascism. Bumhug is of course not a new phenomenon. Demonstrators have always tried to provide fake martyrs of police brutality from the man who died of a broken thigh a fortnight after the clashes between demonstrators and police in Trafalgar Square in 1886 (he was said to have been "murdered" though it was an accident that his leg got broken), to the demonstrators streaming with red dye at the Grosvenor Square demonstration of 1968. Nevertheless red dye displays considerably more bumhug than a broken thigh. Bumhug it would seem is on the increase and bumhuggery seems to be the key vice of a declining Britain.[19]

My other criteria relate to the concept of freedom itself. I would suggest that a free society may without infringing the freedom it seeks to uphold demand, first, that no individual shall be allowed to take any action which would lose him his freedom or that would deny the freedom of others, secondly, that he should make all key moral decisions after due consideration. A totally free society may not demand that its members be good, but it can insist that they remain free. Even if such a society may not determine what an individual ultimately chooses, it can legislate concerning the context in which he chooses in such a way as to ensure a responsible choice. In this way is freedom ensured and reinforced.

Thus a free society cannot for example permit contracts involving slavery, the very negation of freedom, however willing the slaves may be. Furthermore, since the whole basis of an ideology of freedom is the preservation of meaningful free choice for adults, we are forced to discourage actions that are physically irreversible (i.e. that by their nature preclude the making of any future contrary choice) and to have sanctions against those who urge others to take such actions. Thus there is a need to deter drug peddling, euthanasia, duelling, suicide pacts and maiming with consent, because once someone is addicted, dead or maimed he is no longer free (i.e. he can never reverse his initial decision).

In his essay "Morals and the Law of Marriage"[20] Devlin has suggested that divorce proceedings ought to be regarded as consisting of two separate parts, (i) a dispute between the two parties concerning the terms of their separation and (ii) an application for a licence to remarry. The latter he contends should be considered separately as an issue between society and any respondent wishing to remarry (i.e. even a respondent innocent of any matrimonial offence should not be able as of right to marry a second time). The implication of this is that society has an interest in the stability and success of the second marriage and that any decision by the courts should reflect this. Here I feel his approach is right but for the wrong reasons, since it is difficult to see why society should have less of an interest in the stability of the first marriage. A free society concerned with promoting rational and reasonable free choice may rightly demand that before *any* decision as to marriage is made the parties can be forced to discuss and consider the issue very carefully. If this is insisted on in the case of second marriages only, the implication is either that such marriages are prone to failure and in need of such advice, or that the key element for Devlin is not to assist divorcees to a careful second choice, but to punish them for a mistaken first one. The latter aspect is unacceptable but can be removed by giving matrimonial councillors the power to delay but not ultimately to prevent a marriage from taking place. However, they should have this power in all instances, since many categories of first marriages (e.g. those involving teenagers or shot-gun marriages) are just as prone to disaster as the marriage of divorcees. It can be seen from this example that the actual working of many of our institutional procedures might remain very similar if we made responsible choice the basis of the rules whatever the result, rather than goodness *per se*. No doubt some people will argue that this is just as value-laden because it excludes irresponsible choices. I can only reply that I think this sort of procedural morality ought to be enforced, that rules are necessarily value-laden and that it is right that they should be so. Such a move would of course mean a shift from moralism to causalism as the basis for institutional procedures. Under such a system bigamy, where there is no deception, ceases to be morally outrageous and becomes merely an attempt to evade the proper channels of decision-making. It will be the subject of sanctions, not because it is morally offensive, but because it infringes administrative regulations relating to welfare. Bigamy becomes essentially similar to not paying one's National Insurance contributions.

One of the sadder aspects of a free society is the extent to which individuals are unable to use the freedom they are offered. In some cases the individual experiences freedom as *anomie*, as a lack of purpose and meaning in life. He becomes a casualty of the permissive society who would have been happier in a society that offered him a safe routine and a clearly defined and enforced role. In other cases the individual seeks refuge from this moral vacuum in small groups whose internal rules are repressive beyond anything that society seeks to enforce. He is unable to leave and unable to defy. Both these conditions are bad for the individual and in general bad for society, for if the individual drops out of all structured contact with others he is likely to become a liability to himself and a nuisance for society. If he joins a tightly knit gang the purposes of this group are liable to be anti-social. Both these responses are likely to be increasing problems in the years ahead and both are likely to call forth new and more effective methods of social control.[21]

I spent the whole of Chapter 7 discussing the American institution Synanon, not simply because I thought it was interesting and important in itself but because I see it as an increasingly important type of institution in the future. More and more society will seek to encourage deviant individuals to organize themselves into institutions of this kind in order to acquire the moral norms and sense of community that they lack. Such institutions will be total, moralistic, open and congruent with the values and attitudes of the wider society. They will provide a moral environment similar to that of small-scale societies. The casualties of a large impersonal and bureaucratized society will join institutions of this sort while the rest of us enjoy the freedom and diversity that the larger society offers.

In periods of crisis and disorder society often sets up institutions of this kind. The remodelling of the English public schools in the nineteenth century has already been discussed. Another example is the Starehe boys centre in Nairobi in Kenya which was set up to cater for the orphaned, destitute or deliquent boys who were cut off from tribal or family support by the disruptive pressures of urbanization. The centre aimed to provide them with a practical training, with a moral ethos and with a community. It has succeeded so well that now many members of Kenya's African élite send their sons to the centre to be educated. It is as if we in England were to effect a merger between Eton, an orphanage and a Borstal. An institution of this type with even more far-reaching consequences was Makarenko's Gorki institute in the Soviet Union in the 1920s. Urie Bronfenbrenner's description of it reads almost like a visit to Dr Arnold at Rugby:

> In the early 1920s ... Makarenko was handed the assignment of setting up a rehabilitation programme for some of the hundreds of homeless children who were roaming the Soviet Union after the civil wars. The first group of such children assigned to Makarenko's school, a ramshackle building far out of town, turned out to be a group of boys about 18 years of age with extensive court records of housebreaking, armed robbery and manslaughter. For the first four months Makarenko's school served simply as the headquarters for the band of highwaymen who were his legal wards. But gradually through the development of group-oriented discipline techniques and through what can only be called the compelling power of his own moral convictions Makarenko was able to develop a sense of group responsibility and commitment to the work programme and code of conduct that he had laid out for the collective. In the end his Gorki colony became known throughout the Soviet Union for its high morale, for its discipline and for the productivity of its farms, fields and shops.[22]

Makarenko has had a great influence on the development of the Russian educational system and his methods and ideas are widely applied.[23] Instead of a child's peer group being an autonomous force in his life, and often one opposed to the values of the adult world, it is a means of social control used to inculcate the values of Russian society. The child is confronted on all sides with a homogeneous set of values to which family, school and peer group alike insist that he conform. As a result Soviet children grow up obedient, submissive, and yet self-confident, co-operative and competent. What Makarenko had realized was that individuals acquire their moral attitudes and behaviour from small groups and not directly from large formal institutions. In England these groups are autonomous and push the child in many different directions at once. Often the result is that he acquires no moral values at all or a set of delinquent attitudes at odds with the values of the wider society. In Russia the family, the school and peer groups are all controlled and manipulated in such a way as to reinforce one another and this ensures that the values of the wider society are accepted by each and every child.

If we wish to gain greater control of our permissive society then these are the methods we shall have to use. Already many social psychologists such as Bronfenbrenner are urging the merits of Russian methods of education and child-care as an antidote to the ills of American society. Bronfenbrenner is right in the sense that these methods are effective, but I think we want to look more closely at the drawbacks of the Russian system. Russia is after all a totalitarian dictatorship and as such has collective ills that dwarf any problems of individual deviance that we face. Was it really such a good thing that Russian citizens grew up "obedient and submissive" when the society that received that obedience and submission was responsible for the massacre of the Kulaks, the great purges of the 1930s and the vicious anti-semitism of today? Soviet children may not be tempted to attack their neighbours,[24] but what is that when the neighbours may be executed or sent to a labour camp on the slightest pretext. The evils that fanatical collectivism can do are far worse than the results of individual anti-social behaviour. Even in our own society World War I probably wrecked more lives than all the crimes of this century added up.

Nor are the two issues of Russian education and Communist dictatorship entirely separate. Makarenko went on from his Gorki colony to work for the Ministry of Internal Affairs (then the Cheka, later the GPU and the NKVD).[25] These were the very bodies that helped to carry out brutal and lawless murders for Stalin and his successors. It is easy to see that a people trained from childhood to denounce any deviance among their peers grow up to be adults who denounce their neighbours to the secret police. The advantage of such a training is certainly perceived by Soviet educators as we learn from the case of Pavlik Morozov:

A young pioneer during the period of collectivization, Pavlik denounced his own father as a collaborator with the Kulaks and testified against him in court. Pavlik was killed by people of the village for revenge and is now regarded as a martyr in the cause of communism.[26]

Most people in England would rightly be shocked and

horrified at Morozov's action and would sympathize with the peasants who killed him (after all his father was probably killed by the Soviet authorities and the peasants were being deliberately starved to death by the government). Furthermore most English schoolboys would rightly regard a class-mate who reported on a friend for a trivial offence as a wretched little sneak who would be shunned rather than admired. Yet situations like this may be inseparable from a system of social control that works via informal groups as well as laws. Such a system is effective but it is also a denial of freedom.

In the permissive society we are increasingly going to find that we are confronted by the difficult choice between freedom and chaos on the one hand and order and authoritarianism on the other. It is not a new dilemma nor a unique one, for all societies at all times have had to face it. However, we may well find that over the next twenty years or so it will prove difficult to steer between these extremes and yet it is vital to the continued well-being of our free yet ordered society that we do so successfully.

References

CHAPTER 1

1. C.H. and W.M. Whiteley, *The Permissive Morality* (Methuen, 1964), p. 21.
2. Derek Wright, *The Psychology of Moral Behaviour* (Penguin, 1971), p. 67. The distinction is derived from R. Middleton and S. Putney, "Religion, normative standards and behaviour", *Sociometry*, vol. 25, pp. 141–52.
3. Wright, pp. 180–1.
4. Wright, p. 182.
5. James McMillan, *The Roots of Corruption* (Tom Stacey, 1972), p. 61.
6. An index of the changing times was the rise of the pressure group S.T.O.P.P., the Society of Teachers Opposed to Physical Punishment, and the decline of the N.S.R.C.P., the National Society for the Retention of Corporal Punishment, though the latter was replaced by CANE'EM, the Campaign Against New Egalitarian Educational Methods, which modernized its image by referring to the cane as an audio-tactile aid.
7. H.H. Gerth and C.W. Mills, *From Max Weber, Essays in Sociology*, p. 9. The quotations are from Max Weber's *Jugendbriefe*, p. 221, and Gerth and Mills, p. 9.
8. John Wilson, *Reason and Morals* (C.U.P., 1961), pp. 38 and 39–40. There is a further discussion of these issues on pp. 42–57, 78–83 and 128–9.
9. cf. A.C. Kinsey *et al.*, *Sexual Behaviour in the Human Female* (Saunders, 1953), p. 11. "There seems to be no single factor which is more important for the maintaining of a marriage than the determination that the marriage shall be maintained. Where there is that determination, differences between the spouses may be overlooked or forgotton in a perspective which emphasizes the importance of maintaining the marital union. Where there is no such will trivial and minor disturbances may grow until they are important enough to warrant the dissolution of the marriage."

10. Some amusing exceptions to this rule are quoted in Joan Robinson, *Economic Philosophy* (Watts, 1962), p. 138.

11. For a differing view see James McMillan, op. cit., pp. 42 *et seq.*

12. Kinsey *et al.*, op. cit., p. 244.

13. R.S. Lynd and H.M. Lynd, *Middletown in Transition, a Study in Cultural Conflict* (New York: Harcourt Brace, 1937), p. 168.

14. Sinclair Lewis, *Babbitt* (Harcourt Brace, 1922, Signet Books), pp. 185–6.

15. F. Scott Fitzgerald, *This Side of Paradise* (The Grey Walls Press, 1948), p. 63.

16. F.L. Allen, *Only Yesterday* (Harper Bros. and Bantam, 1969), p. 65.

17. James Pope-Hennessey, *Queen Mary 1867–1953* (Allen & Unwin, 1959), p. 513.

18. cf. Mrs Mary Whitehouse, *Who Does She Think She Is?* (New English Library, 1971), p. 20.

19. cf. Harold Macmillan, *Winds of Change* (Macmillan, 1966), p. 185.

20. The need to explain puritanism rather than permissiveness is the theme of many historical and sociological works. See, for instance, Max Weber's *The Protestant Ethic and the Spirit of Capitalism*, or Muriel Jaeger's *Before Victoria*. However other writers see puritanism as the more "natural" of the two. See for instance C.E.M. Joad, *The Future of Morals*.

CHAPTER 2

1. The main changes are listed in P. Richards, *Parliament and Conscience*, (Allen & Unwin, 1970); James McMillan, *The Roots of Corruption*, (Tom Stacey, 1972).

2. cf. statistics in Richards, p. 194.

3. Richards, p. 147.

4. Command 3123, para. 15.

5. Richards, p. 154.

6. Richards, p. 140.

7. Statistics from Richards, p. 183.

8. Hansard Official Reports of Parliamentary Debates, 5th series, House of Commons, vol. 732, col. 1067.

9. Hansard, vol. 732, col. 1154.

10. Richards, p. 97.

11. In Richards, pp. 109–10 the votings on the second and third reading are compared thus:

| | | Second Reading | |
		Yes	No
Third Reading	Yes	116	–
Third Reading	No	10	19
Not voting		99	12
		225	31

12. Hansard, vol. 732, col. 1094.

13. Hansard, vol. 732, col. 1156.

14. Richards, p. 104.

15. Hansard, vol. 732, cols. 1118—19.

16. Hansard, vol. 732, col. 1101.

17. Hansard, vol. 750, cols. 1180 *et seq.*

18. Hansard, vol. 750, cols. 1181 *et seq.*

19. Hansard, vol. 749, col. 934.

20. Hansard, vol. 732, cols. 1118—19.

21. Hansard, vol. 732, col. 1137.

22. Sir John Hobson *et al., Abortion, a Conservative View* (Conservative Political Centre), p. 6.

23. Richards, p. 108.

24. In this instance irreversibility is also a criterion the moralist might adopt for opposing capital punishment on the grounds that it is monstrous to run the risk of (irreversibly) executing an innocent man as a result of an error of the judicial system. For a discussion of the possibility of this happening see Ruth Brandon and Christie Davies, *Wrongful Imprisonment* (Allen & Unwin, 1973).

25. For an earlier discussion of the two kinds of society see E. Durkheim, *The Division of Labour in Society* (Free Press, 1964).

26. Richards, p. 58

27. Hansard, vol. 704, cols. 879 *et seq.*

28. Hansard, vol. 704, col. 881.

29. Hansard, vol. 704, col. 899.

30. Hansard, vol. 704, col. 906.

31. Hansard, vol. 704, col. 964.

32. Richards, p. 56, and statistics on p. 183.

33. Hansard, 5th series, House of Lords, vol. 201, cols. 1189—90.

34. Hansard, 5th series, House of Commons, vol. 548, col. 2634. See also vol. 552, col. 2068.

35. Hansard, vol. 704, col. 902.

36. Hansard, vol. 704, col. 908.

37. Hansard, vol. 704, cols. 939—40.

38. The decline of moralist thinking in Parliament between the 1940s and the 1960s may simply represent the change in the composition of

the Parliamentary Labour party as working-class Members of Parliament are replaced by middle-class trendies. I am inclined to think that though this would assist the change (the working class are more punitive, more attracted by moralist attacks on deviants or moralist slogans) it is not an important factor in causing it.

39. Hansard, vol. 449, col. 1014.
40. Hansard, vol. 449, col. 1016.
41. Hansard, vol. 449, col. 1030.
42. Hansard, vol. 449, col. 1035.
43. Hansard, vol. 449, col. 1053.
44. Hansard, vol. 449, col. 1054.
45. Hansard, vol. 449, col. 1067.
46. Hansard, vol. 449, cols. 1069—70.
47. This tendency to respond to an external threat by an increased moral rigidity is discussed in Milton Rokeach, *The Open and Closed Mind* (New York: Basic Books, 1960), pp. 376 *et seq.*
48. Statistics from Richards, p. 56.
49. Richards, p. 56.
50. Hansard, vol. 704, col. 945.
51. P.A. Devlin (Lord Devlin), *The Enforcement of Morals* (O.U.P., 1965), p. 100.
52. The phrase is of course F. Dostoyevsky's in *The Brothers Karamazov* (Penguin Classics), pp. 883 *et seq.*, where the peasants on the jury found Mitya guilty of murder to the dismay of the trendies.
53. Speech to the electors at Bristol at the conclusion of the poll quoted in John Morley's *Burke* (Macmillan 1887), p. 75.

CHAPTER 3

1. P. Richards, *Parliament and Conscience* (Allen & Unwin, 1970), p. 116.
2. cf. essay by Henry Fairlie on "The BBC" in *The Establishment*, a symposium edited by Hugh Thomas (Anthony Blond, 1959). Fairlie writes: "Of all the voices of the Establishment, the British Broadcasting Corporation is the most powerful" (p. 191). "The assumption that underlies all the BBC's attitudes to authority: namely that it ought to be on the side of authority" (p. 193). "It fears and when it does not fear it despises, non-conformity" (p. 204).
3. cf. Mrs Mary Whitehouse, *Cleaning up T.V.: From Protest to Participation* (Blandford Press, 1967).
4. See press reports, e.g. *Evening Standard*, 25 September 1971.
5. Most of them fit Daniel Boorstin's definition of a celebrity as "a person who is well known for his well-knownness". D. Boorstin, *The Image* (Weidenfeld & Nicolson, 1962), p. 67.

6. *Report of the Commission on Obscenity and Pornography* (USA) (New York: Bantam Books and Random House, 1970), p. 460.

7. *Report of the Commission on Obscenity,* etc., p. 597.

8. *Report of the Commission on Obscenity,* etc., pp. 583, 601, 609–10, 613, 619.

9. *Report of the Commission on Obscenity,* etc., pp. 581, 623.

10. Patrick Devlin (Lord Devlin), *The Enforcement of Morals* (OUP, 1965), p. 108.

11. Devlin, pp. 116–17.

12. Devlin, p. 123.

13. The reasons are discussed in Berl Kutchinsky, *Studies on Pornography and Sex Crimes in Denmark: a Report to the United States Presidential Commission on Obscenity and Pornography* (New Social Science Monographs, November 1970), pp. 99–101.

14. (a) cf. *Television and Growing up: the Impact of Televised Violence. Report to the Surgeon-General, US Public Health Service, from the Surgeon-General's Advisory Committee,* p. 141; e.g. "On the basis of these findings and taking into account their variety and their inconsistencies we can tentatively conclude that there is a modest relationship between exposure to television violence and aggressive behaviour or tendencies." For the mechanism by which television has these effects cf. H.J. Eysenck, *Crime and Personality* (Routledge & K.P., 1964), pp. 182–3.

(b) cf. *Television and Social Behaviour.* Reports and Papers, Vol. III, *Television and Adolescent Aggressiveness. A Technical Report to the Surgeon-General's Advisory Committee on Television and Social Behaviour* (US Dept of Health, Education and Welfare, 1972). See M.M. Lefkowitz *et al., Television and Child Aggression, a Follow-up Study,* p. 84: "On the basis of these cross-lagged correlations, the most plausible single causal hypothesis would appear to be that preferring violent television in the third grade leads to the building of aggressive habits."

15. Another reason for the greater harmful effects of television relative to books is that it is a more visual medium and has more effect on men than on women who are insensitive to visual stimuli. Cf. Corinne Hutt in C. Ounsted and D.C. Taylor (eds.), *Gender Differences: Their Ontogeny and Significance* (Churchill Livingstone, 1972), pp. 81–2.

CHAPTER 4

1. A.C. Kinsey *et al., Sexual Behaviour in the Human Male* (Saunders, 1948). *Sexual Behaviour in the Human Female* (Saunders, 1953).

2. M. Schofield, *The Sexual Behaviour of Young People* (Penguin, 1968).

3. Schofield, p. 223, is source of statistics.

4. Schofield, p. 224.

5. Schofield, pp. 49—50.

6. Schofield, p. 216. E. Chesser, *The Sexual, Marital and Family Relationships of the English Woman* (Hutchinsons, 1956).

7. Derived from figures given in Derek Wright, *The Psychology of Moral Behaviour* (Penguin, 1971), pp. 177—9.

8. Schofield, p. 258.

9. cf. Wright, p. 180.

10. cf. Schofield, p. 180 and p 158.

11. Alan F. Sillitoe, *Britain in Figures, a Handbook of Social Statistics* (Penguin, 1971), pp. 22—3.

12. Sillitoe, p. 23.

13. *Registrar-General's Statistical Review of England and Wales 1969, Supplement on Abortion* plus provisional figures for 1972. Cf. also *Report of the Committee on the Working of the Abortion Act,* Cmnd. 5579, Session 1974—5, Vol. II.

14. Paper on "Abortion and the Unmarried Mother" given at the International Congress of Psychosomatic Medicine.

15. Kinsey (female), p. 244. See also Chapter 1, p.9.

16. Schofield, pp. 230—1.

17. Based on figures in Schofield, pp. 230—1. These are rough estimates on my part.

18. Wright, p. 180.

19. Paper given by Dr A. Gunn, Senior Medical Officer in the University Health Service, to the Royal Society of Health Annual Congress.

20. Bromley Council in closing its list of couples wanting to adopt babies (usual waiting time two years) stated that the pill and the Abortion Act had caused a marked drop in the number of babies needing adoption. Probably also more unmarried mothers, perhaps unwisely, wish to keep their children.

21. Jean Morton Williams and Keith Hindell, *Abortion and Contraception: a Study of Patients' Attitudes* (P.E.P. Broadsheet 536, March 1972) pp. 55—6.

22. Williams and Hindell, p. 55.

23. The proportion of illegitimate births is now fairly constant. For 1967 there were 84 illegitimate births per 1000 live births; for 1968, 85; 1969, 84; 1970, 83; 1971, 84; 1972, 86.

24. *Observer,* 4 October 1970.

25. *Evening Standard,* 10 August 1971.

26. In particular personal utilitarianism differs from my definition of causalism in Chapter 1 in laying stress on the pleasures to be derived from an activity as well as the possible harmful consequences. Thus I

am really now using a utilitarian model which assumes that the giving and receiving of affection can be regarded as of positive utility. I have had to make this modification because individuals are able to assess their own subjective preferences whereas legislators cannot in the same sense know the subjective feelings of the citizens. The legislature can assess what perils the citizens should be protected from but they cannot determine their tastes. For this reason a free market with certain legal restrictions is better than rule by bureaucratic decree.

27. *A Birth Control Plan for Britain* (Birth Control Campaign, London, 1972). Cf. also *The Times*, 17 March 1972.

28. cf. Wright, p. 180.

29. R.S. Morton, *Venereal Diseases* (Penguin, 1966), p. 32.

30. Morton, pp. 13–14.

31. G.M. Carstairs in editorial foreword to Morton, p. 8.

32. Morton, p. 172.

33. There is an interesting parallel with people's reactions to the possibility of a drug that would turn black people into white ones. Causalists approve of the search for and use of such a drug because it would make the day-to-day lives of black people in white societies more tolerable, it would ease racial conflict, and in the long run it would erode colour prejudice. White moralists by contrast heatedly reject the use of such a drug either because they are prejudiced against blacks and like to know one when they see one or because they want to use the plight of the blacks as a stick to beat their fellow whites with.

34. For a more sympathetic view of ritualism in morals cf. Mary Douglas, *Natural Symbols, Explorations in Cosmology* (Barrie & Rockliffe, 1970; Penguin, 1973) and especially Chapter 7, "Sin and Society".

35. For an instance of such a criticism (not the authors') see Williams and Hindell, p. 55, on people's attitudes to women seeking an abortion.

36. J.S. Mill, *Utilitarianism* (Fontana edition), pp. 258–9.

37. K. Walker and P. Fletcher, *Sex and Society* (Penguin, 1955), p. 161.

38. Walker and Fletcher, p. 227.

39. Robin Fox, *Kinship and Marriage* (Penguin, 1967), p. 63.

40. There is a difficulty with the qualification "societies similar to our own" in that if it is interpreted in a very restrictive manner the whole argument becomes redundant, and if it is interpreted loosely the argument may well be false. It does *not*, however, follow that there is no interpretation of this phrase that can provide an argument that is neither trivial nor false.

41. cf. B. Bettelheim, *The Children of the Dream* (Paladin, 1971) p. 212–18.

42. Lionel Tiger, *Men in Groups* (Nelson, 1968), p. 84.

43. Tiger, p. 80.

44. T.A. Critchley, *The Conquest of Violence* (Constable, 1970), p. 175.

45. *Daily Telegraph*, 2 October 1970. cf. also N. Tronchin-James, *The Ministry of Procreation* (Robert Hale, 1968).

46. The Swedish birth rate has fallen from 17·44/1000 in 1949 to 15·42 in 1966, to 13·7 in 1969 and to 13·82 in 1972. This seems to be the result of the pill and the Swedish "pill state of mind". The Swedish birth rate is now lower than when G. Myrdal wrote his *Crisis in Population* in 1934.

47. cf. Schofield, p. 104. Williams and Hindell, p. 34.

48. cf. N. Timasheff, *The Great Retreat* (Dutton, 1946).

49. The failure of the kibbutz can be deduced even from the statements of its supporters: cf. Menachem Gerson "Women in the Kibbutz", *American Journal of Orthopsychiatry* 41(4), July 1971. Cf. also B. Bethelheim, op. cit.

CHAPTER 5

1. Hansard, 5th series, House of Commons, vol. 724, cols. 816 *et seq.*

2. cf. speech by William Shepherd, M.P., Hansard, vol. 724, cols. 814 *et seq.*

3. Mary Douglas, *Purity and Danger, an Analysis of Concepts of Pollution and Taboo* (Penguin, 1970), Chapter 3, "The abominations of Leviticus".

4. Deuteronomy, 14. Authorized Version.

5. Leviticus 11.

6. Leviticus 20.

7. Douglas, p. 54.

8. Douglas, p. 67.

9. Douglas, pp. 69—70.

10. Leviticus 18:23, Authorized Version, as are all the biblical quotations in this chapter (my italics). Cf. also Mary Douglas, op.cit., p. 67 on the term "confusion".

11. Douglas, p. 67.

12. Leviticus 18:22.

13. *Report of the Committee on Homosexual Offences and Prostitution*, (HMSO, Command 247, 1957), p. 30.

14. Genesis 19.

15. Arnold Lunn, "Is Evolution Proved?" qutoed in W.S. Beck, *Modern Science and the Nature of Life* (Penguin, 1970), p. 133.

16. cf. Milton Rokeach, *The Open and Closed Mind* (Basic Books, 1960), pp. 40 *et seq.*, for a discussion of such "primitive" beliefs. Cf.

also R. Brandon and C. Davies, *Wrongful Imprisonment* (Allen & Unwin, 1973), p. 43.

17. K. Walker and P. Fletcher, *Sex and Society* (Penguin, 1955), p. 197 and p. 209.

18. Deuteronomy 22:5

19. Romans 1:26–7

20. Thomas Hardy, *Far from the Madding Crowd* (1874) (Macmillan, 1968), pp. 17–18 *et seq.*

21. Hardy, pp. 454–5.

22. Hardy, p. 453.

23. Hardy, p. 456.

24. Jim Corbett, *The Man-Eaters of Kumaon* (OUP, 1960), p. 77.

25. Corbett, p. 20 (my italics).

26. Gwen Raverat, *Period Piece, a Cambridge Childhood* (Faber & Faber), pp. 113–14.

27. F.E. Halliday, *A Shakespeare Companion 1564–1969* (Penguin, 1964), p. 396.

28. Halliday, p. 224 (my italics).

29. *Report of the Committee on Homosexual Offences and Prostitution* (HMSO, Command 247, 1957), p. 22, para. 55.

30. Hansard, vol. 784, col. 809.

31. Lionel Tiger, *Men in Groups* (Nelson, 1968), pp. 19–20.

32. cf. Robert Lacey, *Robert, Earl of Essex, an Elizabethan Icarus* (Weidenfeld & Nicolson, 1971), pp. 48, 194. Cf. also Lytton Strachey, *Elizabeth and Essex* (Penguin Modern Classics), pp. 20, 99.

33. cf. The Monk of Malmesbury's *Vita Edwardi Secundi*, Edited by N. Denholm-Young (Nelson, 1957), pp. 15, 19, 23. Cf. also C.D. Darlington, *The Evolution of Man and Society* (Allen & Unwin, 1968), p. 521, on the position of Edward and such other homosexual kings as William II and Richard II in England and Henry III and Louis XIII in France. In his historical play *Edward II*, Christopher Marlowe shows insight into the problems created by the king's homosexual relationship with his favourite Piers Gaveston and the reaction of the tough military barons to this. Cf.

Lines 370 *et seq.*

Mortimer senior [leader of the barons] : Why should you love him
    whom the world hates so?
Edward II: Because he loves me more than all the world
    Ah none but rude and savage-minded men
    Would seek the ruin of my Gaveston.

Lines 978 *et seq.*

"*Mortimer junior* [to Gaveston]: When wert thou in the field with
banner spread
But once and then thy soldiers marched like players
With garish robes not armour and thy self
Bedaubed with gold rode laughing at the rest
Nodding and shaking of thy spangled crest."

34. Robert Ashton, *James I by his contemporaries* (Hutchinson, 1969), p. 106.

35. Ashton, p. 114, quoting from Francis Osborne, *Traditionall Memoyres of the raigne of King James the First.*

36. Ashton, p. 13, quoting from Anthony Weldon, *The Court and Character of King James.*

37. Ashton, p. 124, quoting from Godfrey Goodman, *The Court of King James* (my italics).

38. Quoted in Samuel Igra, *Germany's National Vice* (Quality Press, 1945), pp. 37–8 and 40.

39. Igra, p. 40. *Vorwaerts* was a leftish and often scurrilous German newspaper of that time.

40. Igra, p. 37.

41. Tiger, p. 133.

42. Although women tend to be more censorious than men, more men (56 per cent) than women (51 per cent) condemn homosexuality. Cf. *Television and Religion,* Report by Social Surveys (Gallup Poll) Ltd (University of London Press, 1964), p. 82.

43. Hansard, House of Commons, vol. 738, col. 1104.

44. Hansard, vol. 738, cols. 1068 and 1089.

45. Hansard, vol. 724, col. 794, and vol, 738, col. 1081.

46. Hansard, 5th series, House of Lords, vol. 266, col. 647 (my italics).

47. *Report of Committee on Homosexual Offences and Prostitution,* p. 122, para. 11.

48. *Report of Committee on Homosexual Offences and Prostitution,* p. 53, para. 144.

49. Ibid., p. 122, para. 11.

50. Igra, p. 36.

51. Igra, p. 36.

52. One rider to this is the percentage of MPs to vote for and against the bill permitting homosexual activities between adults in private broken down by educational background. Cf. Richards, *Parliament and Conscience* (Allen & Unwin, 1970), p. 185.

Educational Background	Oxbridge	Other Universities	Other Higher Education	No Higher Education	Forces, Sandhurst, etc.
Voting FOR	42·4%	47·8%	56·7%	22·7%	33·3%
Voting AGAINST	11·3%	13·2%	13·3%	22·5%	40·0%

53. The post-war peak in army numbers was in 1952 at 450,000 men with total numbers in the Services nearly 900,000. By 1969 the total number of men in the Forces was down to 400,000 with fewer than 200,000 in the Army. In 1952 11 per cent of the GNP went on defence. By 1969 it was down to 6 per cent. Cf. A.F. Sillitoe, *Britain in Figures, a Handbook of Social Statistics* (Penguin, 1971), pp. 124, 128.
54. *Report of Committee on Homosexual Offences and Prostitution*, pp. 38–9, paras 106, 107.
55. Hansard, 3rd series, House of Commons, vol. 300, para. 1397, 6 August 1885 (my italics).
56. During the imperial period in British history (imperialism was at its height say 1875–1918 and in decline but still important 1918–60) the imperial élite governing the Empire had a decisive influence on the mores and attitudes of the home élite. Perhaps the best descriptions of how this occurred are found in George Orwell's essays.
57. England is an essentially hierarchical country and the mores and attitudes acquired by the home élite from the imperial élite were copied by or imposed on the rest of the population. A small imperial tail thus wagged the vastly larger English proletarian dog.
58. I owe many of the details about the English public schools to Professor J.R. de S. Honey's immensely erudite yet amusing book, *Tom Brown's Universe* (Duckworth, 1974).
59. Thomas Hughes, *Tom Brown's Schooldays* (1857; Dent 1952). Cf. also p. 169 (and footnote): "He was one of the miserable little pretty white-handed curly-headed boys, petted and pampered by some of the big fellows, who wrote their verses for them, taught them to drink and use bad language and did all they could to spoil them for every-thing in this world and the next".
Footnote (in original): "A kind and wise critic and old Rugbeian notes here in the margin: 'The small friend system not so utterly bad from 1841–47. Before that too there were many noble friendships between big and little boys but I can't strike out the passage; many boys will know why it is left in'."

60. cf. Prince Bernhard von Bülow, *Imperial Germany* (Cassell, 1914), or the works of Claus Wagner or von Treitschke.

61. cf. F. von Bernhardi, *Germany and the Next War* (Edward Arnold, 1914). In Chapter 5 the slogan "Weltherrschaft oder Niedergang" is euphemistically translated as "world power or downfall".

62. cf. Spencer's essay, *"The New Toryism"* in *The Man versus the State* (Williams and Norgate, 1884).

63. Details from Igra, pp. 35—6.

64. Details from Igra, pp. 68—70.

65. Igra, p. 46.

66. Igra, p. 47.

67. Details of the sodomite trials are from Igra, Chapter IV.

68. Igra, p. 47.

69. Igra, p. 54 (my italics).

70. London, 1939. Now in Penguin Modern Classics.

71. London, 1935. Now in Penguin Modern Classics.

72. Konrad Heiden, Der Fuehrer (Victor Gollancz, 1945), pp. 235—6.

73. Igra, pp. 72—3

74. Heiden, p. 236.

75. Heiden, pp. 581—2.

76. Heiden, pp. 594—5.

77. Heiden, p. 315.

78. The Japanese experience in these matters is very different from that of most other countries. All general rules fail in Japan whether one is discussing industrial relations, the family or even stage conventions, e.g. The "onnigata" actors of Japan do not fit the earlier generalizations about men playing women's parts on the stage.

79. Heiden, p. 235.

80. Igra, pp. 75 and 89.

81. Igra, p. 87.

82. Igra, pp. 90—1 and 94—5.

83. For data on the Soviet Union cf. K. Millett, *Sexual Politics* (Rupert Hart-Davis, 1971), p. 173.

84. cf. Millett, and the *Report of the Committee on Homosexual Offences and Prostitution*, Appendix III, pp. 149—51. West Germany also abolished its laws against homosexuals in the 1960s. Laws against homosexuals together with militarism and imperialism are so far as Europe is concerned the prerogative of the Communist countries, some of which still spend up to a quarter of their GNP on armaments and maintain very large standing armies based on conscription.

85. *Danish Journal* no. 65.

86. This lack of militarism in English life is best described by George Orwell in his essay "England, your England" in *The Collected Essays,*

Journalism and Letters of George Orwell (Secker & Warburg, 1968), vol. II, pp. 60—2.

87. Simon Raven, "Perish by the Sword" in *The Establishment*, a symposium edited by Hugh Thomas (Anthony Blond, 1959), p. 54.

CHAPTER 6

1. cf. E.M. Schur, *Narcotic Addiction in Britain and America* (Tavistock Publications, 1963).

2. i.e. only those addicts who sold the drug illicitly could be punished.

3. cf. Troy Duster, *The Legislation of Morality: Law, Drugs and Moral Judgement* (Free Press, 1970).

4. Schur, pp. 116—17.

5. N. Imlah, *Drugs in Modern Society* (Geoffrey Chapman, 1970), p. 21.

6. cf. Schur, p. 178.

7. The figures quoted here and in the table below are based on figures given in Schur, pp. 118—19, in D.B. Louria, *The Drug Scene* (Corgi Books, 1970) pp. 59—60; and in M.M. Glatt *et al., The Drug Scene in Great Britain* (Edward Arnold, 1967); and from Home Office Drugs Branch 1974.

8. cf. Schur, pp. 43—4; Louria, pp. 3, 60.

9. Quoted in Schur, p. 164.

10. cf. Schur, pp. 145—6.

11. Duster, p. 181. But see also Schur, p. 140 for a differing view.

12. Schur, p. 229 (cf. also ibid., p. 142).

13. Schur, p. 140.

14. Schur, p. 71 quoting Jeffrey Bishop in Marie Nyswander, *The Drug Addict as Patient* (New York, 1956), p. 150.

15. cf. Schur, pp. 81—5. See also Lord Moran's *Winston Churchill, the Struggle for Survival 1940—1965* (Sphere Books, 1968), pp. 720—1.

16. cf. Imlah, pp. 21 and 41.

17. This was the result of a Supreme Court decision in 1919 which is discussed in Duster, p. 16.

18. Imlah, p. 106.

19. cf. *Ministry of Health Departmental Committee on Morphine and Heroin Addiction Report* (HMSO, 1926), p. 19. Schur, p. 76.

20. Schur, pp. 229—30.

21. cf. Schur, pp. 133—4.

22. cf. Duster, p. 35.

23. cf. Duster, p. 66.

24. Duster, p. 66.

25. cf. Duster, pp. 36 and 109.
26. Quoted in L. Yablonsky, *The Tunnel Back: Synanon* (Macmillan, 1965), p. 375.
27. Based on statistics in Louria, pp. 59—60, Glatt, p. 15, Schur, pp. 118-19 and J. Zacune's "Fifty Years of Opiates", in *Drugs in Society*, June 1972, p. 15.
28. Imlah, pp. 26—7.
29. According to one study—G.V. Stimson and A.C. Ogborne: "A Survey of Addicts prescribed Heroin at London Clinics", (*The Lancet*, 30 May 1970)—37 per cent of heroin addicts interviewed reported that on occasion they sold, exchanged or loaned some of the drugs they were supplied.
30. cf. Louria, pp. 67, 153.
31. cf. Imlah, p. 141.
32. cf. Imlah, p. 39, Louria, pp. 71—87.
33. T.H. Bewley *et al.*, "Morbidity and morality from heroin dependence in a survey of heroin addicts known to the Home Office" (*British Medical Journal*, 23 March, 1968).
34. cf. Imlah, p. 52.
35. Louria, p. 63.
36. Stimson and Ogborne, *The Lancet*, May 1970.
37. cf. Louria, p. 61.
38. No doubt the deceased are also playing a dead role. Come back, Lazarus, all is forgiven.
39. Stimson and Ogborne, *The Lancet*, May 1970.
40. R. Cockett, *Drug Abuse and Personality in Young Offenders* (Butterworths, 1971), p. 2.
41. Cockett, p. 141.
42. Cockett, p. 144.
43. See for instance J. Young, *The Drug-Takers* (Paladin, 1971).
44. cf. J. Willis, *Addicts: Drugs and Alcohol Re-examined* (Pitman, 1973), pp. 107—9.
45. Moran, p. 187.
46. Cockett, p. 144.
47. Many of the details in this section are based on Imlah, p. 101.
48. Willesden is a North London suburb close to Neasden; cf. *The Anatomy of Neasden* (Penguin, 1972).
49. Schur, pp. 235 *et seq.* See also Schur, pp. 203—5.
50. cf. Duster, Chapter 1. See also discussion in Louria of this issue.
51. cf. Imlah, p. 107.
52. cf. Cockett, p. 78; Stimson and Ogborne in *The Lancet*, 1970.
53. cf. "Tobacco—the Demon Weed", *Drugs and Society*, No. 7. vol. 1, April 1972.

54. Reported in the *Guardian*, 30 July 1970, and in the *Evening Standard*, 28 July 1971.

55. Other factors of a cultural nature are of course important, but one of the ways in which these are expressed is through the legislature's attitude to taxing alcohol.

56. cf. *Alcohol Abuse* (Office of Health Economics Papers on Current Health Problems, no. 34, 1970), pp. 19—20.

57. cf. *Alcohol Abuse* p. 29; and Colin Norman, "It's no Crime to Drink", *Drugs and Society*, No. 7, vol. 1, April 1972.

58. Statistics from *Daily Mail*, 31 August 1971.

59. cf. Debate in Hansard, 5th series, Parliamentary Debates, vol. 724, cols. 655 *et seq.*

60. Quoted in Young op. cit., from *The Times* Parliamentary Report, 28 January 1969.

CHAPTER 7

1. I have chosen to discuss Synanon rather than possible British counterparts, simply because more and better studies have been done of this American institution.

2. Daniel Casriel, *So Fair a House: the Story of Synanon* (Prentice-Hall, 1963), pp. 177 and 185. (These claims are disputed by Synanon's critics, notably the American Psychiatric Association and the Consumers' Union; cf. E. Brecher's "Licit and Illicit Drugs" in *Consumer Reports* (Little Brown, 1972).

3. E. Goffman, *Asylums* (Penguin, 1968).

4. cf. Goffman, p. 17.

5. cf. Goffman, p. 18.

6. There are some exceptions. A prisoner can become a trusty, ex-mental patients do return as nurses (and psychiatrists have the largest proportion of any occupation undergoing psychiatric treatment), NCOs do become officers. Nevertheless the barriers are there and create problems. A lack of barriers and an emphasis on internal promotion from the ranks can also lead to problems—the chronic state of the Post Office is evidence of this.

7. For a good historical account of the public schools in this period see J.R. de S. Honey, *Tom Brown's Universe* (Duckworth, 1974).

8. Lytton Strachey, *Eminent Victorians* (Chatto & Windus, 1918), p. 206.

9. Strachey, p. 183.

10. Strachey, pp. 183, 184—5.

11. cf. Goffman on the "underlife" of total institutions, p. 119 *et seq.*

12. There is perhaps a more fundamental reason why men are more

likely to tell jokes about sergeants rather than warders, viz. more men have been in the Army than in jail. Also most men are proud of having served king and country in the armed forces and are willing to talk and joke freely of their experiences. This is not true of jails.

13. The mother-daughter tie can remain very strong in lower-class families even after the daughter has married. Cf. M. Young, P. Wilmott, *Family and Kinship in East London* (Penguin, 1962) pp. 44 *et seq.*

14. I have deliberately only discussed the three *congruent* types of compliance relation, which are the more common and effective institutional examples. For a more detailed discussion see A. Etzioni, "A Basis for Comparative Analysis of Complex Organizations", in A. Etzioni, *A Sociological Reader on Complex Organizations* (Holt, Rinehart & Winston), 2nd edition, pp. 67–8.

15. Casriel, p. 130.

16. Casriel, p. 42.

17. L. Yablonsky, *The Tunnel Back: Synanon* (Macmillan, 1965), p. 82.

18. Yablonsky, p. 209.

19. Yablonsky, p. 258.

20. i.e. All are therapists and all are patients.

21. cf. Yablonsky, pp. 147–8.

22. Yablonsky, p. 254.

23. Yablonsky, pp. 239–40.

24. Casriel, p. 10.

25. Casriel, p. 78.

26. cf. Yablonsky, pp. 254–5.

27. Casriel, p. 74.

28. Casriel, p. 68.

29. Based on a synthesis of data in Yablonsky and Casriel.

30. Casriel, p. 161.

31. Casriel, p. 71.

32. cf. Yablonsky, pp. 249–50.

33. The same basic techniques of humiliation feature in the British institution Phoenix House—a resident who breaks the rules may be forced to wear a placard declaring "I'm a junkie—is that what you like" or "Ignore me please", or forced to sit in a child's chair for a day ignored by all and then ridiculed by the entire community in a meeting. He may experience a verbal haircut or dressing down or a very real haircut leading to a bald head. Cf. Michael Dubois, *The Phoenix House, Junkie Cure*, pp. 3, 4.

34. Yablonsky, pp. 385–6.

35. Yablonsky, pp. 375–6.

CHAPTER 8

1. cf. C.H. and W.M. Whiteley, *The Permissive Morality* (Methuen, 1964), p. 21.

2. cf. Maria Ossowska, *Social Determinants of Moral Ideas* Routledge, 1971), on the distinction between "honorific virtues" and "virtues of benevolence", pp. 61—2.

3. Whiteleys, p. 14.

4. F.L. Allen, *Only Yesterday* (Harper Bros.), p. 85.

5. cf. Pitirim Sorokin on 'The Crisis of our Age' (New York, 1941).

6. cf. Mill, Utilitarianism, p. 258—9.

7. There can be little doubt that this is true today (cf. *Television and Religion*, Report by Social Surveys (Gallup Poll) Ltd., University of London Press, 1964, in the section on sex and religion, pp. 80—6) but I suspect it was always thus. James Joyce's *A Portrait of the Artist as a Young Man* (especially pp. 137—44) or Giuseppe de Lampedusa's *The Leopard* (especially pp. 27—8) give vivid portraits of nineteenth and early twentieth century Catholic puritanism.

8. e.g. S. Freud, *Civilization and its Discontents* (Hogarth Press, 1963); or J.D. Unwin, *Sex and Culture*.

9. Lord Devlin, *The Enforcement of Morals* (OUP, 1965), pp. 27, 28, 30.

10. cf. the distinction between repressive and restitutive law in Emile Durkheim's *The Division of Labour in Society* (Free Press, 1946).

11. Devlin, p. 34.

12. The Pope has declared that income tax evasion is not a sin—at any rate not for Italians; cf. Christie Davies, *The Incentive Case*, (Conservative Political Centre, 1971). For the subtler ethical problems of tax avoidance see A.A. Shenfield, *The political economy of tax avoidance*, I.E.A. Occasional Paper 24.

13. cf. M. Keer, *The People of Ship Street* (Routledge, 1958).

(a) "The possibility of feeling loyal to a group where strong emotion is not generated is outside the scope of Ship Street people." (p. 124)

(b) "When Barbara aged 16 was telling me of her first love, she mentioned that he is at present in an approved school for stealing. I expressed surprise. She promptly replied: 'Ah only thieving from the big stores or the like, he wouldn't rob you or me.' It is interesting that Barbara emphasizes the distinction between stealing from public property and the individual by using different words for the two activities. It is 'thieving' to steal from the 'stores or the like' but it is 'robbing' to steal 'from you or me'." (p. 126)

14. Devlin, p. 32.

15. This case is discussed at length in T.A. Critchley, *The Conquest of Violence* (Constable, 1970), pp. 160—1.

16. Devlin, p. 21.

17. Basil Mitchell, *Law, Morality and Religion in a Secular Society* (OUP, 1967), pp. 34—5.

18. cf. Herbert Spencer, "The Coming Slavery" in *The Man versus the State* (Williams & Norgate, 1884).

19. Details are given in Critchley, pp. 157—9. He notes that "They show . . . how unscrupulous even respectable demonstrators can be . . . in propagating stories of alleged police brutality."

20. Devlin, pp. 61—86.

21. The conflict between the needs of those who can benefit from free, open, impersonal institutions and the needs of those who are penalized by them is clearly outlined in Bernice Martin's "Progressive Education versus the Working Classes", *Critical Quarterly*, vol. 13, no. 4, Winter 1971.

22. Urie Bronfenbrenner, *Two Worlds of Childhood, U.S.A. and U.S.S.R.* (Allen & Unwin, 1972), p. 38.

23. cf. Bronfenbrenner, pp. 165—6.

24. cf. Ossowska, pp. 92, 96—7, for a demonstration that the prevalence of gang hooliganism in a country such as America and its relative absence in Russia is not in any simple way a reflection of differences in economic structure, of differences between capitalist and socialist societies. She indicates that violent gangs of juvenile delinquents are a major problem in Poland but not in Czechoslovakia. Similarly Bronfenbrenner's study indicates that young people create more problems in England than they do in West Germany. There is no simple correlation of delinquency and economic structure.

25. cf. Bronfenbrenner, p. 38. See also K. Millett, *Sexual Politics* (Hart-Davis, 1971), p. 173.

26. Bronfenbrenner, p. 37.

Books for further reading

Bronfenbrenner, U., *Two Worlds of Childhood—U.S. and U.S.S.R.* (Allen & Unwin, 1971)

Cockett, R., *Drug Abuse and Personality in Young Offenders* (Butterworths, 1971)

Critchley, T.A., *The Conquest of Violence* (Constable, 1970)

Devlin, Lord, *The Enforcement of Morals* (O.U.P., 1965)

Douglas, Mary, *Purity and Danger: an Analysis of Concepts of Pollution and Taboo* (Penguin, 1970)

Durkheim, E., *The Division of Labour in Society* (Free Press, 1947)

Fox, R., *Kinship and Marriage* (Penguin, 1967)

Goffman, E., *Asylums* (Penguin, 1968)

Gummer, J. Selwyn, *The Permissive Society: Fact or Fantasy?* (Cassell, 1971)

Honey, J.R. de S., *Tom Brown's Universe* (Duckworths, 1974)

Imlah, N., *Drugs in Modern Society* (Geoffrey Chapman, 1970)

Kutchinsky, B., *Studies in Pornography and Sex Crimes in Denmark* (New Social Science Monographs, 1970)

Report of the Commission on Obscenity and Pornography (Bantam Books, 1970)

Richards, P.G., *Parliament and Conscience* (Allen & Unwin, 1970)

Schofield, M., *The Sexual Behaviour of Young People* (Penguin, 1968)

Schur, E.M., *Narcotic Addiction in Britain and America* (Tavistock Publications, 1963)

Stassinopoulos, A. A., *The Female Woman* (Davis-Poynter, 1973)

Tiger, L., *Men in Groups* (Nelson, 1969)

Whiteley, C.H. and Winifred 'M., *The Permissive Morality* (Methuen, 1964)

Wilson, J., *Reason and Morals* (C.U.P., 1961)

Wright, D., *The Psychology of Moral Behaviour* (Penguin, 1971)

Yablonsky, L., *The Tunnel Back: Synanon* (Collier-Macmillan, 1965)

Index

245

DUDLEY

COLLEGE

OF

EDUCATION